CONTENT IS CURRENCY

Developing Powerful Content for *Web* and *Mobile*

New Strategies in SEO and SMM to Help Grow Your Business

JON WUEBBEN

Praise for *Content is Currency*

"Jon Wuebben has done it again. Yes, we are all publishers today, but most organizations are unclear how to use content marketing within their organization to truly make an impact to both attract AND retain customers. If you want the answers to why... and then how exactly to operationalize content marketing within your business, read this book!"

—Joe Pulizzi, Executive Director, Content Marketing Institute, and
Co-Author, *Managing Content Marketing*

"Who cares about great content? Your customers do! The more relevant, quality content your business can provide, the greater your opportunity to attract, engage and convert visitors to buyers. Jon covers all the bases in *Content is Currency* from personas to SEO to mobile. This book is full of practical tips that you'll be able to "cash in" for better online marketing results."

—Lee Odden, CEO TopRank Online Marketing, and Author, *Optimize*

"Great content is one of the most important parts of inbound marketing, and in *Content is Currency* Jon does a great job of giving you the foundation to transform your company using content to drive your inbound marketing strategy."

—Mike Volpe, CMO, HubSpot

"Social media and content are connected at the hip. If you do nothing but implement Wuebben's chapters on social media optimization and blogging, you'll be light years ahead of your competitors."

—Michael A. Stelzner, Founder, SocialMediaExaminer.com, and Author, *Launch*

"If you can't create a successful, multi-faceted content program for your company after reading *Content is Currency*, you're just not trying hard enough. It's a definitive, detailed guide on the realities of making content drive business results. Bravo, Jon Wuebben!"

—Jay Baer, Co-Author, *The NOW Revolution: 7 Shifts to
Make Your Business Faster, Smarter, and More Social*

"Content rules the web. Producing content is easy. Producing effective content is not. In *Content is Currency* Jon Wuebben leads the reader through the what, why, and how of creating effective content in an engaging way. Large businesses, medium business, *all* businesses should read this book. This is not a volume that is going to gather dust on your shelf; this is a resource you will return to again and again."

—Simon Salt, CEO, IncSlingers

"Content is a critical component of your marketing success. The trick is to make your content more about the value it provides and less about the marketing and sales of your products and services. It's not easy to do and most brands are failing at it (miserably). What does that mean? There is a huge opportunity to understand how content makes your business grow. There is a huge opportunity in figuring out how to create valuable content instead of content that is thinly veiled marketing blather. Jon Wuebben's *Content Is Currency* is your roadmap. Do what he says and your content will turn into money in the bank."

—Mitch Joel, President, Twist Image, and Author, *Six Pixels of Separation*

"Read *Content is Currency* to learn the profitable content strategies you need to make more money online today. It's full of valuable details and real-world examples that can help you upgrade your marketing. I learned a lot reading it and you will, too."

—Scott Fox, Founder, ClickMillionaires.com

"There's a ton of marketing gurus saying to market with content, but they are not explaining how to do it. That's the void *Content is Currency* fills. Highly recommended."

—Bob Bly, Copywriter

"*Content is Currency* should be required reading for small business owners and online marketing staff. It gives a step by step guide to business success through an integrated content marketing strategy."

—Anita Campbell, Publisher of *Small Business Trends*, and Co-Author, Visual Marketing

CONTENT
IS
CURRENCY

*Developing Powerful Content
for Web and Mobile*

JON WUEBBEN

NICHOLAS BREALEY
PUBLISHING

BOSTON · LONDON

This edition first published by Nicholas Brealey Publishing in 2012.

20 Park Plaza, Suite 1115A
Boston, MA 02116 USA
Tel: + 617-523-3801
Fax: + 617-523-3708

3-5 Spafield Street,
Clerkenwell, London
EC1R4QB, UK
Tel: +44-(0)-207-239-0360
Fax: +44-(0)-207-239-0370

www.nicholasbrealey.com

Every effort has been made to contact the copyright holders of the included screenshots.

Printed in the United States of America

15   14   13   12   11   1   2   3   4   5

ISBN: 978-1-85788-573-6

Library of Congress Cataloging-in-Publication Data

Wuebben, Jon.
Content is currency : developing powerful content for web and mobile / Jon Wuebben.
      p. cm.
ISBN 978-1-85788-573-6
   1. Internet marketing. 2. Web sites—Design. 3. Electronic commerce. I. Title.
HF5415.1265.W84 2011
658.8'72—dc23

2011 020201

Contents

PART II

Content for the Web   81

CHAPTER 5
Website Content—Including Case Studies, E-Books, White Papers, and Articles   83

CHAPTER 6
Press Releases and Media/Press Rooms   111

Introduction

Content. It's become a very powerful word in the Internet age, empowering people everywhere to have a voice. Through words, video, audio, and all its other forms, content tells the story of your product or service and propels your brand into the hearts and minds of your prospects, customers, and others. Without content, the web would simply be an empty shell of graphics, meaningless navigational menus, and links that go to empty pages. Good content is critical. *Great* content has truly become a powerful weapon in the web and mobile marketing arsenal of successful businesses around the globe.

What are we referring to when we say "content"? Here is just a small sample of the types of web and mobile content you can produce:

- Blog posts
- Website pages
- YouTube videos
- E-books
- Case studies
- Podcasts
- Webinars
- E-newsletters
- Digital magazines
- Press releases
- Articles
- White papers
- Content widgets
- E-mails
- Autoresponders (a type of e-mail)

Of course, your content serves no purpose if it's not being effectively marketed to your target audience, so a few years ago, *content marketing* was born. Part art, part science, and all focus, content marketing is the lynchpin of all successful online business endeavors. Its pursuit is what many preach, but few practice well.

In my first book, *Content Rich: Writing Your Way to Wealth on the Web*, I taught thousands of businesses, large and small, how to write powerful copy that would get their sites noticed by search engines and motivate their visitors to buy. Since that time (fall of 2008), content marketing has taken this notion into far-reaching places and truly become a strategic play in business, a true phenomenon in commerce and culture. But, it's not just a passing fad or marketing trend, it is clearly here to stay. Through content, you connect. Content is the *currency* that powers the connection. It speaks to us, makes us want to share it, and motivates people to buy. Web and mobile content has a value that can and should be exchanged. Like the tenets of social networking, the effective use of content is not only helping to define the age, but is taking its place in the pantheon of great online business strategies.

In this sequel to *Content Rich*, I build on the lessons I taught then and greatly expand upon them to show you how to capitalize on all types of web and mobile content—not just copy—and leverage them all the way to the bank and back, many times over. I also include the latest research, ideas, and case studies, so you can put web and mobile content to work for your company—today.

When it comes to the web, content has been king for a long time, and it's not stepping down from the throne any time soon. With mobile, new content opportunities are expanding like crazy. The sad truth, however, is that most content is poorly written or produced and doesn't help companies get the results they are hoping for. In fact, most business owners spend all their energy and money thinking about the appearance and the architecture of their sites and invest very little time thinking about the content. Failing to look at content from a strategic point of view, they see their web pages and other content channels as something they need to fill quickly. *Content Is Currency* alerts you to the dangers of this "design myopia" and shows the importance of content from every angle.

In the coming pages, you will learn the important elements of content and content marketing, not the least of which is how to develop content using search engine optimization (SEO), social media optimization (SMO), and call to action techniques that will improve website and mobile performance, search engine rankings, and, most important, connection and sales conversion. Plus, I'll show you how you can achieve these benefits for a fraction of the cost of using an SEO consultant, search marketing firm, or high-priced ad agency.

Optimized Content Works Harder

So, what *is* content development that emphasizes SEO? It is the art and science of producing web content that the search engines (and your site visitors) deem important. If a certain web page doesn't "tell" Google what its topic is, the search engine is left to try to figure it out. Certain things need to be done in order to optimize the content of a web page as much as possible. For any reasonably competitive keyword (the words that people use to find a website), there will be around thirty million to fifty million results. Getting your site into the top ten listings is the goal. If your content is optimized in each important area, you have a good chance of being in this high-ranking group.

Seventy percent of companies that have a website do not know how to accomplish this goal; those that do usually fall victim to that high-priced SEO consultant, search marketing firm, or ad agency I mentioned earlier. This is not to say there aren't some very respected firms out there doing great work, because there are. But there are also many other firms and so called "experts" who make big promises but don't deliver.

As the complete guide to SEO content development, *Content Is Currency* shows you exactly how to optimize the content on your website and how, in the end, to get people to buy. But that's just the beginning. I'll also show you how to produce and optimize content for every conceivable format: blog posts, YouTube videos, e-books, case studies, podcasts, webinars, mobile apps, e-newsletters, digital magazines, press releases, articles, and more. But I don't expect you to be convinced of that quite yet. Just read on, and the lessons will manifest.

What Will You Learn in *Content Is Currency*?

This book is written to help you connect better with your potential online and mobile customers, increase your site's search engine rankings, and/or help you learn the skills of search engine optimized (SEO) web content and content marketing.

Don't understand web content? Aren't good at writing, blogging, or video production? Don't have time to be active in social media? No worries. By reading this book, you'll gain an understanding of the power that the right content can have for your business, and then you can simply hire a qualified service provider to do it for you. *Who* produces it is less important than *what* the content is and *how* it connects you to your target market.

Content marketing is an *investment*. Planned, developed, distributed, and maintained correctly, your content will give you a return on investment in as little as a month or two. That's not bad. Plus, once you achieve higher search engine rankings, social media influence, and increased sales, you will simply need to maintain that level of success—or increase it if you'd like to generate an even higher level of influence. But I don't mean to discount the time required. It is an investment. And it takes a while to get up and running. But once you commit to quality web and mobile content, your business will never be the same.

The Real World

Content Is Currency is full of specific examples, practical advice, and step-by-step instructions that will help those doing business online and in the mobile space to achieve the results they have dreamed about. This book covers the development of all types of online and mobile content, including video, audio, and podcasts, as well as social media content. You will learn:

- What types of content you need for your specific business, target market, and industry, together with the best type of website
- How certain content tricks can influence search engine rankings and sales conversion
- How search engines rank content and why

- How to develop, distribute, and leverage social media content to connect with your target market and grow market share
- How to integrate the unique elements of your web presence: website, landing page, blog, article, e-mail, newsletter, autoresponder, pay-per-click (PPC) ad, and press release copy, as well as online video and audio content
- How content development has affected the online and mobile presence of many companies, using case studies featuring businesses in a variety of industries
- Content development and management strategies for Twitter, Facebook, LinkedIn, YouTube, Flickr, StumbleUpon, and other social networking sites
- Everything you need to know about mobile content in this rapidly developing and promising marketing channel
- Strategies for automating content creation, distribution, and management
- How other businesses have benefited from having a solid content strategy in place

The book is broken up into three distinct sections:

- Part I. Content: It's the Currency
- Part II. Content for the Web
- Part III. Content for Community and Mobile

In Part I, I'll cover what web and mobile content is and why you need it for your business. I'll introduce the various types of web and mobile content and explain how you can generate more traffic and sales through its effective use. I'll discuss how content serves two primary functions: It helps search engines find your pages and it speaks to your customers in a compelling way. I'll review the importance of web and mobile analytics and their role in the content development process.

Next, I'll explain why content works. As you'll see, effective web and mobile content capitalizes on "pull" marketing techniques and the power of "being where people are searching." If you do this right, you can revolutionize your business. Why is effective content so powerful? One reason is that it is one of the most important elements of Google's search algorithm (as well as Bing's and Yahoo!'s); if you produce content that the search engines deem important, they will reward you for it. The other reason, of course, is that your target market wants—and needs—to connect with you.

Analyzing your current content is next. The best web and mobile content in the world is useless if the user can't understand, connect, or access it. I'll walk you through the important elements of your web and mobile presence, key areas that you'll want to check to ensure a positive experience for all visitors. Of course, we'll review important format elements of content such as calls to action, headings and subheadings, and the importance of balancing quality content with quality design.

Content Is Currency then goes into keyword, competitive, and industry research. It is important to conduct these steps correctly in order to make your content as effective and as search engine optimal and socially friendly as possible. In addition, by figuring out what keywords people are searching for and which keywords your competitors are using, you can choose the best keywords for your web and mobile content and ensure you get the exposure you need.

I'll round out Part I by showing you how to optimize your web and mobile content for search engines. Once you have a complete list of keywords and phrases for your site, I'll show you how to place them in the content and meta tags for maximum search engine ranking and effectiveness. I'll also show you how to produce content that simultaneously pleases site visitors and the search engines, a feat many companies find difficult to do.

In Part II, we'll get into all the types of online content you can use to connect with your prospects. At the top of the list is website copywriting, which I deem to be the most important type of online content. Your website serves as the hub of your online marketing efforts, with all other content built around it. For your website, I'll describe the types of pages you must have, based on the type of business you run, and tell you how to produce content that connects with your visitors. This includes specifics for your home page, the company information page, product and services pages, and thank you pages, as well as secondary pages like FAQs, "Why Us," and contact pages.

We'll then get into case studies, e-books, white papers, and articles. This type of content helps establish you as a trustworthy expert in the eyes of others. You can also use this content as a free offer in exchange for visitor contact information. You will learn how to produce case studies, white papers, e-books, and articles that will resonate with your target market and get prospects to contact you.

Next comes the press release. Online press releases serve two purposes: Getting additional first-page rankings in search engines and communicating your company news to the media. In this chapter, you will learn how to write press releases and how to distribute them effectively. This chapter also discusses the importance of a media/press room page on your site to give the media easy access to company information and news.

Building Community

In Part III, we'll cover what I call relationship-building content and content for web and mobile applications. This includes e-mail, autoresponder, or newsletter content. These content vehicles should offer free advice and tools that help improve your customers' lives, build trust, and foster viral activity. I'll show how to take a customer-centric view in the development and distribution of community-focused content in order to build long-term relationships, and we'll examine why autoresponder e-mails are one of the most important tools for building a new relationship with a prospect.

And how about content for social media? Most people realize the importance of Twitter, Facebook, LinkedIn, and YouTube but do not understand how to populate their profiles with substantive content that will increase their influence and authority. We'll get into the major areas of social media optimization (SMO) and show how you can make it work for your brand. *Content Is Currency* highlights the differences in producing content for social networking sites, shows how to automate the process for maximum efficiency, and explains how you can ensure a solid return on investment (ROI). Yes, you can see a return on the time and dollars invested in social media.

Of course, your content marketing efforts will be dead in the water if you don't blog regularly. So, we'll dive into blogging to help you connect with prospects and customers. I'll show you how to write compelling blog posts, get other bloggers to link to you, and build your online community. The interactive and real-time nature of blogs means that you can capitalize on near-instant interaction with prospects and customers on your blog. I'll show you how to use blogs to become an industry expert, launch products, conduct interviews, and perform surveys.

Been on YouTube lately? Yes, and so has everyone else. Video content has only grown in importance over the past few years, and it has become essential for anyone who wants to succeed online. Video is powerful online content that engages the eyes and ears and educates your audience on some important topic. It also motivates people to take action like nothing else, no matter what product or service you sell. Because of YouTube, we are inundated with video content. *Content Is Currency* shows you how to produce, edit, optimize, and launch video content that will get noticed and lead to new relationships—and new sales.

One of the least-used types of content is one that's the least understood: audio content. This includes podcasts, webinars, and teleseminars. Of course, this type of content has also exploded in popularity on the web, although it's dwarfed by video. I'll show you how to produce, edit, optimize, and launch audio content easily and affordably for your business.

We then dive headfirst into mobile content. As you'll see, this quickly growing and very compelling type of content is changing *everything*. And although we are right in the middle of its development and things are changing every day, we'll get into the basics of producing connection-friendly, high-conversion mobile content for your business, whether it's a new app or text message campaign, or simply making your website content "mobile friendly." The key with mobile is finding a way to distinguish yourself from the competition and looking at your efforts holistically with other content channels so you can achieve a consistent ROI. With mobile, your content doesn't always work the first time, but when it does, the conversion numbers can be huge.

Real-World Application

My goal? To be able to effectively provide you with a road map for online marketing success by capitalizing on your content marketing efforts. From content development to content leveraging, content management and curation to content archiving, you'll see how real companies are winning in the content age with compelling, industry-leading web and mobile content. And I'll show you how to make it happen for your own business.

Whether you are a start-up, a growing firm, or a large multinational corporation, I'll provide you with the quickest, most effective ways to develop and distribute content. I'll also show the shortcuts and the automation you can bring to the content development process. I'll review the specific content tactics and strategies you need to employ and I'll discuss the power of *local search marketing* for geographically based businesses that serve a specific community or region.

We'll wrap up the book by setting you on your content development and marketing path. Engaging the content life cycle and your users' specific needs, I'll show how to bring simplicity and quality to all the content you produce. Search engines, social networking, and mobile: How is the content development process tied to these three dynamic areas of the online marketing world? I'll uncover the answers.

Who Is This Book For?

If you have a new business or an existing small business, it's definitely for you. Making sure your web presence connects with your prospects is critical—every lead is important. You never know where your next big customer is going to come from. If you're running a small business, you either:

- Don't have a website
- Have a website but need some improvements in search rankings and social media influence
- Have a website but need help converting prospective customers into sales
- Have a website but need help with search rankings, social media influence, *and* sales conversion
- Are in good shape in all of the above areas, but want to get involved in mobile marketing and need to create powerful content

Whatever your specific content needs, I think you'll find this book very helpful in your pursuit of influence, connection, and sales.

If your small business operates exclusively on the web, then this book is even more important for you. It doesn't matter whether you sell a product or a service, are business to business (B2B) or business to consumer (B2C)—web and mobile content and the effective marketing of that content can help raise your game across the board.

Who else is this book for? Growing midsized companies and large corporations. If you're a growing business, you need to know how you can stand out among your competitors and how you can grow market share by using the power of content marketing. You need to be able to take what you have and build upon your strong foundation. *Content Is Currency* will lead you down the right path.

What if you're part of a large corporation, struggling with content creation and curation? You need to know how content marketing can strengthen your existing position and reduce your marketing costs. Lead acquisition and retention can be expensive. *Content Is Currency* shows you how to leverage the power of content to reduce costs and connect with thousands more potential customers, quickly.

The Purpose of Content

It's important to understand that each type of content you produce serves a specific purpose. The goal of all your content is to connect with those who are interested in what you do (and to be ranked high in search engine results and popular on social sites). But, each individual content type serves important roles in the overall content marketing arsenal. Some companies use only two or three kinds of content and are incredibly effective. Others use many different types, but still miss the mark. Depending on your business and your goals, there are important things you need to know about content before you start creating it.

Let's cover the content on your website first. The goal there is to initiate a connection, to inform prospects about what you do and how you can help them. The content on your site should get visitors to take action—to sign up, enroll, or download something. You want to do business with these people, and at the very least, continue the "conversation" so you can start building a relationship.

Next comes your blog content. The goal of your blog is to inform or educate readers about topics that they deem to be important. If you sell hammocks, you could write a series of blog posts on the best places in the world to enjoy the comforts of and views from a hammock. Or you could write a few posts on the types of hammocks available and the differences between them. Or you could post product reviews. Whatever the nature of your business, I'll cover everything you need to know about blog content in this book.

Case studies, e-books, white papers, and articles also help inform and educate your audience about things they want to know, all without selling your services. Of course, as you'll see, you can softly sell your company, but only at the very end and with a simple call to action. (You would *not* sell your company directly in a blog post however.)

A case study is exactly what you think it is: a review of a successful client engagement for your business. The difference between an e-book and a white paper? An e-book is more informal, casual, conversational, and brief. A white paper is more researched, authoritative, and professional in tone. White papers are typically longer, too. Articles are simply four hundred- to eight hundred–word how-to or explanatory pieces for quick consumption and easy education. We'll get into all the details for these types of content vehicles.

As I mentioned earlier, online press releases serve two purposes: getting additional first-page rankings in the search engines and communicating your company news to the media. But, in addition to these functions, they help you brand your company and build a following. A series of effective press releases, optimized and distributed the right way for your audience, is something that very few companies do. We'll show you how to knock this easy content vehicle out of the park every time, and in so doing, distance yourself from your competition. Like any other powerful branding exercise, press releases can give you tremendous leverage and create the impression that you are a clear authority. Wouldn't you like the media to contact you for your opinion on industry developments instead of you pitching them? It can and will happen when you unleash the power of the press release.

When it comes to content, the easiest to understand is probably the online ad. Obviously, your goal with advertising is to generate interest among new audiences. But are you writing compelling copy? Is it balanced with stellar design? Are you offering something for free? These are all elements of the best online ads. It's shocking to see how much money companies spend on web ads because they simply don't know what they are doing. Hint: The goal is *not* to make Google and other ad networks rich! Okay, I guess it's too late for that, but the bottom line is that you want to use your resources efficiently and get the most bang for your buck. Great ad content will deliver on these objectives, whether it's a PPC ad, banner ad, text link, or video ad.

Your social media content is used to build rapport and grow your community. Like your blog, it is there to share interesting topics, industry research, interviews, product reviews, and more. It also inspires your prospects and customers to talk to each other and to provide you with feedback regarding their thoughts, opinions, and advice.

On Twitter, it's entirely possible that you will hear complaints and frustrations about your company or products. Because you'll have an established presence with some fantastic social media content and will be monitoring it regularly, you'll have the ability to address this criticism quickly to make it go away, which could actually make your customer *more* loyal. That's powerful content marketing in action, and I'll show you how to capitalize on it.

E-mails, newsletters, and autoresponders keep you in a prospect's or customer's inbox on a regular basis. And marketing is all about frequency and recency, right? E-mail content is also about adding value along the way. In other words, as with the other types of content, you will be publishing high-quality content that educates and inspires. Let's face it: There is a lot coming at us all the time. Staying in front of your audience *and* giving them stuff they want can be a very powerful combination.

As you'll see, with video content you are harnessing the power of television and combining it with the power of personal choice. You put spoken words and visual action together, and allow your audience to turn you on or off at their convenience. Through this medium, you are able to show emotion and attitude and motivation; essentially, you have all the benefits of nonverbal communication, something that the printed word simply cannot deliver. We are knee-deep into the online video era, and those who take advantage of the burgeoning medium now will benefit immensely in the years to come.

And what about audio content? You can connect with your target market practically anywhere using this medium—in the car, on the treadmill, or on the subway. The other benefit to audio content—especially webinars and teleseminars—is that it offers a golden ticket to Fortune 500 business. Both in study and practice, corporate America considers webinars and teleseminars to have significant advantages over other types of online learning. Maybe it's the fact that this type of content is usually delivered by an authority. Or maybe it's because this type of content assists in making partnering and buying decisions. Whatever the case, audio content resonates.

Finally, there is mobile content. What are the objectives in the mobile marketplace? Well, plain and simple, you need to be *everywhere* people are. And mobile is where your target market is *all the time*. We *live* with our smartphones! If you can always access your audience, then you have achieved something that few companies ever do: almost total access and attention. Plus, mobile is the great frontier. New developments are happening every day, right before our very eyes, in this exciting content medium. And your company has a chance to help shape the future road with your mobile content.

Throughout the book I'll also let you know about complementary books that I think are outstanding and could help further the cause. One I'll share with you right now is *The Yahoo! Style Guide*; it's essential reading if you want to understand the mechanics of writing and producing online content. It explains sentence structure, shows before and after examples of HTML code, and much more.

FIGURE I-1   *The Yahoo! Style Guide*

And you know what else? I believe in the *power* of content . . . so I'm giving you a big, fat dose of it right here in this book! I really want your company to succeed, so, if you like, call this book a passionate desire to help in any way I can. I love marketing, I love the web, I love my iPhone and my iPad, and I can't get enough! Perhaps you are the same way.

The Content Life Cycle

Part of what I'll discuss in this book is the *ecosystem* of online and mobile content, or what I call the "content life cycle." It's critically important to understand that—unlike traditional marketing pieces such as direct mail and brochures—online content is a living, breathing thing. It's truly evergreen and, in many cases, stays online forever. In other words, your content carries your reputation and your brand with it, in perpetuity. This can be a great thing or a bad thing, depending on what that content is. But the main thing to understand is that this dynamic exists. When you understand that, you can take advantage of content's lasting benefits and get a big leg up on your competitors.

We'll discuss the content life cycle more in coming chapters, but essentially it is this: content planning and strategy, content creation, content marketing/distribution, and content management/curation. This cycle continues forever, and as time goes by, you raise the quantity and the quality of your content with the expectation of reaching more and more qualified prospects and building a relationship with them along the way.

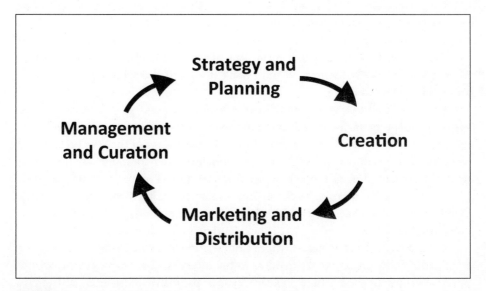

FIGURE I-2   The Content Life Cycle

The Structure of Each Chapter

In the pages that follow, you'll find a standard pattern of information:

- An overview of the specific content type
- Industry trends
- Best practices (and benchmarks)
- How-to advice
- Case studies that detail content put into action

The key to learning is to hit on the most important points and communicate them in a way that's easily understood so that *everyone* learns, as learning styles are different from person to person. Some chapters will be long, others a bit shorter, but I can promise you this: there will be no fluff or excess information.

I don't know about you, but I really don't like it when I'm given ten different ways to do something. I want to know the *best way* to do something and move on to the next thing. In business, our time is limited; we have so much coming at us, every minute, every hour, every day. Content marketing is best accomplished when it's done *efficiently*. Add in the powerful concepts of *automation* and *leverage*, and you'll be well on your way.

Why Am I Qualified to Teach Content?

That's a great question. Allow me the chance to tell you why I believe I can help. As I mentioned earlier, I have passion. Lots of it. As a born writer and communicator, I live to connect with others in meaningful ways. Extend that desire to the online marketing world, pair it with enthusiasm and curiosity, and you have lightning in a bottle, right? My goal, like yours, is *connection*, and I don't stop until I've achieved my objective. You might be able to relate.

I am also well known in the industry as a web content strategist, copywriter, speaker, entrepreneur, and online marketing leader. I love what I do. Although I don't write much web content anymore (thankfully, I have a team of the very best content writers and video editors on earth), I have personally written for more than three hundred web content projects in the past few years. And I feel rewarded, knowing that I helped dramatically improve my clients' business by providing them with compelling, search engine optimized content. It's what fires me up and makes me come back for more: helping businesses take it to the next level in an online environment.

I founded my first business, Custom Copywriting, in 2003. Rising quickly as one of the fastest-growing content providers in the industry, Custom Copywriting supplied web copy for the Fortune 500, small start-ups, many midsized organizations, nonprofits, and individuals. I then wrote *Content Rich: Writing Your Way to Wealth on the Web* in 2008. The reaction to that book was mind-blowing. Everywhere I went, every place I spoke, businesspeople told me how much they had needed a book like this, a detailed, easy to read, how-to manual on writing copy for conversion and for search engine domination. I was humbled and blessed by the book's impact. Almost every day, I received e-mails from people all over the world expressing how much they enjoyed the book. But what really blew me away was what so many of them said:

"Jon, you motivated me to finally start my business."

"I can't tell you how inspiring this book was to me. I am so excited to get out there and start connecting."

"This is the first time I understood what SEO copywriting was. Every other book was too complicated. Thanks Jon . . . so much. You changed my life."

I was truly touched. And I knew that I had found something special. I also discovered something in myself I didn't know I had: the ability to motivate and inspire. My goal when I wrote the book was simply to teach others how to write online content. I came out of the experience with a new passion: to start as many great businesses as possible! I thought, "Let's fire people up!" One of the outcomes of this was the start of my nonprofit, Urban Entrepreneurs, a group that helps the less fortunate in our inner cities start businesses, at no cost to them.

And something else happened after I wrote *Content Rich*: dozens of companies and individuals contacted my company, wanting us to write content for their websites and blogs. With my team of great writers, we were able to do just that. So my company grew considerably.

ContentLaunch.com, the next evolution of my business, began in early 2011. Content Launch is a worldwide provider of online copy, video, and audio content. Eventually, we'll be producing content in eight major languages around the world. I can't wait to see the outstanding content we'll create for these new audiences!

Why else am I qualified to teach this stuff? I speak regularly to business groups across the country on the topics of social media, online content strategy, entrepreneurship, SEO copywriting, and online marketing. In the past few years I have been invited to speak at The Online Marketing Summit, Shop.org Merchandising Conference, Media Relations Summit, New Media Expo, and many other industry events. There is nothing quite like a live performance. For me, it's a thrill to be in front of any audience talking about my passion, whether it's thirty people or three thousand.

I also teach Entrepreneurship and Business 101 at MiraCosta and Miramar colleges in San Diego. So, I'm always out there teaching, helping, and advancing the cause, one on one, face to face, in any way I can. And you can bet that I weave in all the important tenets of content creation, content marketing, and content strategy.

I truly value education, as I'm sure many of you do. After all, you decided to pick up this book, hoping to learn a few things. In terms of my educational background,

I have an MBA in international marketing from the Thunderbird School of Global Management and a BS in management from California State University, Chico. The lessons I learned at Thunderbird (ranked the number one international business school for many years) were absolutely incredible. Going to school with students from fifty different countries around the world is something everyone should experience, especially considering the global business world we live in today. I attended Thunderbird at the dawn of the Internet age—1997 to 1998—so the timing was perfect.

My greatest satisfaction? Helping other businesses improve their online marketing efforts. It's a total thrill. And I continue to have a strong passion for it.

A Few Extra Bonuses for Your Investment

Content Is Currency has been a labor of love, a true extension of my passion for writing, teaching, and helping other businesses succeed. So, like I did with my first book, I'm doing something that few business book authors do: I'm giving you lots of free stuff!

In addition to the contents of this book, and in the true spirit of content marketing, you also get the following free items:

- An audio program that discusses key topics from this book by profiling certain content marketing business case studies
- An online video of a recent performance of the live version of *Content Is Currency*
- Complimentary web content inspection where we review your pages, links, meta tags, and more to uncover areas of opportunity
- Twenty percent discount on any marketing consulting and/or seminar programs when you contact us for a content project

So, there you have it, a few freebies that will further help you with all your content marketing endeavors. Access to our audio program, live *Content Is Currency* video, and other free online bonus items are included in your book order. Simply go to www. contentiscurrency.com and register your name and e-mail address.

I'm excited to have this opportunity with you! I think you're going to really enjoy the topics covered in the book. I can honestly say I've enjoyed researching, writing, and editing it. Like my first book, it has been a lot of work, but a lot of fun, too.

After you finish the book, feel free to send me an e-mail at jon@contentlaunch. com and tell me what you thought, or feel free to review it on Amazon. I always like to know what made the biggest impact on people and what could use some improvement. It's the only way we get better.

A couple of other things: Connecting with content is mostly about being consistent and getting the basics right. Of course, you want to produce great content and be as original, authentic, and thought-provoking as you can, but it really comes down to making a commitment. So, I'll show you how to best integrate content and content marketing into your existing routine so you can get it done efficiently and make it a lifelong habit.

The other thing I want to be sure I do? Fire you up and get you content-inspired! I want to enable you to extend your passion for your products or services into the hearts and minds of people everywhere. . . . And I want to show you how you can turn the *power* of content into a rich database of loyal customers and a fistful of recurring revenue.

So, let's get started. . . . Why is content the "currency" of the web and mobile?

PART I

Content: It's the Currency

What Is Content Marketing, Why Do You Need It, and How Do You Maximize Its Effectiveness?

Now you know what to expect from *Content Is Currency*, but how will the lessons apply to your company? How can you capitalize on the information? It all starts right here, with the fundamentals of content marketing.

Readers of this book will no doubt reflect a wide range of online marketing capabilities, from the rookies who are starting their very first business to the more experienced marketers who are seeking a few new strategies or insights into the latest techniques. We'll assume that most people reading this book are at the novice level, so as to not miss anyone. From what I've seen out there in the business world, gleaned from speaking, consulting, and working on websites, 80 percent of businesses know only a limited amount about web and mobile content and how it affects them, no matter what they may think they know. The good news is that there is an upside to being in this situation. Your biggest online success is in front of you!

In the past seven years, I have had Fortune 100 companies as clients, and even *they* have made mistakes with web content. Yes, it's true. Just because you are large and well established doesn't mean you have your finger on the pulse of content marketing. Number one on the list of challenges for these large companies? Not using metadata and keyword research correctly. Number two? Not believing in the power of social media. More to come on these points.

One of the first things we learn about website development is that simply building a website or establishing your social media presence does not ensure that people will come. You have to register your website with the search engines. You may need to open an account on Google Places. You'll want to build inbound and outbound links. For your social networking activities, you'll need to reach out to others in your community, provide value to the group, and stay involved. And yes, you have to create compelling, value-added content and get it distributed—smartly.

So, we've established what web and mobile content are and that you need them, but what is content marketing? **Content marketing** is the act of sharing tips, advice, and other value-added information as a means of converting prospects into customers and customers into loyal, lifelong, repeat buyers. Utilizing the power of opt-in permission to deliver content via e-mail, RSS feeds, social media channels, and other methods, your goal is to become a valued resource for hundreds and thousands of people who, in time, will want to buy what you sell. Over a period of weeks, months, and years, you'll build a solid relationship with them and earn their trust. You don't want to sell them once and never see them again. You want to make a friend—a friend who enjoys buying from you—for life.

So, there you go, plain and simple. That is content marketing in a nutshell. But, how do you make it work for you? Stay tuned . . . it's all here.

Marketing in the Pre-Internet Days

It's been said many times before in practically all the important online marketing books out there, but we need to mention it here as well: the historical context of this medium called marketing. What did companies use in the years before the Internet? Most common were "interruption" marketing techniques such as television commercials, radio ads, or direct mail pieces, which tended to annoy many people and were difficult to measure. Today, these traditional media vehicles, including print advertising, are in decline. And the reasons are self-evident: it costs too much and doesn't connect with prospects as well as it once did.

Back in the day, the large corporations that owned popular magazines and newspapers were essentially database companies that collected detailed information about their subscribers; as a result of this power, they could get top dollar from companies that wanted to advertise. The best web and mobile companies are now doing the same thing, but with much more customer data—right down to the things they like to do in their spare time. It's a marketer's dream!

As you'll see, content marketing is very different from the interruption techniques of the past, and involves delivering requested information with independent value that creates trust, credibility, and authority—and, in the end, more sales and more satisfied customers.

Content marketing is about doing lots of things right: having a blog and establishing a platform. Check. Having a social media presence on Twitter, Facebook, YouTube, and other sites. Check. Providing free content in exchange for contact information. Check. Getting people on your autoresponder list and regularly sending them informative tips and advice about things that are important to them. Check that, too. In essence, you want to leave no stone unturned, showing up everywhere and anywhere your prospects may be hanging out online (and on their mobile devices, too). Wherever they go, there you will be as well, with their permission, of course. They won't be able to miss you. And you won't be able to miss them. Casting a big net that covers every area of your target sea will help you find all types of fish you've never seen or even thought you'd see. And that's the key.

If you start to feel like a publisher with all this content marketing stuff, well, then you'll know that you're doing things right. Like it or not, everyone is a publisher in today's business world. You business veterans out there, just take a look at all the marketing activities you have done up to this point—it feels a lot like publishing, doesn't it? Like a magazine or television station, you need to produce content—all types of content—for your consuming prospects. Before, you were just a provider of products and services. Now, you are a trusted expert resource for your customers!

How do you create compelling content? By focusing on delivering relevant, valued information that people will notice. When you do this, you'll generate trust, credibility, and expert status in your particular industry, and people will come to you when they are ready to buy. That's it. Some people will be attracted to your content immediately. Some will only want the free stuff. Others will be "just looking." And some will have the big bucks and want to spend it with you (hopefully).

And what about this thing called SEO, or search engine optimization? You may have heard it mentioned, but how does it fit into the content marketing world?

> Search engine optimization is the practice of using a variety of techniques to improve a company's ranking of all its content types on search engines. These techniques may include editing or adding to HTML code, working with site navigation features, employing linking strategies, and including compelling web page content.

The words and phrases you choose in your copy, the clips you choose for your videos, and the way you sound in a podcast all contribute to the overall picture of your web success. But you have to tag and optimize them so they don't go unnoticed.

And what about SMO, or social media optimization? It's equally important. Below is Wikipedia's definition, which I think is solid[1]:

> Social Media Optimization (SMO) or Social SEO is the methodization of social media activity with the intent of attracting unique visitors to website content. There are two categories of SMO/Social SEO methods:
>
> (a) Social media features added to the content itself, including: RSS feeds, social news and sharing buttons, user rating and polling tools, and incorporating third-party community functionalities like images and videos
>
> (b) Promotional activities in social media including: blogging, commenting on other blogs, participating in discussion groups, and posting status updates on social networking profiles

---

[1] Wikipedia. "Social Media Optimization." Accessed 2/18/11. http://en.wikipedia.org/wiki/Social_media_optimization.

It all starts with setting up your profiles on Twitter, Facebook, YouTube, LinkedIn, and other social media sites. SEO and SMO will be a big part of the content you develop. They are tools in your online marketing tool chest, and you'll want to use them consistently so search engines and social media networks pick up your content. If you produce great content, but the search engines can't "see" it or those in your social networks aren't spreading it, well, that would just be a big ugly shame, wouldn't it? Yep.

Why Do You Need Great Content?

Well, besides what we've already mentioned, great content ensures your long-term success and helps build your brand. What is brand building? It's the notion of establishing a familiar presence, having a standard way of doing things, and establishing a certain level of confidence in the minds of your customers. They'll always know what they're going to get with you, and in return for that peace of mind they'll spend their money with you. You need great content because great brands always communicate very well. They don't just keep pace, they *set* the pace. And really well-produced web and mobile content can do that for your business. Think Starbucks. Think Apple. These companies are leaders for a reason. Through their powerful brands, they are champions of content and content marketing.

Effective web and mobile content also capitalizes on "pull" marketing techniques and the power of being where people are searching, which can clearly revolutionize your business, especially for those who are still operating from a "push," or pre-web, strategy. Effective content is powerful because it's one of the most important elements of Google's search algorithm (as well as Bing's and Yahoo!'s); if you produce content that the search engines deem important, they will reward you for it. And let's not forget the social media networks and mobile devices. The same goes for them.

Content also makes you *really interesting*. It puts you in the driver's seat. You set the pace for your industry. People come to you for editorials and feedback, and your content establishes you as an authority. The media will want you. Your clients will want you. People will retweet your tweets, "Like" you on Facebook, and give you a thumbs-up on StumbleUpon. They will want to come to your party. Doing content right is a no-holds-barred, one-way ticket to industry dominance.

And guess what? You usually get to name your price when it comes to selling your goods and services to these satisfied content consumers.

Maximizing Its Effectiveness—The Content Marketing Machine

In my seminars and talks, I frequently mention the "three pillars" of web content success: content, design, and usability. Essentially, these pillars are what your content says, how it looks, and its ease of use. This is a good place to start with what I call your content marketing machine, otherwise known as your *total* content marketing effort.

It relies on certain inputs and steps that build upon each other and slowly but surely create a perpetual, automated lead-generation and business-growth machine.

Using the three pillars as your foundation, you need to consider three things:

- What types of content you produce
- How you put your content in front of your prospects and customers
- How you are supporting your content

In terms of the content you produce, think of it divided into three channels. The first is the content that makes up your site: your home page, your services pages, your case studies, your blog. Next, is the content you use for lead generation. This could be content that's on your site or off your site, but it includes materials like white papers, webinars, and free e-books. This is the type of content that most companies have yet to discover. Finally, there is your off-site content. This would be your tweets on Twitter, your PowerPoint presentations on SlideShare, your status updates on Facebook, your videos on YouTube, your mobile apps, and more.

It is really the careful practice of producing content in all three of these areas that will grow your influence and your brand. And, as we have mentioned, you need to produce all types of content: hard-hitting copy, powerful audio, and visually appealing video. The secret is in automating your process and leveraging it with tools like HootSuite and others. More to come on that!

Next is how you get your content in front of your target audience. One of the best ways is through a blog. Like a must-read newspaper—think of *The New York Times* or *The Wall Street Journal*—your blog is a perfect way to build a strong base of support for your mission, capturing those all important eyeballs and building a solid relationship with your target market. The search engines love blogs because of the fresh content. Your audience will love you because you are making their lives more interesting, their brains smarter, and their pocketbooks a little heavier with your great ideas. And here's where it gets really good: They sign up for your RSS feed, your newsletter, and/or your autoresponder series. That's when you *have them*!

It's also where you use content marketing fundamentals to start creating a relationship. Obviously, you still deliver terrific quality. You teach and entertain more than you sell. You use metaphors and stories to make your writing conversational and easy to read. But you also use subtle techniques to create an audience of buyers, not just loyal readers. You begin to call on your content bag of tricks, adding more persuasive elements to your writing, your videos, and your other content. All the while, you're getting more and more information about your audience, their likes, their dislikes, where they live, how they buy, and more.

Essentially, you're building your case, establishing trust, and making your target market fall in love with you. On that magical day when they're ready to buy (and it will come), send your loyal reader to a well-crafted landing page on your website. As I'll explain later, a landing page is a very specific page that gets visitors to do just one thing. Of all the web pages you have, your landing page does the most explicit selling, with a great offer and a clear, direct call to action.

Once customers buy the first time, chances are very good that they'll buy again and again and again, especially if they are happy with your product or service. They'll tell people about you. They'll follow you wherever you go. And *voila*! The content marketing machine has done its job. But you can't rest on your laurels. . . .

The Seven-Prong Approach

To get the most out of your web and mobile content, and to support it in the best way possible, you'll use a seven-prong approach. Once you are performing and staying active with all the important content marketing activities—your blog, your videos, your Facebook fan page, and so on—it's time to back up your efforts to give it a boost. How do you do it?

First, you want to leverage your client testimonials or positive reviews. If you provide a service, perhaps offer a portfolio of sample work or several case studies. For companies that sell products, include product reviews. What's that? You don't have any? Okay, well, you know where you need to start. Pick up the phone, send some e-mail surveys, and ask happy customers for a few reviews of your work or your products. If you can include the reviewers' full names, the companies they work for, and a photo, even better. Every website that sells a product or service should include client testimonials. It's a no-brainer. And it's a solid way to support all your great content. By the way, testimonials and reviews themselves are great content, one of the best kind: *user generated*. With regard to displaying your client work or product reviews, it's just a matter of putting up a new page on your site that includes this material. If you need to get your web designers to do it, work closely with them to make sure they do it right.

Of course, you'll use all the great rules of SEO to guarantee top placement in the search engines. Nothing can support your content marketing activities more than this. You'll be sure to do your keyword research (see chapter 3) and use the important keyword phrases in your meta tags and page content. You'll ensure you tag your videos and construct the right URLs for your blog posts. And you'll do many, many other things to ensure total SEO across the board. Optimized content is smart content. And smart content means lower costs per lead. More about SEO in Chapter 4.

Next, you further support your content building process by enticing prospects with a free trial service or small product sample to start things off (pitch this when you think they are ready to buy). If they like what you offer, you'll complete the rest of the project, deliver the rest of the product, or get them on a full subscription and get paid for it.

You want to guarantee your products and services, and if something goes wrong you need to make it right. This will further strengthen the trust your customers have in you and get them to refer you to others. Let's face it: Issues will come up; it's part of being in business. The question is *how you deal with them*. If you provide customers with a total guarantee, you create a strong sense of confidence and further empower your content marketing.

You'll also want to **monitor the competition**. What types of content are your competitors producing? There are always a few great competitors out there that are leading the charge, no matter what industry we are talking about. Are you the follower or the leader? See what everyone else is doing and *become* the leader. You can do it. And your content will thank you for it.

To further support your content marketing machine, you'll want to **actively pitch the media**. Send out press releases and develop relationships with members of the media who cover your industry. Find them with great resources like Help a Reporter Out (HARO), Pitchrate, and Profnet. Become active on all the important blogs in your industry. Be sure they know about you, all the time, every time. If you get the media on your side, they will do the promotion work for you! That's user- (or partner-) generated content at its finest!

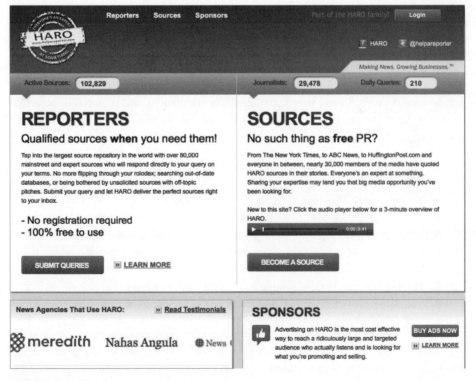

FIGURE 1-1   Help a Reporter Out (HARO)

Finally, you'll want to **build partnerships with others in your industry** to further support your efforts, your growth, and, yes, *to share* your content. This is probably the number one problem I see with most small businesses today: They are afraid to reach out to others. Some of them hide behind their online personas or brands and never get out to do any good old-fashioned networking. In a Web 2.0, social media world, face-to-face meetings and handwritten letters can work wonders. And these more traditional efforts can really support the online and mobile content marketing you do.

So, there you go; you have all the support pieces of the content marketing machine. Whether because of oversight or ignorance, other books on the subject of content marketing don't describe these ideas, but it really is a very important distinction that shows what separates the best companies from the mediocre ones. Content and content marketing is only *a part* of a very big business picture. It does not exist independently or, as they say, in a vacuum.

Another easy way to view what you do with content is to see it in *three distinct phases*: what you are doing, how you are doing it, and how you support it. For example, what you are doing is creating content for lead generation, you are doing it by writing a series of autoresponders and e-books, and you are supporting it and backing it up with your case studies, client testimonials, and service guarantee.

How does your company size up?

Eight Steps to Content Success

There are many ways to look at online and mobile content and many strategies that can be employed. With any new learning, I like simple lists and sequential steps that communicate the concepts in a quick, easy-to-understand way. With that in mind, let's review what I call the eight steps to content success. These are:

1. You learn who your customer is and where the pain points are.
2. You develop consistent, relevant content in multiple channels.
3. You let go of all control, and let your ideas spread.
4. People share your ideas and link to your content.
5. People find your content through social media and search engines.
6. Prospects and customers start relying on your expertise—the relationship begins.
7. You become the trusted solutions provider in your industry.
8. Your customers tell others about you.

By embracing these steps and following a certain order, you can make a big impact very quickly. The difficult thing for some companies is step three, letting go of control. But here is the reality: In the content age, consumers are in a position of great influence. On the web, they have the chance to say anything they like about you; whether it's true or false is only part of the issue. If they can get people to rally behind them, they can become a real force—either a positive force that helps your company or a negative force that could potentially destroy your company. It's important to understand this dynamic, and we'll discuss this topic in greater detail later. Of course, step two, developing the content, is also a challenge for many companies, but after reading this book you'll have a much easier time ensuring that you have solid content development and that you are connecting on every level.

Content Strategy

Content strategy is the disciplined practice, used by many forward-thinking online marketers, of planning the **development, delivery, and management of web and mobile content**. It's a process-driven activity, one that is made up of scheduling, creating, distributing, and following up on all the content that is published. It includes strategizing for all the content types we've brought up so far: website copy, e-books, social media content, web videos, technical sales sheets, and more.

Your tactical activities, of course, make up the strategy. If you're like many companies, you'll have your main website, a blog, your social media profiles, and maybe a digital newsletter. Perhaps you'll have much more than this, but if you have these basic building blocks, you can start constructing a unified and directed *content strategy* around them. In other words, you are going to tie certain goals and results to these content tactics. Here are some examples:

- Grow our Twitter followers to three thousand in the next three months
- Publish one web video every week for the next six months
- Blog three times a week from now on
- Fully optimize our website for our keyword phrases

Development

What types of content will you create? What will it look like? Where will it be found online? Who will put it together?

Delivery

How will the content get populated online? Who will upload it? How will users, visitors, subscribers, and customers see it? How will you ensure they see it?

Management

What happens after the content is launched? Who will follow up on inquiries, comments, replies, and requests for service? How will the content get revised or updated when the time comes? Who will be in charge of curating and archiving content?

Make sure, as you put together a content strategy, that you follow through with all of these important steps. It is a commitment and a process that involves a group of dedicated team members. You'll need time for planning and management of your strategy.

We All Hunger to Connect

Humans are pack animals. We need each other—some of us a little more than others, some of us a little less. And whether we live in the backwoods of Georgia or the middle of Manhattan, we all connect and interact and desire the attention of others. It's the plain and simple truth. And its ramifications are highly relevant in the content marketing space.

I know some of you are saying to yourselves, "Yeah, so what does this have to do with content?" Well, I think it's important to take a step back and see the bigger picture of how we humans are wired. The fact is that your content is going to connect you with others for a number of different reasons. What are the great motivators?

- To be liked, appreciated, right, secure
- To be attractive, sexy, comfortable
- To be distinct, respected, happy, and healthy
- To feel important or gain knowledge
- To make money or save money or save time
- To make work easier
- To have fun or gratify curiosity
- To make things convenient
- To eliminate or reduce fear, greed, or guilt

As you create and market your content, ask yourself, Which human motivation am I connecting with? Am I fulfilling a few of these, or just one?

Be careful: If your content is too self-serving, you may not be connecting with any of them. Perhaps you are trying to make yourself feel important or communicate how great your company is. Oops! Time to start over.

Just look at how people everywhere, especially the younger generation, took to text messaging. Some teenagers send two hundred texts a day! It's crazy. But you know what? They love doing it. Some of the behavior might be excessive, but the fact is, they *need* to connect. Through their connections, they better understand the world around them and they better understand themselves.

The importance of content and the idea of connection can best be understood by looking at what's really happening in the world. A *New York Times* article from November 2010, titled "Growing Up Digital, Wired for Distraction," expressed it well:

> Technology has created on high school campuses a new set of social types—not the thespian and the jock but the texter and gamer, Facebook addict and YouTube potato. The technology amplifies whoever you are.

For some, the amplification is intense. Allison Miller, 14, sends and receives 27,000 texts in a month, her fingers clicking at a blistering pace as she carries on as many as seven text conversations at a time. She texts between classes, at the moment soccer practice ends, while being driven to and from school and, often, while studying.[2]

So, our challenge as marketers is really twofold: to meaningfully, authentically connect and to stand above all the other content "noise" out there.

The growing importance of web and mobile content parallels an interesting change in culture: We used to primarily be *consumers* of products and services; we are now consumers and *communicators*. Think about it: The big corporations used to tell us how things were going to be and we accepted it. Now, we all tell *each other* about ideas, concepts, and available choices, and we all consume only the best stuff. The democratization of commerce has finally taken over! The culture is changing right before our very eyes, and companies like Facebook, Apple, and Google are leading the way.

Another way of looking at the content age is to see the current environment as made up of two groups: creators and consumers. If you want to see the consumers up close, just go to your local Walmart or shopping mall. If you want to witness the creators in action, you might have to look a little harder; they congregate in areas populated by software and other technology companies, in places like Silicon Valley; Austin, Texas; Seattle; Raleigh-Durham; and other hotbeds of new commerce. Creators are also found among the thousands of small, home-based businesses throughout the country, the individuals who built empires from blogging, eBay stores, e-commerce sites, and the like.

If your company has always simply "sold stuff," then you will have an immediate challenge. Being a creator (of content) requires a new mindset. How do you blog about something cool when a blank page is staring back at you and you've always had a "me" mindset? How do you engage a video camera when you have nothing to say? *Content Is Currency* will help you get over the hump.

Meanwhile, many of the big, old-school corporations are stuck in the traditional marketing paradigm, still spending millions of dollars on high-priced ad agencies, creating self-indulgent corporate content.

Yes, content is "the currency." In the online world, content is the preferred method of exchange and it has significant value. The actual definition of currency is "something that is used as a medium of exchange." Because the winners of the online world are well versed in the ways of quality content, they are the ones who are truly rich. Through leverage and thought leadership, they gain compound interest and increase their "holdings." The online rich are truly getting richer. The good news is that the playing field is open to all. You can become one of the new "content rich" rich as well! And if

[2] Richtel, Matt. 2010. "Growing Up Digital, Wired for Distraction," *The New York Times*, November 21. Accessed 2/19/11. http://www.nytimes.com/2010/11/21/technology/21brain.html.

you are a small company or a start-up, no worries. Six years ago, the online industry powerhouse, HubSpot, didn't even exist. Now it has thousands of clients, all over the world. Why? HubSpot tapped into a real need—inbound marketing software—and delivered valuable content and great service to satisfy that need.

The lesson? If you are a small company, you can compete with the big guys. And you can become the industry leader. Just ask Zappos.com, the billion-dollar online shoe company. Or Groupon, the exciting new online juggernaut that is revolutionizing the way we buy local products and services in the communities where we live and work.

Your Content Marketing Goals

Every company has a unique set of goals when it comes to content creation and content marketing. Some of the more sophisticated marketers out there, the ones who already have a basic understanding of the concepts I've discussed so far, may be looking for the latest statistics, research, and real-world content case studies. I'll definitely deliver on these goals, so stay tuned!

Others of you may need to be convinced of the potential these strategies hold. You may have tried blogging, but got discouraged after a couple months because you felt like you were blogging for no one. You may have tried some e-mail marketing, but couldn't find the time to get it done every month. Whatever your challenges, they can be surmounted with the tactics and strategies I discuss in the upcoming chapters. What I ask you to do at this point is to list your top ten goals for your content marketing program.

Let's take a closer look: What are some possible content goals? How about, "Establishing a presence on Facebook, growing it to three thousand fans in the next six months, and updating my status every day with one piece of valued-added, substantial content." Another goal might be "Developing a user-friendly Drupal website that includes separate pages for each of my services, is totally optimized for search, and includes my social media links and a free e-book that discusses the benefits of software outsourcing." If this is one of your goals, you'll be producing lots of quality content to get it done.

Whatever your content goals might be, the key is to write them down, and then to relentlessly pursue them like never before.

Other Important Considerations . . .

The areas we covered in the previous section are the most important to focus on, but there are other things you'll want to consider as well. Let's get into a few of those now.

Content Serves Two Masters

With web and mobile content, it's important to know that you are serving two masters. The two masters we are referring to, of course, are the search engines and the potential customer who has found your site. Each has unique needs. The search engines are asking you to use certain keyword phrases a few times, in a few specific places, and on a few different pages.

The customer is asking for benefits—What is this country club going to offer me if I join? How is the video game Rock Band going to enhance my life if I buy it? Customers couldn't care less whether you've used a certain set of keywords five times. Make sure your content is always serving both masters at the same time. With practice, it will become second nature.

Some would argue that a third master exists in the form of social media networks, but I would say that it's really your fans, followers, and friends who are helping to shape this channel for you (with your help, of course).

Aligning Your Content with Your Business

If your business is a law firm, do you need a shopping cart web page? Probably not. Likewise, if you are operating a business that manufactures guitars and you have a network of retailers, do you need to write web copy that discusses pricing of certain models? Not really. Let the retailers do that. If you are running a Japanese restaurant, do you need to use SEO articles and press release copy? Probably not. The fact is that every company has unique needs with regard to its content. There's no "one size fits all." Be careful, though, that you don't disregard a new type of content just because at first glance it looks like it's not applicable to you. Most of the content I describe in this book can find a way into your online marketing activities.

Remember How We Interact with Online Content

The way information is processed on the web is unique. If you look at the studies (and examine your own behavior), you'll see that we "scan" content on the web and on our mobile devices, unlike the way we read a newspaper, a magazine, or a book, where we are reading for more detail. People are busy and don't have the time to read every word. And there's no need to read the whole page if you can get the meaning by scanning it in a quarter of the time. So, make sure the content you produce is simple to scan for information.

In addition, online shopping is not a true browsing experience. Yes, we look around and surf from site to site, but the experience is unlike shopping in brick-and-mortar stores, where we can window shop, go in, and pick up an item and touch it. Online shoppers really are "directed." People go to a site and use the navigational menu or search box to find specific products. Knowing this, we want to make our content succinct, segmented, and specific so we can help the customer to buy quickly and eas-ily. It's a little tough to employ this concept at first, but it's helpful because we need to be reminded to tailor the content we produce to the way people behave and interact with the technology.

Measure—Survey and Make Necessary Changes

Through the content marketing process, you'll want to be sure you measure the consumer's response to the content you distribute. How many "Likes" did your new e-book get on Facebook? How many responses did you get to a particular blog post? How many views did your recent YouTube video receive? All of these things can be measured, and it's important that you do this. It's the only way we understand what our prospects think about the content we publish.

You can also use simple tools like Survey Monkey, Wufoo, or SurveyGizmo to get the opinions of your customers and prospects. All you need to do is come up with some good questions to ask and then send a survey out to your database. The insights you receive could be very helpful, and they may give you the specifics you need to make improvements to your content. Of course, these folks aren't always right about everything and no one knows your business like you do, but they can definitely inform the process.

Let's face it, most businesses never survey their customers. Just the act of putting the questions together and showing interest in your customers' opinions could spark a fire and get some quality interaction going. The bottom line is this: Measuring response will bring efficiency to the process and make your content creation job a whole lot easier. Think about it. If you have a list of the top fifty topics your customers most want to know about, you've already completed the first step in the content life cycle.

For your website or blog, you can use Google Analytics to get a detailed view of how visitors are interacting with your website and mobile content. More on this later.

The Ultimate Goal: Viral Spread of Your Content

"Viral" used to have a pretty negative connotation. It almost always referred to sick-ness and disease. Now, it is usually heard in the context of the web. When something "goes viral," it spreads across the web like wildfire, getting the attention of millions of people everywhere. When it comes to the viral spread of content, 95 percent of the time it happens by accident. You really never know when a YouTube video or a free e-book is going to catch fire. But when it does, you better hold on to your hats and glasses and enjoy the ride! Yes, going viral is a bonanza for online or mobile content, but a more realistic goal is to simply create high-value content across multiple channels (search engines, social media, and mobile) that connects you with a few thousand interested people or companies. If you can do that, you'll be in great shape.

If you can empower yourself to use the fine arts of leverage, automation, and outsourcing to gain further efficiencies, even better! The key with your content is to stay consistent, be authentic, provide valuable information, and find a way to give back. If you do this, people all over the world will beat a path to your door for as long as you want them.

Places to Find Content Ideas

Here are some fantastic sources of relevant, timely topics, whatever your company's content needs might be:

- Google Trends
- Google Insights for Search
- Twitter Search
- Technorati Charts
- BlogPulse Trend Search
- Industry association sites
- Competitive blogs
- Compete.com
- Quantcast
- comScore
- Your customers

Stuck for content ideas? Check out a few of these resources to power up the inspiration! Then brainstorm your way to content development.

FIGURE 1-2   Google Trends

FIGURE 1-3   Compete.com

Think Like an Artist, Execute Like a Samurai

Artists will tell you that inspiration can strike at any time. They never know when or where, they simply need to make sure they are ready to capture the magic when it does eventually come. Of course, you won't be painting the *Mona Lisa* or sculpting *David*, but you will need to come from a creative place if you really want to stand out with your content. Consider a simple and popular content type: a blog post. The title that you give your post will determine whether a paltry 10 percent or a robust 70 percent see it and comment on it. The title has to be unique and compelling. It needs to act as an entryway to the rest of the post.

In addition to being creative, you also need to be two other things: a great synthesizer and an original thinker. Synthesizing will come into play when you look at the ten other blog posts or articles that you may draw from to create your new post. The original thinking will display itself when you add your own ideas, opinions, and forward-thinking comments to your piece.

Unlike some artists, who fail to act on their inspirations and create their art for public consumption, you will need to *execute like a samurai*, putting together your copy, adding your keywords, logging on to your blogging platform, and getting your work out there. Of course, you'll also need to monitor reader comments and reply as soon as possible. Yes, there is a lot to do to generate just one blog post, but the rewards can be immense. Done right, your blog post will come together in beautiful synergy to the great satisfaction of your many subscribers. And you will be happy. Later on, maybe you'll sell some stuff, too.

One thing none of us can deny, however, is the lack of time we have to create great content. In "Why Brands Are Becoming Media," respected marketing mind Brian Solis said, "One of the greatest challenges I encounter today is not the willingness of a brand to engage, but its ability to create. When blueprinting a social media strategy, enthusiasm and support typically derails when examining the resources and commitment required to produce regular content."[3]

Solis stressed the importance of publishing calendars, editorial oversight, content performance analysis, and cross-discipline collaboration: "New media necessitates a collaboration between all teams involved in creating and distributing content, including advertising, interactive, communications, brand, and marketing—with an editorial role connecting the dots." I couldn't agree more.

The Undeniable Power of Web Content

Consider this statistic: Search marketing was a $19.3 billion business in 2011. Wow. The number just grows and grows. (It was up from $14.6 billion in 2009.) If this doesn't tell you that you should be focused on search engine and social media optimized content and content marketing, I'm not sure what will. What's the number going to be next year or the year after? This train has left the station and I don't care what's going on in the economy, if you are online and performing all the great techniques of content marketing, there is no downturn in *your* economy!

Current Trends in Content Marketing

So, what's hot right now in the content marketing space? Let's take a look . . .

1. **Social media marketing gets huge.** In corporate America, it has taken a long time for social media to get any respect. Conditioned to the idea that sales and profitability are the be all and end all, the entire justification for a company's existence, businesspeople have found it difficult to break out of this mindset. Companies everywhere are now migrating to social media, some because they are faced with no choice. Their prospects are there and they must be a part of the exchange. As part of this evolution, social media is extending throughout organizations, including customer service

---

[3] Solis, Brian. 2010. "Why Brands Are Becoming Media." Mashable, February 11. http://mashable .com/2010/02/11/social-objects/.

departments, to address customer issues head on. Social media advertising is also becoming more sophisticated and providing stronger results as this new advertising platform starts to take shape. Now, metrics are becoming more important than ever, and companies like Radian6 are helping us get there.

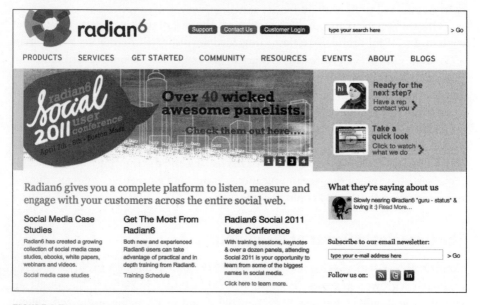

FIGURE 1-5   Radian6.com

2. **Mobile marketing becomes the real deal.** The mobile interactive extension continues to boom because people's time has never been more constrained and convenience has never been more valued. Forrester Research forecasts that 75 percent of marketers plan to include mobile in their marketing mix.[4] This is not surprising, as smartphone adoption is happening at a lightning-fast rate. Recent data shows that 30 percent of cell phones are smartphones.[5] Along with ease of use, e-mail and texting is possible with a smartphone. The average user has twenty-seven apps on his phone. The ability for your site to be found and optimized on mobile search is also very important. Currently, mobile queries make up 10 percent of all queries made on Google, and this number is growing. Quick Response (QR) codes—two-dimensional barcodes readable by smartphones—and mobile payment capability are growing quickly as well. And apps for these functions are available or soon will be for all platforms.

[4] VanBoskirk, Shar. 2010. "Internet Marketing Channels to Watch in 2010." Forrester Research, October 5. Accessed 2/11/11. http://www.forrester.com/rb/Research/interactive_marketing_channels_to_watch_in_2010/q/id/57594/t/2.

[5] Kellogg, Don. 2010. "iPhone vs. Android." Nielsen Wire, June 4. Accessed 2/12/11. http://blog.nielsen.com/nielsenwire/online_mobile/iphone-vs-android/.

3. **Content marketing expands into new venues.** Content and the practice of content marketing is everywhere now. It's not just downloaded, accessed, read, and stored on your PC anymore. It's on your laptop, your smartphone, your social media networks, and of course, your iPad (the tablet has sold more than twenty-five million units since its introduction (as of August, 2011). And Amazon has sold more than eleven million Kindle e-readers, further ensuring that content is a part of our hour-by-hour activity. One of the benefits for companies this development brings is the ability to sell content to a targeted audience, a goal that requires an analysis of content consumption habits. Roughly two-thirds of consumers have paid for some form of online content, including digital music, software, cell phone and tablet apps, digital games, news articles or reports, and videos, movies, or television shows.

4. **Online retail continues to take market share from other channels.** Consumers want *easy* shopping. With more and more people trusting online purchasing and enjoying the fact that they can buy from the comfort of their own homes, brick-and-mortar retail continues to slide. J.P. Morgan forecasts that U.S. online retail will continue to grow at a 12 percent annual growth rate from an estimated $166 billion in 2010 to $235 billion in 2013.[6] Also, group buying using Groupon is growing and will continue to expand as long as marketers see a decent return.

5. **Integrated marketing comes of age.** Integration across marketing platforms is an important part of any advertising and branding program, as evidence by the big social media campaigns of 2011, including Dos Equis Beer's "Most Interesting Man" and Conan O'Brien's "Team CoCo." Social media marketing works hand in hand with mobile marketing, while mobile marketing works with off-line marketing like television. Executed well, these channels can work together seamlessly, providing a strong synergy and an even stronger connection with target markets.

6. **Location-based services are growing.** As the company's website states, Foursquare is a "location-based mobile platform that makes cities easier to use and more interesting to explore." It's also become one of the hottest things in the online space. Essentially, users "check in" via a smartphone app or SMS, sharing their location with friends while collecting rewards points and virtual badges from the store, restaurant, theater, or other venue. Users can bookmark information about venues they want to visit. Companies are using Foursquare and other location-based services to attract new customers as well as to reward loyal ones.

As of April 2011, Foursquare had signed its ten millionth user, and the location-based network has grown by more than 3,400 percent over the previous year. Despite those impressive numbers, the service still has some distance to go before it can claim to be mainstream. But it's on the move and will affect content marketing in big ways.

---

[6] Cohen, Heidi. 2011. "7 Top Online Marketing Trends for 2011." ClickZ, January 10. Accessed 2/14/11. http://www.clickz.com/clickz/column/1935424/online-marketing-trends-2011-included.

7. **Target market segmentation and targeting are driving more dollars to content marketing.** Online marketing is getting more sophisticated. Going after the exact market you want to reach is easier than ever. An eMarketer survey, "Factors Driving the Move to Digital Marketing,"[7] showed that "better audience segmentation, customization and reach" is a key factor in allowing companies to touch the audiences they're targeting (30 percent indicated it as such). Also high on the list was "more targeted, behaviorally driven, niche media channels." If you can reach the people you need to reach online and do it for less money, it's not surprising that the web and mobile are the places to be. They deliver more content and better content to more people.

8. **Quality content is more important than quantity—it really makes a difference now.** I remember seven years ago, when article marketing was so hot. The idea was simple: Put out as many articles as you can with links back to your site to improve SEO. In many ways, it worked pretty well. But those articles were typically of marginal quality, and some of them were just plain bad. Fast-forward to 2012, and you have a very different scene. It's the great content—the long, research-based blog posts; the fifty-page, value-added e-books; and other types of super-high-quality content—that are getting all the attention. And that's not surprising. People gravitate toward the good stuff. They don't want to waste their time. In the content age, it's all about *quality* content.

9. **User experience is becoming more important than ever.** Whether through live chat, live events, virtual sales characters, or virtual environments, the human side of the user experience is very important right now and it is growing in use with each passing week. Users have high expectations and they want to have a truly interactive experience with your company. Look for more developments in this area over the coming two to three years.

10. **Content marketing is super hot.** After reading the last nine trends, this one is a forgone conclusion, right? It's all about content right now. And maybe that's why you're reading this book. The how and why and when of content are everything. If you don't connect, you don't sell, and that's the bottom line. Companies need to *give* before they *get*, and right now, they need to give a lot. Done strategically, methodically, and intelligently, content marketing can provide the greatest return on investment ever. Just keep reading, and you'll see why.

After you finish *Content Is Currency* and you are ready to begin planning your content marketing, use these trends to light your way. Using the strategies in this book, take a comprehensive approach and always look at the analytics (including social media and mobile metrics). If you do it right, you'll certainly be able to compete effectively in the content age.

---

[7] Nicole Perrin. December, 2010. "11 Trends for 2011," E-Marketer.

Current Research on B2B Content Marketing

As a devoted marketer, I read everything I can to stay abreast of the ever-changing web and mobile marketing space. It's a challenge, for sure, but over the years, I have found the best resources for staying up to date. One of them is MarketingProfs.com. Another is my friend Joe Pulizzi's Junta42 group. Last year, MarketingProfs.com and Junta 42 came together to publish a great report, "B2B Content Marketing: 2010 Benchmarks, Budgets and Trends."[8] I want to share the best of the report with you now:

1. They found that nine in ten organizations market with content, regardless of size or industry. Most popular tactics:
    a. Social media (excluding blogs)—19 percent
    b. Articles—78 percent
    c. In-person events—62 percent
    d. E-newsletters—61 percent
2. B2B marketers employ many different online tactics to achieve their marketing goals. The top eight in rank order:
    a. Social media (excluding blogs)
    b. Articles
    c. E-newsletters
    d. Case studies
    e. Blogs
    f. White papers
    g. Webinars
    h. Videos
3. Fifty-one percent reported that they plan to increase their spend in content marketing in 2011
4. Marketers, on average, spend more than a quarter of their marketing budget on content marketing
5. Marketers report that content marketing supports multiple business goals, led by:
    a. Brand awareness—78 percent
    b. Customer retention/loyalty—69 percent
    c. Lead generation—63 percent
6. Web traffic is the mostly widely used success metric (56 percent), followed by direct sales (49 percent)
7. The challenges they face:

---

[8] Pulizzi, Joe. 2010. "B2B Content Marketing: 2010 Benchmarks, Budgets and Trends." Content Marketing Institute, September 15. Accessed 2/5/11. http://www.contentmarketinginstitute.com/2010/09/b2b-content-marketing/.

     a. Producing the kind of content that engages prospects and customers (36 percent of respondents)

     b. Producing enough content (21 percent)

     c. Budget to produce content (19 percent)

8. Practices of best in class

     a. They allocate more of the marketing budget to content marketing than others (30 percent versus 18 percent)

     b. **They consider the "stage in the buying cycle" when developing content**

     c. They get lots of buy-in from the company's executive team

I emphasized with boldface type the best practice that I think is hugely important. Targeting and strategizing with your content appears to be a significant differentiator between those who succeed with content marketing and those who don't. As you read the rest of this book, keep this point in the back of your mind. Ponder your various customer groups, think about how they flow through the sales and qualification funnel, and determine which types of content they need to see to help them make the decision to use your company. This, I think, will be most beneficial to your overall content plan.

Another thing that was clear from the study: Marketers are not as confident as they should be regarding the effectiveness of content marketing tactics. There is a lot of hoping and guessing going on. Understandably, many marketers are reporting to a higher-up, and their reputation is on the line. To that I would say: It's the companies that allow their employees to fail that will ultimately be the most successful, especially in the online marketing area. We are charting a new course here, and mistakes are going to happen. But so are unprecedented surprises and incredibly great things, like new customers, lower marketing expenses, higher sales, and company expansion. It's the bold marketers, the ones who are piggybacking off best practices, applying the tactics to their own challenges, and never relenting in their quest to build connection, who will blaze a new trail and win in the end.

Summing It Up

So, what is content marketing? It's a means of communicating confidence and integrity on behalf of an online business. It's fully utilizing the immense power of the web and mobile to unleash a fury of connection and conversion. It's doing everything right online and through the mobile channel, when most of your competitors are doing everything wrong.

All of the important factors can be addressed through the content development process. The articles and e-books you write, the videos you produce, and the mobile apps you develop hold a great deal of power. What's the best way to communicate a positive image of your company in your prospective customers' minds? You'll find out.

An incredible connection with your target market is up for grabs. And it's yours for the taking. You can start today.

Content marketing means a lot of different things to a lot of people. Those in the know understand how powerful it can really be. Whatever the success story, there are thousands being told. Good content has meaning. Great content can help you connect and convert.

The next step is *analyzing* your current content.

CHAPTER 2

Analyzing Your Current Web Content and Mobile Presence

A nalyzing your current web content and mobile presence is an important first step in your epic quest to maximize the effectiveness of your content and put the content marketing machine to work for your business. For some, it will be a fairly simple exercise because the only thing they have that could be considered "content" is the copy on their five-page website that was developed ten years ago. For others, especially larger corporations, the analysis could take weeks or even months to perform.

The process is pretty straightforward:

1. Take inventory of the content you currently have in place
2. Review the content for quality (writing/production)
3. Review it for search engine optimization
4. Analyze its social marketing potential
5. Rewrite or rework it to correct any mistakes
6. Brainstorm a list of additional content items you may need

Remember, the strategies you learn in this book will go a long way toward helping you complete these tasks. What could you do right now? Step one, the inventory piece. Put together a simple spreadsheet that lists the content type, the title of the page or piece, the date it was created, and a column for notes. That will get you started.

What most of you will find during this process is that there is a lot of work to do. The majority of companies will find they have about 5 to10 percent of the total job done with their current content. The tasks that will take the most time? Creating new copy, videos, and other content, but that comes later. For now, you just need to get a handle on what you have and how it could be used moving forward. Remember, your content is supposed to *serve a purpose*; actually, it should serve a few purposes, in most cases. You don't want your content to be something that just fills up the home page or that site visitors glance at real quick and that's it. You want your content to be **compelling**

to readers, visible to search engines, linkable to partners, shareable through social media, and transferable to mobile devices.

The areas where most of the holes will be? Blogging content, social media content (and profile setup), and, of course, mobile content, which very few companies have in place at this point. Others may not have any lead-generation content—e-books, webinars, white papers, etc. And don't be surprised if you are missing practically all of the major forms of content. You are in the majority!

Don't forget to inventory all of your **printed materials** and company marketing collateral, including brochures, sell sheets, hard copy presentations, old VHS tapes (and company DVDs), and any other marketing material. Some, if not most, of these items could be turned into digital materials. There could be lots of value in those fifteen-year-old videos.

There's a Lot of Bad Content Out There

To illustrate just how big the opportunity is for content improvement, consider the websites you visit every day. You randomly search the web, check out a friend's site, or review a potential partner's blog. After reviewing the content, analyzing the context, and looking at the design of a few sites, what is it that you notice? Lots of bad websites, right?

The fact is that there are thousands, perhaps millions, of websites that look just plain awful. Add confusing navigation and stilted, corporate copy, and it's clear that we have a major problem on our hands. As someone who has worked in web development for more than eight years and has a large team of copywriters and video editors working on content, I see it every day. Actually, *many* times a day.

So, we've established the problem: The majority of companies out there do not have the basics down when it comes to producing content that is compelling to readers, visible to search engines, linkable to partners, shareable through social media, and transferable to mobile devices.

By the way, website *design* is a whole other story—that's even worse! I don't know about you, but I'm in favor of establishing official content and design standards that all websites would need to meet before being allowed on the web. That would solve a lot of problems—and make for a better searching experience for all of us!

The bottom line is that bad content means *fewer conversions and fewer sales*. That's how important it is. Don't discount it. It's critical that this piece gets done right. One other point: An impressive site design can never rescue poorly written copy, sloppy videos, or boring webinar recordings. There are lots of beautiful websites out there that have unreadable content. They usually end up being just a "nice to look at" site that serves no real purpose. And forget about being found in the search rankings. It's not going to happen unless you understand how to write metadata and optimize your pages, which I'll discuss later in detail.

And *why* is there so much bad content out there? For one, generating fresh, interesting content is not easy. It takes a lot of work. It takes a lot of time. Second, content is seen as a *commodity*. Companies don't realize what they have. They don't understand the power that their web and mobile content can generate. After all, if you've never gotten any leads from natural search, how do you know what it feels like? I'll tell you what, it feels pretty darn good! (And it's so inexpensive, too.)

In addition, our standards are really low. Bottom of the barrel. We don't know what "good" looks like! And we certainly don't know what *great* content looks like. *Content Is Currency* will help you with all of this.

The final reason that there is so much bad content out there? **Because no one takes ownership of it.** Every business process needs a champion, and, chances are, there is nobody is your organization who is responsible for the arena of web and mobile content. Even marketing departments fall on their faces here. What do they do? They like to outsource this step, hiring a cheap freelancer on Elance.com, one who has no clue about SEO or social media. Or, worse yet, the marketing department may hire writers from India, where English is a second language, to put together their all-important web content. That's just craziness! Running a one-person show? Well, then, it looks like you're the champion!

How to Approach Your Web Content Analysis

In this chapter, we'll look at what I believe is the most important type of web and mobile content: copy. I'll show you the most important elements to look for, how to produce the highest quality copy, and examples of the good and the bad. (Note: All of the other types of content, including social media content,videos, photos, audio, and mobile content will be covered in their respective chapters.)

So, how do you look at your site or lead-generation content with a new set of eyes? What's the process a copywriter goes through when she is rewriting a site? Good questions. There are lots of different methods and approaches, but when you're trying to fix those broken sentences and phrases you should look at three areas separately:

- Quality of the copy
- Formatting and usability
- How the content relates to the design

Overall Quality of the Copy

The first thing to look at when you're analyzing a web page is the copy itself, naturally. So, how does it look? Really. Take a step back and seriously think to yourself, What would the average person think of this content? Does it make sense? Would I understand what the site is all about if I was visiting for the first time? Remember, when considering your site's web copy, that people scan the text; they don't take in every word. And second, the meaning is better understood when the copy is written the way people speak. Things have changed a lot for the written word over the last fifty years or so. There used to be much more structure and formality to writing. It was expected. There was also a stricter adherence to grammatical "rules," like you can't end a sentence with a preposition or start one with the word *and*.

But you know what? That type of formal language is horrible to read! It's boring and uninteresting. It takes all the creativity away when you have to follow a set of strict rules. Did you know that some of the greatest composers of popular music couldn't actually *read* music? Paul McCartney is among them. He and his buddy John Lennon violated many "rules" of music composition on their way to writing the most beloved songs of all time. But that's what made their music *distinctive*. They figured if it sounded good, then why not? For those music folks out there, you know that many of their songs have chords that are not even in the key of the song, but they work *for all the right reasons*. Well, it's the same thing with writing. Rules can get in the way.

Don't get me wrong. There are guidelines for the basic structure of content on the web and in the mobile channel—that's what we're discussing in this chapter, after all, but they shouldn't *handicap the expression of thought*. They are merely the frame of the house; the words you write make up the rooms and truly make it a home.

So why not write the way people speak? It just makes more sense. It connects you with regular, everyday people, some of whom didn't do that well in their high school English classes anyway! It doesn't mean you're less intelligent when you write this way—far from it. The very fact that you have a functioning website has already addressed that point.

Check out the way this book is written. If you take a look, you'll see many rules of grammar broken. And I started as a copywriter! Other professional writers say that same thing.

Voice, Tone, Personality, and Style

We've all heard the expression, "its not *what* you say, it's *how* you say it." Well, in the web world, **voice and tone** are how you express your thoughts. And just like every individual has his own *tone of voice*, so too will you have a certain way of delivering your words, videos, and other web content. If you read Stephen King or Tom Clancy or any other fiction author, you know that each has his own writing style. This is a pretty good analogy of what you should be after with your web content: your own way of getting points across. Good first questions to ask when writing content for your site are, "Who are we?" and "What makes us special?" Your individuality as a company will naturally flow out of this exercise.

Consistently delivered across all of your content vehicles, your voice and tone can dramatically improve your branding effort as well. In fact, some companies use the voice and tone of their communications as a clear competitive advantage. The goal of any company with a web presence should be to develop its own distinct voice. As I've mentioned before, so much of the content on the web sounds exactly the same: that bland, boring, long sentence after long sentence "corporate speak" that no one wants to read. This is *not* an example of voice and tone. It's an example of pure crap. Just think about all the other elements that make you unique as a company: your logo, your tag line, your website design, your merchandising—shouldn't your content be thought of in the same way? Absolutely.

Whatever you do, be sure you don't sound like your competitors. And do not, I repeat *do not*, lift content from your competitors' sites and place it on yours. This is a big no-no, but I think most people understand that. And you know what? It's about time that your words, videos, and other content get the respect they deserve. After all, don't they take up the most real estate on your website? Your web presence is totally driven by words.

What's the difference between voice and tone? Voice expresses your site's general personality, which could be cool, professional, trendy, authoritative, practical, etc. Tone expresses the mood or feeling of the voice: friendly, appealing, upset, enthusiastic. As far as content *style* and content *personality* are concerned, these are pretty much the same as voice, but I wanted to use them here to help you understand what we are talking about. *Your* personality is different than your *best friend's* personality. Make sure your content is, too.

Reflection of Your Brand

I'm going to say a few more words on branding for those folks who may be a little rusty . . . a brand is **the image that you project and that your customers know you for in the market place**. It's what makes you stand alone and gives you your uniqueness. It's also a promise that you make to your customers, an expectation that they have of you. There's a comfort level and a certain degree of standardization, wrapped up in personality and devoted loyalty, that gives you a strong brand.

For example, at Starbucks you know you will get a high-quality cup of coffee every time you visit, no matter where you are in the world. The store and its merchandising will look the same from place to place, and even what the barista says to you when your coffee is ready is very similar at every store. (This observation hit me just recently!) So, yes, Starbucks is a strong brand.

And this carries over to the company's website content. Here is how Starbucks expresses its brand[9]:

> We love coffee and everything that goes with it. Good books. Great music. And what's more, we love sharing our favorites with you. What makes a Starbucks coffeehouse such a vibrant and inviting space? A philosophy of community and

---

[9] Starbucks Coffeehouse. Accessed 2/7/11. http://www.starbucks.com/coffeehouse?sms_ss=blogger.

environmental responsibility. Community means we're better together. In our stores and the world at large. Chat, connect and get involved.

Notice that it does not say:

Starbucks is an international coffee roaster and retailer that specializes in the finest coffees around the world. Our team is dedicated to providing you with a quality experience and providing you with a great place to meet with friends or work on your laptop.

UGH! That, my friends, is *corporate speak*.

The Power of Storytelling

Most of us still recall a few good childhood stories. Whether our teachers or our parents told us the stories, one thing was clear: They fired up our imaginations and provided great satisfaction. I know it was true with me. From *Charlie and the Chocolate Factory* to *Peter Pan* and *Where the Wild Things Are* to *The Giving Tree*, these indelible stories will be with me forever.

Like a good song, stories are mesmerizing because they touch us in lasting ways. In business, and specifically content marketing, the power of storytelling is underused. There are huge, undiscovered opportunities to weave stories in and around your brand to build rock-solid identification and loyalty in your customers.

And you know what? People never outgrow their love of good stories. The key is finding a way to tell a story with your products, services, and company as a whole. What are the values that drive your business? How can you connect to your target market in emotionally enriching, mutually beneficial ways?

With all the "noise" and interruption, you need a way to break through the clutter, a way that will impact people and help them understand where you are coming from. You need a way to help customers appreciate the authentic space that you live in within your industry, to present your content in a way that will absorb them and get them to want more. In the business environment, and specifically with content marketing, you should embrace and nurture storytelling. When you do, your audience will feel like they are a part of your story. And because you took the time to connect with them in a unique and sincere way, *the way that they remember from stories of long ago*, they will find ways to connect with you in meaningful, long-lasting ways.

Why are executives like Steve Jobs and Walt Disney so legendary? In large part because they were able to *engage people's emotions*. Within the confines of your online and mobile content, you can do the same thing. Creating scenarios of possible future events, using personal anecdotes, and talking about experiences can truly get people— your potential customers—to stand up and take notice. So those products and services you offer? They will be much more interesting and engaging when presented within the context of a story.

Accuracy of the Content

Once in a while, I'll get an e-mail from someone telling me to check some copy on one of my web pages. It could be a misspelling, a fact that is actually wrong, or something else. Although we'd like to think we are perfect, we know that this type of thing happens. After all, if you are managing hundreds or thousands of pages or have dozens of different *types* of content out there, all with a few dozen samples, then the errors will happen every now and then. The important thing is to correct them as soon as possible and reupload whatever changes are necessary.

Why? You could mislead or confuse visitors. You could expose your company to embarrassment or ridicule on the blogs. You could also have a potential legal issue on your hands. Not good. Get those mistakes fixed ASAP.

The biggest problem with content accuracy? Dead links. Get those links corrected and then be sure to check all your links every few months to ensure they always work.

Is the Content Interesting?

Does the copy grab you? Is it interesting and informative? Does it address your needs? And does the content have a certain rhythm to it? It should. Is there variety in the writing? Are all the sentences long, with multiple adjectives and adverbs? The goal is to combine short sentences with a few long ones. The trick is to make the copy flow. Using fragments is not a bad thing, quite the contrary, actually. The occasional fragment or sentence that starts with "But" or "And" can capture reader interest and keep the writing lively. Try it out. You'll like it. And your customers will, too! (See how effective it is?)

Do this: Go to a few of your favorite websites and try to remember what it was that you liked about them the first time you visited. You may be part of their online community. Maybe you post comments to their blog. Do you like buying from them? Or is it the way the copy reads that first captured you? Even though you may not have realized it, the copy probably was something that made you decide you liked the company.

Strong Word Choice and Sentence Structure

An easy-to-read, compelling, and strong communication style can give you a huge advantage over your competitors. Most of us know it when we see it. In literature, it's called a "page-turner." On the web, it's the home page that explains what you do simply and effectively. After twenty seconds, your visitors know who you are and what you can do for them. It's the e-book that explains the benefits of outsourcing or how to make great-tasting smoothies using captivating words and compelling pictures. It's the e-mail that not only gets read but that gets a response. That's powerful words and sentences in action, my friends.

And remember, more than 40 percent of U.S. adults have low literacy skills. You don't want to leave all those wealthy, "reading challenged" prospects out of the picture! Also, in this ever-diverse society, many people speak English as a second language. You don't want to leave them out either.

If you don't know how to write an effective sentence, or if you struggle to put together a compelling and grammar-balanced paragraph, you may want to leave the copywriting to someone who has a natural way with writing. Don't get me wrong, you can *learn* to write stronger sentences, but it could be a struggle for some people. Entire books have been dedicated to this topic. For our purposes, let's review the most important points for crafting good sentences.

First, **keep your sentences simple**. If they are running five lines and have multiple prepositions and conjunctions, cut them up into digestible pieces. Again, many people out there are slow readers with remedial-level comprehension. You need to communicate at a sixth-grade level so all potential prospects clearly understand. One thing about those slow readers, though: There are probably a few millionaires among them. And they may want to buy your product or service.

Next is **the word *you***. Get used to using it! Your content should be all about "you": "We want to help YOU find a better way to get from point A to point B, and we want YOU to help us understand future product needs better." I think YOU get the idea!

Keep your paragraphs short. This helps people digest the information. Think of all the junk mail we get. You see how these letters are structured? They usually have two- to three-sentence paragraphs. This helps break up the message and get unique points across. Same goes for your web content. Long paragraphs scare people away. They don't have the time or inclination to read the whole thing. And they never will. Think simple.

Make your action in the verbs, not the nouns. If you are trying to get a point across, why not communicate it in the clearest, most direct way possible? You don't want to make prospects reread your content because they don't understand what you are trying to express. You want them to reread it because they are thinking about buying from you! Here is an example of what I'm referring to:

Good verb
*The judge directly **explained** the verdict.*

Bad verb (noun hiding verb)
*The judge's explanations for the verdict **were direct**.*

Also, clear out the words that are unneeded. If you look at practically any sentence, you'll find words that serve no purpose, other than making the sentence longer.

Example:

Before:

*If you **previously** selected a movie, then you are ready to watch it.*

After:

If you selected a movie, then you are ready to watch it.

Get Rid of the Clichés and Cheese

Almost everybody uses clichés, jargon, and cheesy sayings in their normal, everyday speaking. Some of us probably don't even know what they are, but we rattle them off all the time. Expressions like "think outside the box," "tried and true," "off the shelf," "raise the bar," etc. These are all overused, trite, generally bad ways of communicating. Essentially, they are poor phrase choices, whether they are spoken *or* written. So what do you do to make the change? Substitute a simple, direct word.

Example:

Before:

The new software has all the bells and whistles, including off-the-shelf plug-ins that make a big difference in usability.

After:

The new software has all the features you need, including plug-ins that make a big difference in usability.

Are You Asking for the Sale?

The call to action is an important part of any content that is trying to sell. Now, not all content will serve this purpose, but eventually you'll be using it. You'll use it on your landing pages; you'll use it in a sales presentation. You'll use it at the end of some of your webinars, perhaps.

So, what types of call to action are you using? Are you simply presenting information or are you trying to build a relationship with a customer? If your website is a "brochure" type of site where you aren't trying to sell anything, then it's probably all right if you aren't asking for the sale. But, the majority of sites out there do want the user to take some type of action.

What do you have in the language that will prompt visitors to do something? On your website's home page, you should have content that motivates the visitor to go deeper into the site, for example, "Find out all the details of the special fall sale on the women's clothing page!" And then hyperlink "women's clothing" to that page.

Your product descriptions should have more than just a list of features and an "Order Now" button. Get the benefits in there, up front. Let customers know what else they receive if they buy right now, for example, "Get your choice of a free belt or handbag when you buy a dress today!" Compel them to take that next step! If you are trying to sign people up for your newsletter, do you just have the obligatory "Sign Up for Our Newsletter" and a place for them to type in their e-mail address? Or do you have some copy there that tells them why they should sign up and encourages them to do it?

FIGURE 2-1   Newsletter Sign-Up Box

AIDA

When you take a look at your site's copy, are you using AIDA? AIDA stands for attention, interest, desire, and action. Some have heard this before, maybe in a high school or college English class, but many people have not. Essentially, it's a style of writing that helps grab readers' attention, build interest, and create a desire so they will take action, in that order. It reflects the way people like to be sold. If you're selling something over the phone, the same steps apply.

You really need to ask yourself, "Am I writing this content for me and the way I like to write, or am I doing it for readers, reflecting the way they respond to written words?" Ask yourself: Am I closing the deal with my customer? This is the ultimate goal of lots of content (definitely not all of it, though). Make the reader do something: fill out a survey, submit a request, sign up for a service, or buy the product.

Think of it like this: *People buy more frequently when they are asked to buy.*

Ensure That Your Content Is Readable

Not sure how readable your content is? Put it to the test, the Flesch Reading Ease test. You can find this test using Microsoft Office Word 2010. To use the test in Word:

1. Click the File tab, and then click Options.
2. Click Proofing.
3. Under "When correcting spelling and grammar in Word," make sure "Check grammar with spelling" is selected.
4. Select "Show readability statistics."

After you enable this feature, open a file that you want to check, and check the spelling. When Word finishes checking the spelling and grammar, it displays information about the reading level of the document. The test checks syllables per word and words per sentence, scoring on a one hundred-point scale. The higher your score, the easier the copy is to understand.

Putting It All Together—Harmonizing Your Content

When you finish writing your content, how do you ensure everything looks good, sounds good, and generally "works"? Performing all the separate pieces—making sure you write about product or service benefits, including a good headline, and implementing keywords—is one thing, but how do they all fit together? As I've mentioned, you'll want to have others read your work and provide their opinions.

So, what are some simple little rules to remember as you write, so you can harmonize the content while you are writing it? First, use **variety** in the language. Use a simple sentence followed by a more complex one, followed by a fragment, or some other unique combination. What you are trying to get away from is boring, uniform copy. Using contrast is a good idea; it makes things stand out. By making the sentence structure varied, you make it interesting. By making it interesting, you provide good contrast. By giving your copy a good dose of contrast, you motivate people to buy. See how I did that? Look at the last three sentences I wrote and you'll get an idea of how to implement style, contrast, and interest!

You also want a **unified thought process**, so the entire section of content has a good rhythm and flow to it. If you feel like you are rambling with the content, you probably are. Make every sentence count. All the while, be looking for *link opportunities*; you want to use linking on some of your keyword phrases—both internal and external linking. More on that in a bit.

If you are a retailer and do most of your business in the community where you are located, you'll also want to **think local** for the language you choose and keywords you use. Place the most important information, the feature/benefit story, near the top. Wherever people start reading is the perfect spot for the information you want them to remember.

One other technique that can really make a difference in your content: **Showing instead of telling**. Using this little nugget of content gold can be difficult for a lot of people, because so many spend their lives doing more talking or writing in a "telling" kind of way. So, how would you show instead of tell in your content writing? The Starbucks example we used earlier is perfect.

Telling:
Starbucks is an international coffee roaster and retailer that specializes in the finest coffees around the world. Our team is dedicated to providing you with a quality experience and providing you with a great place to meet with friends or work on your laptop.

Showing:
The second you walk through the door you can smell it—the rich, unmistakable aroma of java, the air so thick with it you can almost taste it. At Starbucks, we love coffee and everything that goes with it. Good books. Great music. And what's more, we love sharing our favorites with you. What makes a Starbucks coffeehouse such a vibrant and inviting space? It's the people that come here—they smile, they laugh, they do business, they relax. And they appreciate our philosophy of community and environmental responsibility.

See the difference?

Formatting and Usability

The words you use on your site are important, but what it looks like and the way visitors get around is also critical. This is also an area of huge opportunity for most companies, especially those that have a website that's outdated or not as effective as it once was.

Using Headings and Subheadings

Headings and subheadings help break up the page and give the eye something to focus on. As you scan web content, your eyes need brief moments of rest. They also need to take in specific information. Using headings and subheadings helps make this process easier. The major purpose, from a purely functional view, is that they tell the reader what the page is about, and more specifically, what that section of the page is about. This is great for quick reviewing. If you are going from page to page on a site, seeking only information about a company's services, the headers can provide that information. Break up the page into digestible parts. Your customers will thank you for it with more sales.

Using Bulleted Lists

One of the other important things to consider is the use of what's called *white space* on your web pages. This is the area of the screen that is blank, that has nothing populated in it. It's the white area all around your content. Be sure you have some. A long, uninterrupted string of sentences that make up a massively long paragraph is the direct opposite of what we are looking for, but you see it on the web all the time.

So, how can you break up your copy and get people's eyes to focus? Use bulleted lists. The copy shouldn't be in standard block paragraphs like you see in books and magazines. Remember, you're competing for your visitor's time. If they don't get the information they need quickly, they'll jump to the next website.

How should you use this formatting technique? In the middle of the page is a good spot. It looks more balanced in this position and the list can be used to communicate some of the most important information on the page, maybe the benefits your customers will receive if they buy your product. Numbered lists are great, too, like "Top five uses for our product" or "Top ten services we can assist you with." People's eyes are naturally drawn to these types of copy techniques. Using bulleted lists may be the most underappreciated and underutilized formatting technique, but it can really help communicate the content. As you'll see, it's also good for your SEO effort.

Using Blocks of Content

Is the copy broken up into readable/scannable sections? Or is it copied and pasted on the page haphazardly, without regard to the visitor's perception? You need to ensure your content can be scanned in thirty seconds or less. Remember, we're dealing with short attention spans. In addition, studies have shown that it can be 20 to 30 percent more difficult to read from a screen than to read print, so you need to account for that difference.

Contrast Between Text and Background

Although this seems like an obvious usability point, you'd be surprised how many companies are still not doing this step right. Have you ever see a website that had a black background and purple text? I have. How did a site like this get published? What were they thinking? Bottom line, if you can't see the copy clearly or have to squint to see it—it's not working. A safe alternative? White background and black text. That's how most of the best sites are set up anyway. Your text and background choices are not the place to be creative; save that for your company logo or tag line.

Proofreading and Testing

There is nothing worse than good web content that misses the proofreading or testing stage. I've seen it happen many times: the copy starts off great, the first paragraph is sounding perfect, I understand exactly what they are talking about, and then—boom— a big misspelling or a missing word. It looks so bad. And it's really unfortunate because it came so close to being perfect.

The problem is that some people get so turned off by bad grammar that they decide they won't do business with you, based on this reason alone. Very unfortunate. They probably assume that if you can't get little things like your content right, maybe you'll make mistakes with their service. So, you want to be sure this step gets done right.

Although it's a simple step, it usually gets missed or glossed over because it's the very last one in the process. Note: Using the spell-checker in Microsoft Word is *not* enough. It can't tell whether words are used correctly in their context (like *your* versus *you're*). It also won't tell you whether a word or part of a word is missing.

The bottom line is that you want to inspect your content three times, every time. And have someone else look at it too. If you can find a third person, even better. A good way of accomplishing this is by printing the copy out and reading it that way. It gives you a little different perspective. Reading out loud helps, too. So does giving yourself some time after you write it. Let it breathe and then come back to it thirty minutes later, ready to check it.

Error-free content is tough, but if you can get this step right, you'll appear professional, reliable, and credible to everyone.

Grammar, Spelling, and the Rest

The best advice I can give you is to take a look at *The Yahoo! Style Guide*. It is a fantastic resource for this topic.

How Content Relates to Design

All web content, just like all print content, is made up of words and pictures. On the web it's called content and design. These two work hand in hand, and cannot be separated from each other. Every once in a while, you'll see a site that is all words and has no graphics or design treatment, but it's very rare. And I would say "UGLY" if I were to judge it. Of course, you also see websites that are all images, especially sites in the fashion industry. But these sites have different goals when it comes to online marketing. These companies don't use their sites for lead generation, but rather to brand and to communicate an image. For our purposes, we are using content to do it all: provide lead generation, brand, and communicate an image.

Copy does not exist in a vacuum. And neither does design. They are forever linked, and really should be. But how do they balance each other? How do they work together?

Recently, my company was working on a website content editing project for a financial services company. The firm was having a conversion problem. They had no issue getting traffic to the site—they just couldn't make people buy once they got there. After taking one look at their site, we knew the problem was obvious. The copy was just thrown on the page with no variation in font sizes, font types, or eye-appealing contrast. There was no customization to the site and nothing to focus on. I think there was only one paragraph break in the twelve hundred–word home page "manifesto." And other pages on the site were the same. It also looked like they had used a website design *template*, which is another bad idea.

Their competitors' sites were very different. They all employed easy-to-read charts, testimonials, and other interesting design elements. My client had none of these. Obviously, something had to change, or his conversion rate would continue to suffer. Here are some of the things you want to look for when you consider your website copy and how it relates to the design:

- Is there contrast in the style of fonts, the size of fonts, and the colors used? Some of the most eye-catching websites use a few contrasting fonts; different-sized fonts for the headings, subheadings, and body copy; and a complementary color palette. This approach wraps the content up into a great-looking package and truly brings it to life.
- Are the areas of the page that you want your customers' attention drawn to clearly visible? If you're using a "Learn More," "Buy Now," or other clickable button, is it obvious? Make sure it stands out on the page and can't be mistaken for something else (by the way, don't use "Click Here"—it's overused and looks amateurish).
- Is the design simple and easy to navigate or is it cluttered? Some of the best websites are really very simple in appearance, even if they have lots of content. The rule here is to spread the copy out, creating a unique page for every topic. Besides the obvious aesthetic reasons, it's also great for SEO purposes. Don't "drown" your copy in a complex design structure or have a million different web pages on your menu. Remember, white space is important. Let the content breathe!

Usability Analysis

Much of what we have learned regarding website usability comes from researcher and writer Jakob Nielsen. Called "the best-known design and usability guru on the Internet," Nielsen holds a Ph.D. in human-computer interaction, and the insights that the Internet community has gained through his studies have vastly improved the user experience. Almost all of the findings have a correlation to content, so it's important that we look at some of the key takeaways.

Probably the most fascinating of Nielsen's findings has to do with how people read on the web. In Nielsen's groundbreaking eye-tracking study from 2006,[10] he recorded the reading behavior of 232 users. The users viewed thousands of web pages, and Nielsen found that their reading behavior was pretty consistent. It didn't matter what the site or task was, there was a definite outcome. What did Nielsen find? That the dominant reading pattern looks somewhat like a large letter "F" on the page. His findings:

---

[10] Nielsen, Jakob. 2006. "F-Shaped Pattern for Reading Web Content." Useit.com, April 17. Accessed 2/2/11. http://www.useit.com/alertbox/reading_pattern.html.

- Users first read in a horizontal movement, usually across the upper part of the content area, which forms the F's top bar.
- Next, users move down the page a bit and then read across in a second horizontal movement that typically covers a shorter area than the previous movement. This forms the F's lower bar.
- Finally, users scan the content's left side in a vertical movement. This last element forms the F's stem.

It should be noted that sometimes users read across a third part of the page, making the pattern look more like an E than an F. Other times, the reading pattern looked like an inverted L. What are the implications for your content? Place the most important copy in the areas where the eyes scan.

Writing in the Style of Inverted Pyramids

We know that people are *scanning* your content. So given these findings, how do we ensure that they get the information you want to communicate? We do this by writing in the style of an "inverted pyramid." What this means is simply putting the most important information, your major points, first. Follow with supporting information and end with the least important details—background, maybe answers to a couple of popular customer questions, etc.

You also want to place the most important content in the upper left area of your pages. Make sure you emphasize the most important information with prominent headings and boldface type. And, as you'll find out in a bit, placing your important keyword phrases in these locations is also critical.

Easy Navigation—Make the Content Simple to Follow

How many clicks does it take, on average, for your customers or prospects to find what they need on your site? Have you ever looked? Check out your website analytics program and see what the numbers are telling you. Follow their path from start to finish. This data is invaluable—and it can help you redesign and/or rewrite your pages if necessary. How many clicks should it take for visitors to get to what they are looking for? Probably fewer than five, but it's less about the number of clicks and more about providing an intuitive, easy-to-follow path, no matter what they are trying to find.

Talk to your customers about this. See what they are telling you. Ask them point blank if they think your website and other types of content are confusing. Is the copy and navigation holding them by the hand or backing them into a corner? Get a handle on this, and you are on your way toward improving the overall content experience.

Patterns, Alignment, and Consistency

Whether it's your e-book series, your autoresponders, or your website, you want to take a look at your pages, individually and collectively. Do they have a consistent look and feel? Does the content have the same voice and tone? They absolutely need to. If you see major differences from page to page, your content will not only look bad, it will throw your readers off and sometimes make them stop reading altogether. I know I have done it many times.

Other things you want to check? The location of graphics, the site search box, your menus, etc. There shouldn't be any variability with these site design elements. If you see problems here, you should seriously consider redesigning. If you notice that your copy needs a complete refresh as well, then this is a good time to do both. A total facelift is much easier than making design changes one year and copy changes the next!

CASE STUDY: Improving Usability for Crazy Egg

Crazy Egg is an analytics company that creates heat map data visualizations, showing website owners where visitors click most frequently. As Crazy Egg looked at its own visitor behavior, the company realized it could do a better job of converting site traffic into new customers.

To accomplish this goal, the company partnered with SlideDeck, a website development firm in San Diego, to design a **custom product tour** that would walk visitors through a series of graphic slides that explained product benefits. It would conclude with a compelling call to action inviting visitors to find out more. They hoped this new, easy-to-use website module would provide better conversions for the site, perhaps lifting sales 8 to 10 percent.

What they ended up with was something even better. It seemed that the custom product tour was just what prospects wanted to see. With the redesigned home page of CrazyEgg.com now prominently featuring a compelling product tour as the main point of visitor interaction, potential customers felt closer to the product. Through story and pictures, they were able to see the benefits of Crazy Egg, right on the home page. After a few weeks, *conversions were up 21.6 percent over the previous site design.*

What was the takeaway? That improving site usability for visitors can sometimes be a simple exercise that leads to significant sales improvements.

CHAPTER 3

Performing Keyword and Competitive Research

Keyword strategy is part art and part science, and is probably the least understood and most overlooked part of companies' web and mobile strategies. Of all the things I have witnessed in the past seven years, the lack of knowledge in this area has been by far the most surprising.

Most companies simply don't appreciate the importance of this critically important task. Begin by asking yourself what search phrases people could be using to find your website. You'll want to really brainstorm this one, coming up with general phrases, specific phrases, and "long tail" phrases (three- to six-word phrases).

If you are a pet groomer in Monterey, California, then you'll probably want to use "pet groomer in Monterey, California" as a keyword phrase. If you are a .net development services firm, you'll want to use ".net development services," but you'll also want to use ".net development company," ".net development provider," and others. Of course, there is a lot more to the keyword research process, so let's get into it.

The Essential Practice of Keyword Research

Did you know that more than half of the people out there think that the companies listed at the top of the search engine rankings are the top companies in their field? It's true. I start off with this startling statistic because it has dramatic implications. It also talks to the power of keyword phrases and search engine optimized content.

Lots of consumers use the web to investigate before they buy, but at the same time, there are many people who are ready to buy when they log on. If you are on the first page of the search results for the keyword phrase they are using, and they click on your listing, they are definitely aware of you. More than likely, they will believe you are a company that they should consider purchasing from.

So, being on that first page of Google results for your important keyword phrases could be a gold mine for your business. Google, like all the other search engines, looks for keywords when it is "crawling" the web to determine search engine rankings. If you use your keywords in certain strategic places, Google will usually notice it. So will people who are searching for your products and services, end up on your site, and complete a contact form. And you know what? These leads *are prequalified*. That's incredibly powerful. And for some of them, the odds are very good that they will purchase soon. So, the lesson here is if you do your SEO content correctly and get your site optimized, you will go a long way toward building your brand awareness.

The first step is determining who your audience is. How do they behave? What's important to them? Are they all pretty much the same or are they made up of several distinct groups? Chances are, they are probably a diverse group of people. Remember, if you are serving a global audience, the web pulls from all over the place. So think broadly. If you are a local company, serving only your community, then this wouldn't be the case, of course. Your keywords will be geographically based.

Once you know your customers, you can start understanding how they search for you online.

What Words Are Potential Customers Using to Search for You?

Here's a key question: Do you know which keyword phrases your customers are using to find you? You'll probably be able to guess at a few. But most of them, you won't know right away. The reason is that there are probably a hundred (sometimes hundreds or a few thousand) phrases that people could use to search for you. There are *always* more keyword phrases than you think. Even if you are a small company and only sell one product, there will still be dozens of potential phrases that you can optimize for.

What's one way of learning these phrases? Ask customers. Some may not remember the words they used, but many will, especially if you ask them on a web form or talk to them on the phone right after they visited your site. This is valuable information. Be sure you keep an ongoing log of what they tell you. As the first step in gathering keyword intelligence, it's easy and it doesn't cost you a thing.

Be aware, too, that keywords people use do change and evolve over time. They may be searching for "power boats" now, but when a new technology comes out, let's say a new thirty-two-valve turbo engine, they may start using "turbo engine power boats" too. Just be aware of what those keyword changes may be.

How can you get help in determining appropriate keyword phrases? I thought you'd never ask. This is the other important step that you want to take. Let's face it, the key to doing anything on the web—whether it's getting help with design, determining the databases you want to use, or learning about SEO content development—is finding the right information so you can do it yourself, or locating the right organization so you can partner with or outsource to them. I say, focus on your core competencies and find quality partners for the rest. Well, for the most part, you don't have to do that with SEO content—you *can* do it yourself. But you can also send the work out. So, back to the topic at hand: getting help with your keyword research.

Measuring Demand *and* Competition

Most of the information in this chapter refers to measuring the demand of your keyword phrases. But let's not forget the level of competition either. Essentially, this is the number of sites that are using a particular keyword phrase on their pages. The best way to find out is to simply search for the phrase in a Google search and see how many pages are using it. The number will be in the top right corner of the search results page.

You'll also want to click on a few of the listings on the first page to see how the top sites are optimizing for the phrase. This will give you some insight into why they are ranked as high as they are. If you find a phrase that is really popular—and you will— don't think you can't rank for it, too. It will probably be very difficult, but you don't want to simply cede to the competition. Get out there and beat them at their own game!

Keyword Discovery

For a subject as sophisticated and dynamic as Internet keywords, we need all the help we can get. This is an art and a science, after all. Anything that combines those two disciplines is bound to be complex. The good news is that there are some great resources that deliver on their promise of comprehensive keyword analysis.

Keyword Discovery, a great keyword research tool, has been on the scene since 2004. It's been adopted as the best keyword phrase analysis tool by many of the top search marketing industry gurus. At $69.95 per month, it's well worth the investment. And it's available as a free trial. Make sure you do it! The tool uses historical data from 36 billion searches conducted via two hundred search engines and uses search logs from the engines as well. It also offers a year's worth of data, so you can spot seasonal variations in keyword use. This can be valuable information, especially if you are a clothing retailer or have a cyclical type of online business.

If you are looking for a super-robust tool, be sure to check out Keyword Discovery. Remember, uncovering only ten to twenty important keyword phrases can alter the landscape of your business very quickly. This is as good as gold when it comes to your SEO content effort. Harness the power.

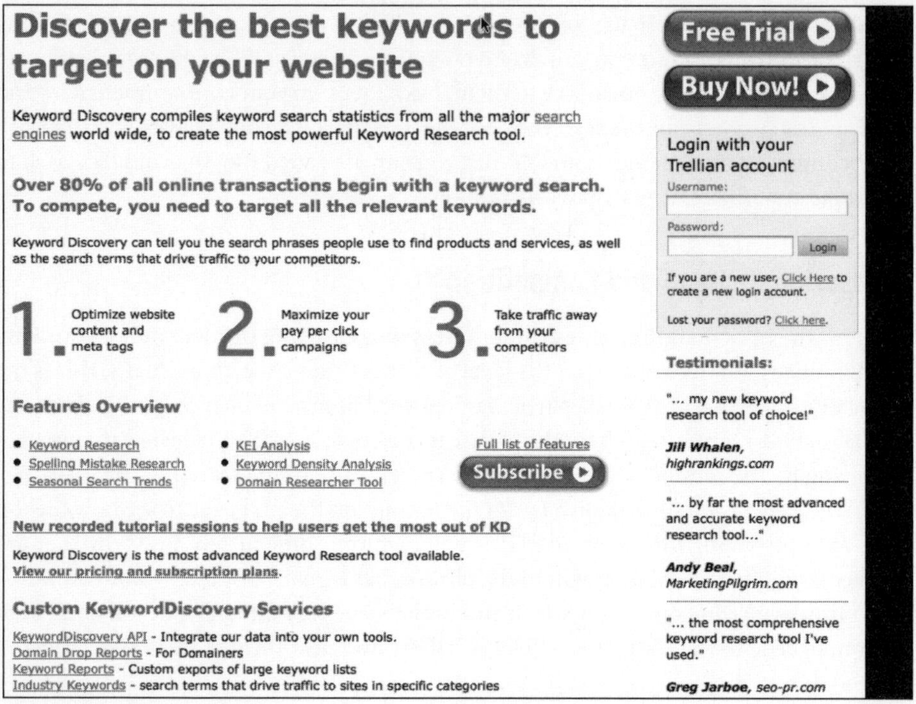

Discover the best keywords to target on your website

Keyword Discovery compiles keyword search statistics from all the major search engines world wide, to create the most powerful Keyword Research tool.

Over 80% of all online transactions begin with a keyword search. To compete, you need to target all the relevant keywords.

Keyword Discovery can tell you the search phrases people use to find products and services, as well as the search terms that drive traffic to your competitors.

1. Optimize website content and meta tags

2. Maximize your pay per click campaigns

3. Take traffic away from your competitors

Features Overview

- Keyword Research
- Spelling Mistake Research
- Seasonal Search Trends

- KEI Analysis
- Keyword Density Analysis
- Domain Researcher Tool

Full list of features

Subscribe ▶

New recorded tutorial sessions to help users get the most out of KD

Keyword Discovery is the most advanced Keyword Research tool available. **View our pricing and subscription plans.**

Custom KeywordDiscovery Services

KeywordDiscovery API - Integrate our data into your own tools.
Domain Drop Reports - For Domainers
Keyword Reports - Custom exports of large keyword lists
Industry Keywords - search terms that drive traffic to sites in specific categories

Free Trial ▶

Buy Now! ▶

Login with your Trellian account
Username:

Password:

Login

If you are a new user, Click Here to create a new login account.

Lost your password? Click here.

Testimonials:

"... my new keyword research tool of choice!"

Jill Whalen,
highrankings.com

"... by far the most advanced and accurate keyword research tool..."

Andy Beal,
MarketingPilgrim.com

"... the most comprehensive keyword research tool I've used."

Greg Jarboe, seo-pr.com

FIGURE 3-1   Keyword Discovery

Wordtracker

Wordtracker been around since 1997 and is recommended by many leading search marketing firms. As the "first mover" in the keyword analysis space, this tool pioneered a unique way of looking at the words we all use to find things on the Internet. Although it's been fourteen years since Wordtracker first came on the scene, it is still highly regarded and does a very good job for thousands of companies across the globe.

It uses what the company calls a "keyword effectiveness index" (KEI) analysis. KEI is a formula that compares the popularity of a keyword phrase (the number of searches that contain the keyword phrase) to its usage popularity (the number of actual web pages it is found on). Although a little confusing at first, it does tell an interesting story. When you go to the site, you'll see that it offers a free trial. Do this. It's a great first exercise for any business looking to get a leg up on its online competitors. Or if you just want to know more about how to optimize your website.

When you try Wordtracker out, it asks you a few questions and goes through a simple process of coming up with a target list of keywords. You'll see the "count" of each keyword. This is simply the number of searches performed for the keyword. You'll also see a KEI for each keyword phrase. Be sure to take some time analyzing what this is telling you. But don't put all of your faith in it. Wordtracker's KEI analysis will tell you that certain keyword phrases are too competitive or popular and steer you away from using them. This isn't always the best advice.

As I mentioned earlier, you want to be found for those wildly popular phrases. Sometimes it will take a while, but you need to face your competitors head on. As we know, there are a lot of things you can do to further optimize your content so that you can *own* that popular keyword phrase! Don't just give up and let your competitors beat you out.

Wordtracker can help determine how many competing sites are using the keywords you're looking at and can identify the phrases that have the greatest traffic potential. Some other things that Wordtracker can help you determine are keyword variations, word variants (example: *dog tags* versus *dog tag*), and managing keyword lists. The cost to use the service is $69 per month or $379 per year, as of November 2011.

How does the tool get its information? Wordtracker periodically compiles a database of over 330 million search terms, which is updated on a weekly basis. All search terms are collected from the major metacrawlers—Dogpile and MetaCrawler. Why do they use these two and not Google? It's because many people use Google to check their rank for a keyword phrase, so it's not a totally accurate measurement of the keyword's popularity.

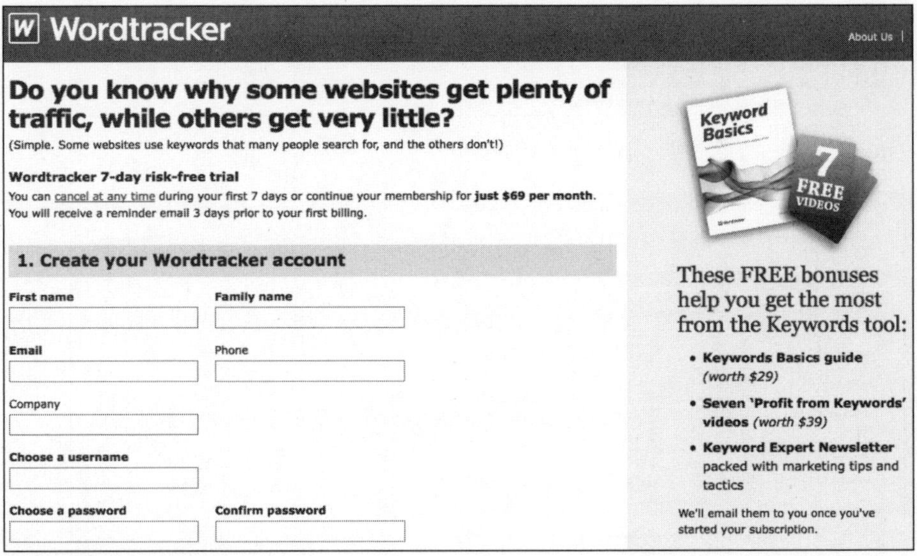

FIGURE 3-2   Wordtracker

Free Keyword Research Tools

There are a few adequate keyword research tools that are free. These include Google AdWords Keyword Tool, Google Insights for Search, and Aaron Wall's Free Keyword List Generator (Located at www.seobook.com). You may also want to check out Aaron Wall's Advanced Keyword Research Tool. Note that with the AdWords tool, you don't get keyword demand. Rather, the tool shows you an estimate of the number of clicks you may receive with an average bid. It does, however, support languages around the world, which appeals to an international audience, especially those interested in paid search.

The others mentioned above are all really cool and worth checking out—you can never have too much information on your keywords.

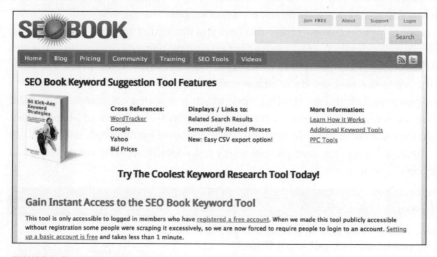

FIGURE 3-3   SEO Book Keyword Tool

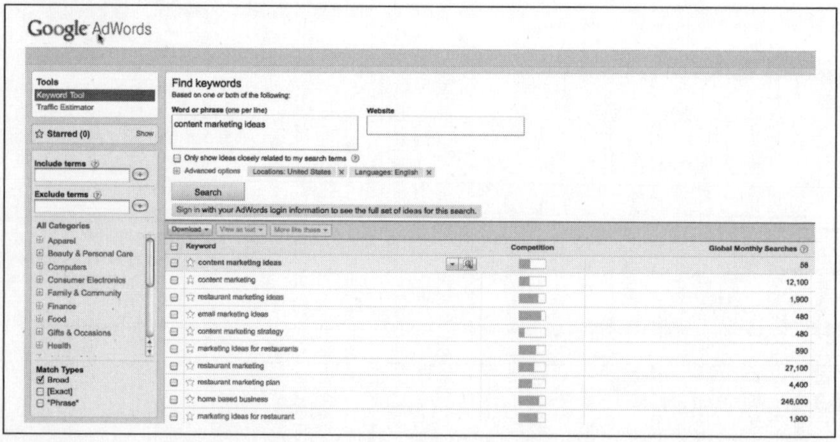

FIGURE 3-4   Google AdWords Keyword Tool

Your Site Search Box

Companies that have that little search box on their sites—the one where you can type a word or two to find things that match those words on the site—have an ulterior motive. Yes, they want to help you find relevant information on the site. But, guess what? They also look at which words people type in that box for keyword research purposes. Knowing what and how visitors query can pay big dividends. I highly recommend you use this strategy on your own site.

FIGURE 3-5   Site Search Box Example

Checking Web Server Log Files

Are you using Google Analytics, WebTrends, ClickTracks, or some other log file analysis software? Mine it! This is great stuff to know. If you are new to this type of software, you should be aware that it can tell you which key phrases users typed into the search engines to find you. No guessing here, no asking users what phrase they searched to find you. Right there in the files will be all the search terms they used. And this is just the tip of the iceberg with these types of software products. If you don't have one installed, seriously consider it. It's another item that's well worth the investment.

Keyword Strategizing and Brainstorming

Talking to your management team about their keyword ideas is a great idea. Get everyone in a room and make a list of potential keywords. Have a lively discussion. One thing is for sure: The list will be longer than the one you wrote out. There are always hidden or forgotten keyword phrases that may be relevant.

Next, you want to get into the strategizing part of the exercise. The first step here is to come up with a complete list of all the keyword nouns. Be sure to remember the basic breakdown: product category, segment of the market, brand names, and individual model names. An example of this would be "truck" (product category), "full size light duty" (segment of the market), "Ford" (brand name), and "F-150" (individual model name). Now, look at the corresponding adjectives for these nouns. And be sure to look at the full spectrum of adjectives, including comparison adjectives (tough light duty truck), qualifier adjectives (heaviest light duty truck), function adjectives (fastest light duty truck), attribute adjectives (2 ton light duty truck) and action adjectives (buy light duty truck).

Finally, think from a creative place. Try to get inside your customer's head; maybe it's someone who has never bought a truck before and is totally new to the truck buying experience. What's going through his mind when he is getting ready to go online and perform a search? What problem is he trying to solve? What does he really want? What will he use in his search? Does the industry use certain jargon or clichés? If you call your product one thing and your customers call it something else, you need to be aware of this. This dynamic is a very common issue. Don't let it happen to you. Uncover the unknown.

Semantically Related Phrases

This is one step many companies miss altogether. Think about other words and phrases that are similar to your main keyword phrases. Words have relationships to other words, so when you think in terms of semantics, you might come up with something like the following: *auto, car, vehicle, motor vehicle, automobile*. These are all semantically related. You could even take the process a step further and look for words and phrases that appear totally different but are very much related. For example, for the main keyword "SEO," you might come up with: *search engine optimization, website promotion, online marketing, search, submission, high ranking*. To see what related terms might be relevant for your products or services, use the Google AdWords Keyword Tool.

How Popular Are Your Keyword Phrases?

Using Google once again, I search for "cars," a very generic one-word keyword phrase. At the top right of the search results page, it says there are 811 million results for "cars." Wow—it would be tough to get ranked well for that keyword phrase, right? Yep. Really tough. Fairly impossible. And how many times was "cars" searched last month worldwide? Millions of times. Another humbling number.

Next, I searched for "family camping tents." I found 618,000 results, which would be much easier to rank for. If you sell tents and need to get a website up, there is hope! Last month this term was searched 6,500 times. Finally, for a full picture of the popularity or lack of popularity of keyword phrases, I typed in "Chesnik Kaleidoscopes." The results there were a whole lot lower: only 530. Super easy to rank for that keyword phrase, but, of course, you wouldn't choose a phrase like that for your optimization efforts because it's the name of a business and its product. But I think you get the idea.

How does this concept apply to your company and your keyword phrases?

Align Keywords with the Customer Buying Cycle and Role-Based Keyword Searches

This is a step that few companies ever take. Of course, we all know that not everyone who jumps on the web or a mobile device is going to buy the very first time. Consumers are really doing one of four things:

- Gathering general information
- Trying to learn about a specific product/service
- Shopping
- Buying

The key thing to know is that for each point in the buying cycle, consumers have a likelihood of using a unique type of keyword phrase. For example, if we are talking about buying a car, a keyword phrase prospective customers may use in the education step would be "2012 best cars." At the shopping stage, they may use "car dealerships in Atlanta." At the buying stage, they may use still another unique keyword phrase, like "Toyota Camry in Atlanta," or they may go back to the dealership's site and buy a car right off the website. Be aware of the customer buying process when you optimize your site's content.

Role-based keyword searching behavior is another interesting SEO dynamic. Basically, it breaks down to this: Who is searching—the president of the company, the market research guy, or the salesperson? For example, what does each use as her keyword phrase and why? You need to align your keyword phrases with the type of people who are seeking you out. Some websites even categorize their product pages by customer role; it just depends on your specific customer set. This concept is worthy of mentioning because it may be a great opportunity for you to write more targeted and specific pages tailored for a particular type of customer.

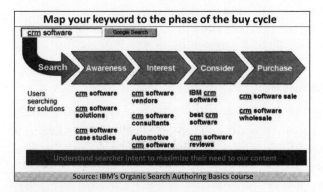

FIGURE 3-6   Mapping Keywords to Buy Cycle

Keyword Density

This represents the percentage of your keyword phrases in your web content. The goal is to make keywords 2 to 4 percent of the total words on the page. This is what Google likes to see. Less than 2 percent, and you probably don't have enough density; above 4 percent, and you could trigger the spam filter. Stay away from that!

Stemming

This is an important concept in keyword research—and also one of the least used and most misunderstood Why? Because Google values sites that use different forms of a certain keyword. And most people are unaware that this is part of the ranking algorithm. What does stemming look like? For *walk*, the forms would be *walked*, *walking*, *walks*, and so on.

The other reason to use stemming is that the same phrase repeated three or four times in the body copy tends to look bad. It's also boring. So, spice up your content with a little stemming.

Look for Emerging Keyword Phrases

We live in a super-fast, turbocharged world. Things are changing all the time. Your competitors are moving, some of them very quickly, to dominate your business. Online, they are going to be coming after you fast on the SEO front. So, ask yourself this question: What are my customers searching for *today* to try to find me? That's the million-dollar question. You'll find that keyword searching evolves over time and new trends can influence the process. What your prospects typed in the Google search box one day might be different the next.

So, what are the emerging keyword phrases for your industry? Stay on top of your competitors' source code and site copy to see what they are using, and then use your due diligence on Keyword Discovery and Wordtracker to see what the latest trend is. Another good idea is to use Google Insights or Google Trends. These are fantastic resources for finding out about the very latest developments.

Keyword use is a moving target. You'll need to optimize your copy based on emerging keyword phrases. Don't let your competitors do it first!

Optimize for Long Tail Keyword Phrases

The "long tail," as popularized by *Wired* magazine editor Chris Anderson in 2004, is defined as this: the idea that companies sell small numbers of hard-to-find items to diverse customers. So, it's selling less of more. What's a long tail keyword phrase? A phrase that is made up of three to six words. Here are a couple of examples: "large inexpensive oil painting" or "grain fed beef from America." There are probably a few dozen or more that would apply to your business. Find out what they are by using the keyword research tools listed in this chapter.

The really great thing about optimizing for long tail keyword phrases is the *high conversion rate*. Because they are so targeted, and people who use them are usually making a buying decision soon, long tail keywords can literally translate to a 30 percent or higher conversion machine for your site. That's the power. Long tail keywords are matching consumers with exactly what you are selling. Plus, they are both descriptive and specific, two key attributes of keyword phrases. And by using long tail keywords, you'll give your site that added variety that Google likes to see.

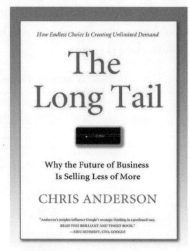

FIGURE 3-7   *The Long Tail* by Chris Anderson

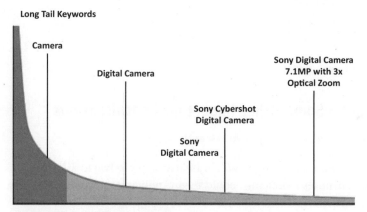

FIGURE 3-8   Long Tail Keywords

Establish New Phrases That No One Is Using Yet

You also want to try to establish new keyword phrases that you can build content around. This could be a phrase that isn't yet used by searchers. Your goal is to build a following around the phrase, so that when it is eventually searched, all the searches will lead right to your site and nowhere else.

The well-regarded online marketing software company HubSpot did this very well with a keyword phrase they coined: "inbound marketing software." Within a few months of launching their site, people were searching for that phrase and HubSpot came up every time, all the time. Pretty cool.

Which keyword phrases lead to conversions? Great question. Check your site analytics program (Google Analytics is great) and logs, and ask your customers. Information is power.

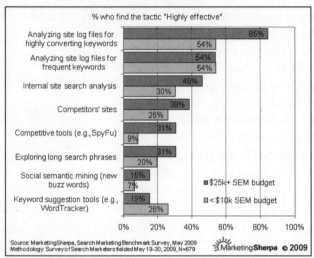

FIGURE 3-9   MarketingSherpa's Tactics for Keyword Research

Keyword Nuances—Some Other Important Considerations

Be aware of these often overlooked keyword research issues:

- Multiple audiences: a certain keyword phrase may apply to two totally different industries or purposes ("policing" could mean "policing the community" or "policing the Internet")
- Related meanings: avoid a broader term ("warranties") when a more specific one is accurate ("home warranties")
- Acronyms: beware of double meanings in your keywords; spell them out as often as possible (use "Internet Service Provider" not ISP)
- Use synonyms and other related words
- Plural/singular issues: "trucks" and "truck"—there are differences; when in doubt, optimize for the plural form and that will capture the singular form too
- Multiple intents: "hotel" and "lodging"—they may mean the same thing to you, but according to some studies, the term "hotel" will have a higher conversion rate
- Boldface type: helps visitors see the phrases they searched for and may be recognized by Google, too; don't overuse it though, just a few times is enough

Finally, in your goal to harmonize your content, you want to always be thinking "keywords." Look for those general nouns like "balloons," "cars," and "rings," and think, Is there a more descriptive way to describe these things, maybe a way that incorporates a keyword or two? How about "hot air balloons," "formula one race cars," and "diamond solitaire engagement rings"? Presto, you've just used your keyword phrases. Now do it again and again.

One additional note: Keyword research is an ongoing process that never ends. It's always evolving. And if you start offering a new product or service, be sure to do new research to account for this.

Keyword Relevant Content for e-Commerce

If you run an e-commerce site, you have probably struggled with search engine optimization (SEO). With all your content-light navigational pages and product pages, which are prone to content duplication, it's challenging to give Google the relevant, unique content it wants. Throw in the fact that many of your affiliates or partners are using the same content on their sites, and you start to have a real problem. There are things you can do, however, to develop content that connects with both your prospects and the search engines. What are they?

1. **Write category descriptions.** Let me guess: Your category pages have little or no content, right? If you are like most e-commerce sites, these pages are populated with lots of images and links but limited copy.

How do you correct this? Write descriptions or introductory copy for each category. Whether this shows up above or below the product listings doesn't really matter. Google needs to see solid keyword-influenced content on these pages. And be sure to use your primary or more general keyword phrases here. Make this happen, and you are well on your way to fixing the issue.

2. **Rewrite product descriptions.** Remember our earlier discussion of "long tail" keywords? These are phrases like "large dog bones for great danes" or "safe toys for young children." Your product pages are a great spot for these types of keyword phrases. You want to eliminate the manufacturer-provided descriptions that so many e-commerce sites use. This is duplicate content in the search engines' eyes, and they don't like it.

So, take some time, rewrite your most important product pages with unique product descriptions, and optimize them for those extended keyword phrases. You could see some huge SEO improvements in short order.

3. **Write buyer guides.** Your customers want to know everything about your products before they buy. If they get that information from your site, chances are, they'll buy from you. How can you best accomplish this? Write a bunch of buyer guides for your most popular products. What do your customers need to know? How can they

use the product in their lives? Answer these types of questions in your buyer guides and then be sure to optimize them for primary or secondary keywords.

4. **Include expert product reviews.** Product reviews drive solid rankings in the search engines. Why? People are *looking* for reviews. They get a great deal of information from them, especially when they are researching a product. If you can have your best customers write keyword-targeted content for your site, you could get dozens of new pages ranked fairly quickly.

Competitive Research

There is lots of stuff that you'll need to do to monitor your competition, much more than this book covers. But from a content perspective, there are things you'll want to stay tuned into and be aware of so you can respond or make changes to your site, blog, or social media profiles as well. After all, you don't want to be late to the party if there is a new industry development.

Having said this, I want to reiterate something: Focus more on developing what you are as a business, stay on task with your content plan, and move forward assertively to stake your claim. Focusing too much on the competition can become an obsessive practice and can take your eye off the ball.

The factors you'll want to be dialed into, however, are the following:

- How your competitors rank in the search engines
- What types of free (and paid) content they use
- Webinars and other lead-generation content they use
- Their social media presence
- Their blog

All of this can help you in your quest to dominate the space!

Analyzing Your Competitors' Keyword Phrases

This is something we have done ever since we opened our doors. If you want to increase your sales and improve your business, you've got to know what your competitors are doing with keywords, right? As you make changes to your offerings, so do they. Things are always moving, positions are always being jockeyed for, new markets are always in play. At the same time, your competitors may make some mistakes, as you could too. The nice thing about the web is that it lends itself very well to checking your competitors' keyword phrases (and other important items)!

How do you do this? Just jump on a competitor's site, right click on the home page, and click on "View source code." Near the top of the code that pops up, you'll see "Meta tags." You'll want to look at these, especially the title, description, and keyword tags. This is where you'll see the keyword phrases your competition is optimizing for on the page. Check all their pages. If they are using the same meta tag phrases on all their pages, then you have an advantage, because that's a big mistake (and one we see a lot).

If it's your first time checking a competitive site, you'll be surprised how easy it is to acquire this information. You couldn't do this with your competitors in the pre-Internet days. In addition to checking their HTML code behind the scenes, you also want to be diligent in checking their inclusion of keyword phrases on their site. See where keywords appear and how often they're used.

A couple of things to keep in mind: Your competitors don't always know what they are doing. They could be making the same mistakes you are. Or, they could know exactly what they are doing. Are they checking you out? Assume they are, because it probably is the case. The other word of caution is to check more than just a couple of competitors. I would check nearly everyone on the first three pages for your most popular keyword phrases. It just makes sense to do a comprehensive job in this area. What you find out could be very interesting and could help you compete more effectively in the content age!

FIGURE 3-10   View Source Code Pop-Up Window

```
<!DOCTYPE html PUBLIC "-//W3C//DTD XHTML 1.0 Strict//EN" "http://www.w3.org/TR/xhtml1/DTD/xhtml1-strict.
<html xmlns="http://www.w3.org/1999/xhtml" xml:lang="en" lang="en" dir="ltr">

<head>
<meta http-equiv="Content-Type" content="text/html; charset=utf-8" />
 <title>Web Content Development | Web Copywriting | Content Marketing Services</title>
 <meta http-equiv="Content-Type" content="text/html; charset=utf-8" />
<meta name="description" content="Content Launch is the leading web content development firm worldwide.
<link rel="shortcut icon" href="/sites/default/files/content launch favicon.png" type="image/x-icon" />
  <link type="text/css" rel="stylesheet" media="all" href="/sites/default/files/css/css b492b1536eca6327
<link type="text/css" rel="stylesheet" media="print" href="/sites/default/files/css/css 135d0364dc21d388
<!--[if IE]>
<link type="text/css" rel="stylesheet" media="all" href="/sites/all/themes/content_launch/css/ie.css?a"
<![endif]-->
<!--[if lte IE 6]>
<link type="text/css" rel="stylesheet" media="all" href="/sites/all/themes/content_launch/css/ie6.css?a"
<![endif]-->
  <script type="text/javascript" src="/sites/default/files/js/js 5a67bae24b3122a3f4f1b35d8653651d.js"></
<script type="text/javascript">
<!--//--><![CDATA[//><!--
jQuery.extend(Drupal.settings, { "basePath": "/", "googleanalytics": { "trackOutgoing": 1, "trackMailto"
//--><!]]>
```

FIGURE 3-11   Source HTML Code for a Web Page

Keyword Density and Prominence Analyzer

Ranks.nl is a fantastic tool for these important keyword research activities. Essentially, you can use this tool to "spy" on your competition and find out which phrases they are best optimized for. When using the tool, you want a keyword prominence of 80 percent or more to help determine the appropriate topic for your page.

Ranks.nl has had one of the best page analyzers on the web since 2001, and is recommended by many in the search marketing industry. For more experienced search engine optimizers, it's great for verifying the work you have done. For beginners, it's a great tool that helps show the reasons that a page is ranking well—or not.

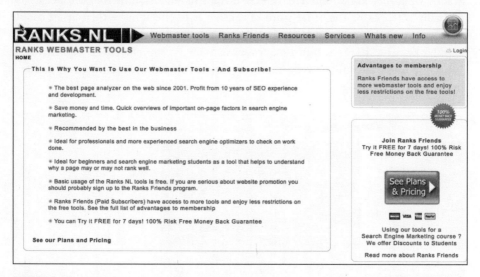

FIGURE 3-12   Ranks.nl

CASE STUDY: The Power of Keyword Research and Optimization for a Local Company

Dan Walton and Joanne Connerty, co-owners of Studio Blue (www.studiobluepdx.com), a Pilates studio based in Portland, Oregon, weren't seeing much search engine "love." When they did a search in Google for terms like "Portland Pilates," their site was nowhere to be found.

At first, Walton and Connerty turned to PPC and Citysearch, spending over five hundred dollars per month on advertising. Because Studio Blue was a new studio (launched in 2007), the company had limited advertising funds and was looking for creative solutions.

Walton and Connerty had heard about search engine optimization (SEO), but the costs were prohibitive for their small business budget. Vendors were quoting monthly contract prices of four hundred dollars or more, on top of the money they were spending on PPC. Rather than hire a vendor, they decided to learn more about SEO and see if they could handle it in-house.

One of their clients happened to be SEO copy expert Heather Lloyd-Martin, CEO of SuccessWorks. Lloyd-Martin realized that making small changes to Studio Blue's content could mean big ranking changes. The site's original content contained very few keywords, reducing the opportunity for a prime search engine position. For instance, the web copy read "our classes" rather than "our Pilates mat classes." Conducing keyword research and rewriting the content, as well as creating keyword-rich, clickable titles, would increase Studio Blue's search engine position.

"Many small business websites have great web copy—it just isn't written with SEO in mind. Revising the copy and adding key phrases can result in huge ranking increases, as well as increases in conversion rates," said Lloyd-Martin. Walton and Connerty took Lloyd-Martin's online SEO copywriting training class and learned how to write effective SEO copy. Specific changes they made included:

- Creating a keyword list before they started writing. Walton and Connerty assumed that people were searching under "Pilates," but they didn't know that they'd have to make their keywords geographically specific ("Portland OR Pilates"). Keyword research also helped them find other related keywords, such as "Portland mat classes."
- Making sure that each page was "themed" around related keywords. Once they had their keyword list, Walton and Connerty matched keywords to related pages and included those words or phrases in the content. For instance, Walton and Connerty used the keywords "Portland mat classes" on the "mat classes" page.
- Creating highly "clickable" titles. The first opportunity for conversion is the search engine results page, so Walton and Connerty knew that how the title (the blue clickable link on the search engine results page) appeared to the reader was extremely important. They spent time creating benefit-rich titles, including phrases such as "Free Pilates mat classes." This helps their listing stand out on the search results page (and encourages people to click).

(continued)

CASE STUDY: *Continued*

Today, Studio Blue ranks in the top ten for a variety of keywords, including:

- Pilates Portland
- Reformer classes Portland
- Mat classes Portland

Now, approximately 80 percent of all new clients find Studio Blue through a search engine, resulting in approximately thirty new clients every month. Additionally, because Studio Blue was doing so well in Google's organic listings, Walton was also able to reduce his PPC and advertising costs by 50 percent. Most important, when Walton and Connerty redesigned and relaunched their site, they were able to write all the copy themselves—and feel confident while doing it.

So, what's stopping you from attaining higher keyword rankings? Well, nothing is stopping you now. You have the bible of online content right here in your hands. But, hang on, there are a few more important steps. Now you know which keywords you want to use, but how do you place them in your website content? Good question . . . let's get right into that. Time to optimize!

CHAPTER 4

Optimizing Your Web Content

There's no doubt about it: the search engines, especially Google, have revolutionized global commerce in the short fifteen or so years they have been around. Everything—absolutely everything—about business has changed in their wake. From starting a new business to marketing your business to growing your business, it all is much easier than it ever was before. And we have Google to thank for that. Its rise has been the stuff of business folklore. Like Apple and Microsoft before it, and Facebook and Twitter in recent years, Google came out of nowhere. It was fueled by little more than great ideas, a revolutionary approach, and two very smart guys from Stanford.

But understanding how rankings work is challenging, even for the most experienced search engine marketers. And with mobile coming on strong, it's even tougher to get a handle on all this stuff. Producing the content is one thing. Optimizing it so it shows up in search engines is something altogether different.

Here's the deal: When you put a piece of content together, it doesn't do any good unless people see it and act on it. This is what the search engines do—*they get content to the people*. They are the distributors of your content!

What can be ranked in search engines? Well, remember that list we started the book with?

- Blog posts
- Website pages
- YouTube videos
- E-books
- Case studies
- Podcasts
- Webinars
- E-newsletters
- Digital magazines
- Press releases
- Articles
- White papers
- Content widgets
- E-mails
- Autoresponders
- Newsletters

Practically all of these can be optimized for search! Note: The only ones that aren't subject to optimization are the last three: autoresponders, e-mails, and newsletters. These are sent out through your e-mail marketing program or CRM system.

It's true that not everyone will find your site or other web content through search engines. Some prospects will find out about you through an event or from traditional advertising like a TV commercial or a magazine ad. Many people will find your content through social networking sites. This channel of "first discovery" is growing rapidly, of course. And some have even predicted the demise of the search engines because of the time and attention that people devote to Facebook, Twitter, and the like. I say NO WAY. There is absolutely no indication that Google will be stepping aside any time soon. In fact, it is finding ways to take market share *away* from Facebook, though alas, that's a topic for another book! There's never a dull moment in the digital marketing space. So let's get into the heart of SEO. We covered it early on, but for our purposes here: What exactly is search engine optimization, or SEO, and what are we talking about when we say "optimizing" web content?

> With search engine optimization, you use certain techniques to improve the rankings of your site, blog, articles, e-books and other web content on search engines. These techniques may include editing or adding to HTML code, working with site navigation features, employing linking strategies, and including compelling web content.

In this book, I cover all of the details of the web content piece of SEO, which I believe is the most important. Why? Because it all starts with content, it will always be about content, and content is truly the way we connect with other people. We don't connect with them through HTML code (at least directly).

And here is the link missing from other books in this genre: you cannot, I repeat cannot, have a discussion about content, content marketing, content strategy, social media marketing, or mobile marketing without talking about SEO. It's just that simple. The problem is that almost all other books simply gloss over the topic. Some actually leave it out, which is a big mistake. In *Content Is Currency*, you'll find everything you need to know so you can compete more effectively with your content!

The goal for your website? To rank on the first page of Google (and the other search engines) for **fifty** of your top keyword phrases. In fact, this goal is so important that I want you to write it down and pin it up on a bulletin board so you can see it every day. This means that if, for example, you sell dog and cat toys, you're going to be on that coveted first page of Google's search results for "dog and cat toys," "fun toys for dogs," "soft toys for dogs," "toys for pets," "puppy toys," and forty-five other phrases.

The mission has been assigned. And you won't stop until you get there, right? Okay, good. I'm happy. (Note that the primary focus in this chapter will be the optimization of your *website content*. For all other content types, we discuss specific SEO (and SMO) strategies in their respective chapters.)

Search Engine Ranking Factors—SEOmoz Study

When it comes to content optimization, a good place to start is with a study[11] that SEOmoz did in 2011. It has been widely used, quoted, and talked about, just like it was in 2009 when they published their first version. SEOmoz, led by industry veteran Rand Fishkin, is one of the leading SEO software providers, and Rand is a true thought leader in the space. Essentially, the study looked at all the potential search engine ranking factors. Here are the five most important ones:

1. Page level link metrics
2. Domain level link authority features
3. Page level keyword usage
4. Domain level keyword usage
5. Page level social metrics

This simple, five-point list should be nailed to your wall somewhere; it's that important. Like others, I've done the research, too. I have used these tactics with our clients. And the bottom line is that it's the current gold standard for content optimization. I recommend visiting www.seomoz.org to review it in detail.

FIGURE 4-1   SEOmoz Search Ranking Factors

---

[11] SEOmoz. "Search Engine 2011 Ranking Factors." Accessed 6/14/11. http://www.seomoz.org/article/search-ranking-factors.

When you look at the list, what you see right away is the word *link*. It's the *top two* points on the list. Clearly, it's really important. When other sites post links to your site, they are, in effect, casting a vote for your site. But what *is* a high-quality external link?

> An external link is a hyperlink that points at your domain from another site, a site that is relevant and highly ranked by the search engines.

And how about "keyword-focused anchor text"? What's that? Essentially, it means using a keyword phrase that's important to you as the hyperlink itself instead of using your URL or other text. If "*content management software*" is the most important keyword phrase for you, then this is what you would want an external site to use when they link to you. When someone is on that site and is intrigued by "content management software," she would simply click on the link and within two seconds be delivered to your site. Isn't the web great?

Figure 4-2 shows an example of an anchor text link that takes the reader to a specific page when she clicks on it.

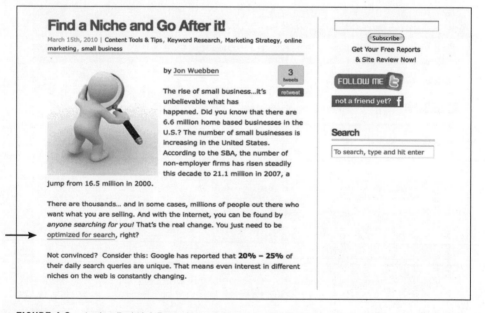

FIGURE 4-2   Anchor Text Link Example

The challenge, of course, is that getting links like this can be really tough. It is, in fact, the most difficult part of the online marketing game. But here is the secret: **Great content will bring the high-quality links *to you*!** So, that's exactly what you are going to do: After reading this book, you're going to produce some incredible, link-friendly content.

Writing for the Search Engines *and* for People

Keep in mind, you are still doing two things at once with your content: writing for the search engines *and* writing for people. Google is looking for certain things on your site that humans are not—that's just the plain and simple truth.

But how are people's and search engines' needs different? How do you write for both at the same time? Why do we have to be concerned? These are all questions that we will answer. Know that if you are looking for one golden rule of content development on the web, it is this: Develop for people first, search engines second.

Let's take a minute to understand how search engines work, exactly.

The ABCs of SEO

How do search engines work? I'll put it to you plainly first, and then we'll get into some technical detail. I think it's pretty important to understand this stuff, inside and out. And again, I'll say it once, and I'll say it again: I am shocked to see how few businesses know these details about search engine optimization. Whether I'm at a Chamber of Commerce event or a trade show, or am interacting with prospective clients online, I see a huge "knowledge gap" when it comes to SEO. So let's settle that right now.

The basic process:

1. Search engines analyze words on web pages
2. The engines record these words
3. When people type words into a search field, the engines try to match the words typed with the words they recorded, delivering a list of relevant sites
4. The engines provide a list of what they believe are the very best matches for the search based on certain criteria

Your goal? To be one of those sites the engines provide. You can ensure this by taking the steps I outline in this book (among many other things, such as link building). Remember, **people usually don't go past page three in the search results**. So if your site is listed on page four (or page ten), you probably won't get much traffic. That's why we are going to teach you how to get on page one. Your two best content strategies to accomplish this are:

1. To have valuable, interesting content that people like and want to link to
2. To understand which words (keywords) people use in their searches to find you, and then to use those words in the content and in the metadata.

Because we know that links are really important for your SEO effort, it's helpful to understand where you could do some easy linking research. The best thing you can do is use Yahoo! Site Explorer (http://siteexplorer.search.yahoo.com) to find the sources of your *competitor's* links. Reviewing this will show you where you should get links, too. It will shorten the process and get you started quickly.

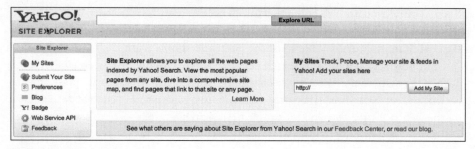

FIGURE 4-3   Yahoo! Site Explorer

Filtering and Ranking

The search engines—Google, Yahoo!, and Bing—are huge players in the overall Internet industry. Everything they do (especially Google) impacts the web in big ways. Fifteen years ago, they were practically nonexistent. Today, they are not only the key movers and shakers on the web, they are giant multinational companies that wield great power. So what do you need to know to understand how to work with the search engines? How do they set the rules of the game?

Your first priority, of course, is to get your site ranked. This can be a challenge if you're just starting out. I remember when I launched my first site way back when, not really understanding SEO at the time. My site designer didn't know much about the optimization process either. So my site wasn't optimized, and because I didn't use keyword phrases in my copy, it didn't rank. At all. I would search over and over again, week after week, and wonder why my site wouldn't come up. I finally woke up one day, discovered search engine optimization, and changed my entire strategy. I rewrote my site copy, changed designers, and came out with a totally new site. Within a few weeks, I was ranking for "seo copywriting," "website copywriter," and others.

Once you finish your site and it gets indexed by Google, Yahoo!, and Bing, you are in the game. Then it's all about making it better, improving your rankings as much as possible. So, what are the criteria the search engines use to make decisions about which sites get placed where? They do this by using *filtering and ranking*.

With filtering, search engines decide which pages are in the search results and which are not. If you meet their criteria, you will be filtered into the results. Essentially, the search engines filter by language, character, and country. They also filter by picture, image, presentation, and so on. If you are writing English content for your website, you don't have to be too concerned with filtering.

With ranking, search engines order results by relevance to decide which pages get to be at the top of the list. Because ranking issues are so important when it comes to content, this is the area we'll discuss the most.

The Ranking Algorithm

Without getting into too much detail, a search engine algorithm is a complex mathematical formula that determines how web pages are ranked. So if you have a site that sells handbags, and "handbags" is the keyword, how does Google's ranking algorithm deal with it? Well, it will look at all the indexed pages for the word "handbags" and determine which pages are the most relevant or "important" for that word. The ones that are the most relevant will end up on the first page of the search results. What factors go into the algorithm? That's a closely guarded secret within the hallowed halls of Google's corporate headquarters. And it changes all the time.

There are probably more than a hundred factors that go into the final equation. Most of them, you don't have to worry about—you wouldn't know what they are anyway. But, there are many well-known factors that you can influence directly through the power of optimized content. The list from the SEOmoz study at the beginning of this chapter summarized it, but let's take a deeper dive.

Factors That Help Your Page Rank Well

Yes, the search engines can be a mystery, but there are many helpful guidelines to keep in mind as you seek to rank well with them. What are the important factors?

PageRank

Google's "PageRank" is the most well known page factor. If you aren't aware of it, it's the little horizontal bar on the Google Toolbar that displays a web page's importance, shown by a strength indicator in the bar that ranks from one to ten. A score of ten would be assigned to a very important site, a score of zero to a totally unimportant one. A page that has good PageRank would have a score of five or six. A site like Yahoo! or Amazon would have a score of ten. By definition, "page" factors consider anything the search engine knows about the page, the site, and the other sites that link to that page.

PageRank is not as popular as it used to be, and even Google downplays it, but I believe it is still a helpful tool to look at when you are wondering if a certain site is a "fly by night" company or one that is truly the "real deal." Here is what Google says about it:

> PageRank relies on the uniquely democratic nature of the web by using its vast link structure as an indicator of an individual page's value. In essence, Google interprets a link from page A to page B as a vote, by page A for page B. But, Google looks at more than the sheer volume of votes, or links, a page

receives; it also analyzes the page that casts the vote. Votes cast by pages that are themselves "important" weigh more heavily and help to make other pages important.

Now that you know this, let's get into the specific content-related factors that will help you.

The Query Ranking Factor

Why is it called the query ranking factor? Because the search or "query" that someone types into Google determines what pages come up. You, in turn, can do certain things on your page with your content to make sure your page is ranked high. The most important and most basic thing to understand? The keyword phrase has to be used in certain places on your page in order for the page to rank.

So what are all the other query factors that play an important part in your site content?

Keyword Frequency

Keyword frequency refers to the number of times your keyword phrase occurs on the page. Typically, you are looking for the keyword phrase to be used at least three times throughout the page (assuming 250 to 400 words per page). You'll probably have a couple more keyword phrases that you'll want to use, too, so if you have a total of three keyword phrases, that makes nine places that you'll be using your phrases on a certain page.

On the other side of the equation, don't use your keyword too frequently—that's called keyword *spamming*. Not only is it a bad idea, but people reading the content will be turned off; worse yet, it could get you banned from the search engine.

One little secret, and this is something you don't hear about often: You don't want to repeat the exact keyword phrase time after time throughout the content. Rather, you want to use some *variations* on the phrase. What do I mean? If your keyword phrase is "portable poker tables," you want to also use "poker tables that are portable" and maybe "poker table portability." One caveat, however: Your first priority should be to use the complete original phrase, but you can work in the variations as well and still get search engine ranking benefits.

Keyword Density

Taking the idea of keyword use a step further, let's consider keyword density. The density is the percentage of the total words on the page divided by the number of times the keyword phrase appears. What do the search engines look for on keyword density? Between 2 and 4 percent. So, if you have three hundred words on the page, you'll want the keyword phrases to occur two or three times. When working with your keywords in the copy, make sure all those keyword phrases are spaced out well. You don't want it to look forced.

Remember, you want your copy to read as if the prospective customer is having a conversation with you. If the keyword phrase is "Christmas wreaths," you definitely wouldn't write this on your site:

> We sell decorative Christmas wreaths that are guaranteed to last thirty years or more; our Christmas wreaths are made from the finest materials and our Christmas wreaths are shipped to your door within two days. Would you like to buy one of our Christmas wreaths?

I think you get the point.

Aligning with the Searcher's Intent

If you search for "iPod product guide," you'll probably get a PDF document in your search results. This is Google trying to match the results with what you intended to find. People search for a variety of reasons, but if you were to break it down to the most essential reasons, they would be:

- For information
- To purchase or perform a transaction
- To navigate, looking for the home page of a certain site

You want to try to match your intention for a particular page with the searcher's intention. This can be done very easily if you write the content with the searcher in mind. As time goes on, there will be more and more emphasis on this type of personalization and customization with the search engines.

The Process for Page Optimization

The basic process for page optimization is this: Choose your page, write the content, analyze the page's performance, and then improve the page if necessary. If you continue to be unsatisfied with how it is doing, just keep tweaking it until you have what you want.

Of course, you'll need to put it in perspective. If you are going up against some tough competition with a popular keyword phrase, you may never get to the first page of the search engine results. You need to be realistic. It can be a frustrating process, but one that could provide great rewards. With my first site, it took a long time to get to the top spot on Google for "website copywriting," but once I did, it was a great feeling. Once we got there, we stayed in the top spot for more than five years, which brought in lots of new business—for free!

Optimizing a Web Page

So, how do you start? First, look at your keyword phrases. You probably have a list of at least a hundred. If you are a large company with many products or services, you could have several hundred. You'll have *general keyword phrases* and *more specific* phrases. You'll see phrases that seem like they would go together, and some that are more popular than others.

If you are a watch retailer and you're working on your home page, you'll optimize for "watches," "watch accessories," and "watches for sale." If you are writing the products page, you might optimize for more specific types of watches like "Rolex watches," "Tag Heuer watches" and "Breitling watches," for example. Some keywords will appear on multiple pages. If you are an exclusive Rolex watch retailer, "Rolex watches" could appear on the home page and on the products page.

There will always be a phrase or two that won't seem to fit on any page—just because the phrase came up as a potentially good one during the keyword research process does not mean you have to use it. One thing you can do is search for that phrase on Google and see how other sites are using it; this may help get the ideas flowing. If you can't find a way to make it fit, don't force it. If you can create a new page, however, and find enough to write about around that phrase, then definitely do it. You could generate new traffic to your website in a very short amount of time using that keyword phrase.

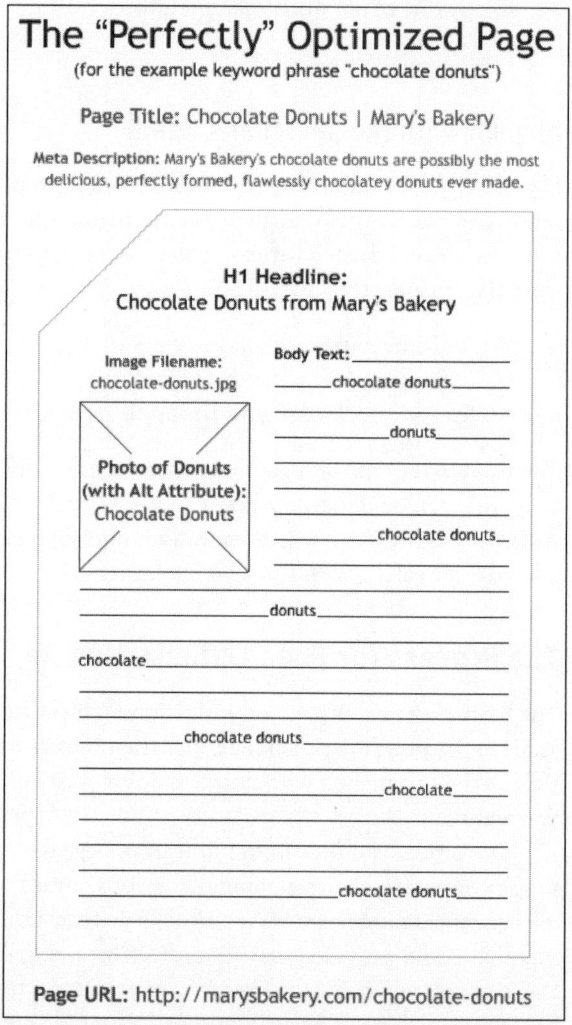

The "Perfectly" Optimized Page
(for the example keyword phrase "chocolate donuts")

Page Title: Chocolate Donuts | Mary's Bakery

Meta Description: Mary's Bakery's chocolate donuts are possibly the most delicious, perfectly formed, flawlessly chocolatey donuts ever made.

H1 Headline:
Chocolate Donuts from Mary's Bakery

Image Filename: chocolate-donuts.jpg

Photo of Donuts (with Alt Attribute): Chocolate Donuts

Body Text: _____
_____chocolate donuts_____
_____donuts_____
_____
_____
_____chocolate donuts__
_____
_____donuts_____
chocolate_____
_____chocolate donuts_____
_____chocolate_____
_____
_____chocolate donuts_____

Page URL: http://marysbakery.com/chocolate-donuts

FIGURE 4-4 Web Page Showing Important Placement of Keywords

One of the goals is to match a set of keyword phrases to what that page is specifically about. If you are a fish market and you have a product page on shellfish, you want to use the same shellfish-themed keyword phrases like "fresh lobster," "soft shell crab," and "fresh ocean shellfish" all on that page. The more general keyword phrase "San Diego fish market," for contrast purposes, would go on the home page.

Keyword Extensions/Building Out More Pages

If you want to really give your keywords power and you have lots of one type of item, be sure to build out additional pages to support all the variants of a keyword group.

Example: If you are a retailer of all types of beauty products, here is a sample list of keywords you could use to build out new pages:

- Facial cosmetics
- Cosmetics for teens
- Women's cosmetics
- Men's cosmetics
- Organic cosmetics
- Hypoallergenic cosmetics

All you need to do is build a unique page for each and then on the facial cosmetics page, for example, use even more specific keyword phrases within that phrase, such as "facial cleansing cosmetics," "facial exfoliating cosmetics," etc.

It's all about starting from the very general keyword phrases (reserved for your doorway or entry pages like home and products pages), and then getting more and more specific with the keyword phrases as you work your way down the site navigation layers.

Headings and Subheadings

Besides making headings and subheadings short, snappy, and memorable, as we learned in an earlier chapter, you'll also want to use keyword phrases here and bring up a benefit if possible. If you can do all that, you are doing well.

For blog posts, heading tags (tags act just like keywords) help you to structure the content of your blog post. The main benefits of using these tags are to inform search engines about the topics you covered in your post. Your reader will also have a nice, scannable title to see. Bottom line: If you use keywords in your heading, whether it's a blog post or web page, you will definitely attract visitors as well as search engines.

Example:

Blog Title Example: *How to Use Keywords Effectively in Your Blog Posts*
"Use Keywords in Blog Posts" is the keyword phrase.

Bold and Italicized Keywords

Have you been on a site and observed that some of the words are boldfaced and/or italicized? These actions help a little bit because the words stand out to visitors, which in turn motivate the search engines to give them more consideration, too.

So what's the strategy here? Try it out. Boldface a few of your keyword phrases or other important words. Don't go overboard, though. You don't want to highlight too many words, or they won't stand out.

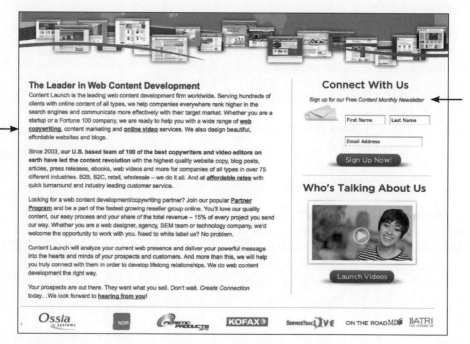

FIGURE 4-5   Web Page Showing Use of Internal Linking, Boldface, and Italics

Internal Linking

Internal links are links that lead from one page on your site to a different page on your site. They are commonly used in main navigation. These types of links are useful because they:

- Help users navigate your website
- Establish information hierarchy for the given website
- Improve your SEO efforts by providing "link juice"

The reason internal links help with SEO is because they help the spiders do their job of crawling through the site. Search engines need to see content in order to list pages in their index. With a crawlable link structure, using internal links, they can find all of the pages on a website. So, if you are a paint retailer, you want to provide internal links on your home page to "residential home painting" and "commercial home painting" in the body text of the page. These could be important keyword phrases for your retail products and for the services that you provide. Doing this will help the search engines to "see" the pages.

In terms of the first point—internal links are useful because they help users navigate your website—you'll want to consider your linking strategy. You could use internal links to:

- Drive users to tasks that support fulfillment of business objectives
- Steer users toward additional, related information that may support their decision-making processes
- Offer relevant pieces of information that will further engage the user in your brand experience
- Encourage users to join an online community, participate in a social media channel, or comment on a blog[12]

We discussed writing good call to action content in Chapter 2, but it's worth mentioning here because, typically, your call to action will come toward the end of the page, which is a great place for keyword phrases.

Metadata

Meta tags are one of the most misunderstood parts of the optimization process. For the sake of clear understanding, we're going to make it very simple. First, what are they?

> Meta tags are code that is found both in the HTML pages of your site architecture *and* in what you see displayed on the page when you do a search.

There are two important meta tags: the title tag and the description tag. The title tag uses two to three keyword phrases and/or benefits to tell the searcher what the page is about. It can read almost like a headline—this will motivate people to click on it. If you are thinking about using your company name in the title, you should reconsider; this is valuable real estate. Are people searching under your company name? Most likely not.

The description tag goes one step further and explains in a little more detail about that page and what the company is offering. Two important points on meta tags: Every page should have unique tags, with unique keyword phrases, and you want to write them with the idea that you are trying to "sell" that person on clicking to find out more. Basically, it's a little ad that is out there on the web, bringing your clients

---

[12] Halvorson, Kristina. 2009. *Content Strategy for the Web*. New Riders Press, Berkeley, CA.

in. Often, it's the first thing people see about your site, so you want to make sure your tags are right.

Want to see something interesting? Jump on to Google and type in "site:www.yourdomain.com"—fill in "yourdomain" with your site's URL. What pops up are all your titles and descriptions for pages indexed by Google. Are they all the same? That needs to change! Every page needs unique titles and descriptions.

To illustrate the use of meta tags further, here are the home page meta tags for my company, along with what actually displays in Google and Yahoo! for that page:

Home page:

META TAGS

<title>Web Content Development | Web Copywriting | Content Marketing Services</title>

<meta name="description" content="Content Launch is the leading web content development firm worldwide. Offering web copywriting, blog posts, articles, press releases, web content marketing & strategy services, online videos and more, our high quality, search engine optimized content converts prospects into customers. Get your free content marketing kit and website analysis today.">

Google:

Web Content Development | Web Copywriting | Content Marketing Services

Content Launch is the leading web content development firm worldwide. Offering web copywriting, blog posts, articles, press releases, web content marketing . . .

www.contentlaunch.com/—Cached

Yahoo!:

Web Content Development | Web Copywriting | Content Marketing . . .

Content Launch is the leading web content development firm worldwide. Offering web copywriting, blog posts, articles, press releases, web content marketing & strategy . . .

contentlaunch.com—Cached

Experiment with your tags, and don't stop until they are working well for you. Getting these right is going to make a big long-term impact on your site—and on your online profits! And remember, make your keyword phrases very specific. If you currently say "our vacation packages," use "our Bahamas island vacation packages" instead. If you are selling "day spa services," use that as your keyword phrase instead of simply "services."

Snippet Content

The "snippet" is the text that appears underneath the title on the search engine results page. Some people read snippets, others scan them, and some don't look at them at all. But you know what? If it's written well, this little group of words can get people to click on the link to your web page/site. Google and Yahoo! usually just take a small chunk of text from your page and use that as the snippet. Google's are usually shorter than Yahoo!'s, and Yahoo! will often use the description tag. Bing's snippets work like Google's.

One way you can influence snippets is by writing solid content on the page: benefits-oriented, keyword-rich content that can convert as well as be great description tag copy. Influencing the snippet copy is one of those things people usually miss when they are thinking about improving their website.

How else can you influence your snippet? For Yahoo!, place your keyword phrases together near the beginning of the description. For Google, do the same thing, but in the body text, or main copy section of the page. How long are snippets, usually? Around 150 characters.

One last secret: Place a benefit statement next to your keyword phrase in the snippet. Here's an example for the keyword phrase "art supplies":

The most extensive art supplies online

. . . Stop searching. All your paintbrushes, oil paints, and other art supplies are available in one place. Free shipping! www.NelsonBrothersArtSupplies.com/ 35K—Cached

"Free shipping" is, of course, your benefit statement/call to action. Try this technique out!

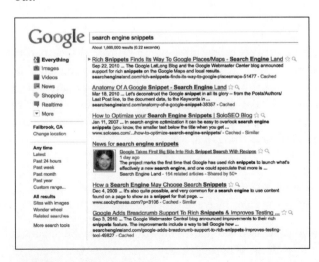

FIGURE 4-6   Snippet Example

Alt Text and Text Hidden in Images

You know those big, beautiful images you see on the fashion or department store websites? Did you know that they are almost always invisible to the search engine spiders? It's true, and most people don't realize the impact. They may even be using their keyword phrases on the site. But it's not going to do them any good with the search engine spiders.

How can they change this? The web designer or webmaster, whoever that might be, needs to code these keywords *as headings, not images.* That will solve the problem.

Alt text is descriptive text for images on the page. This is another one of those areas that people forget about. Many images don't have any text to describe them. This can be fixed by simply writing some copy, using a keyword phrase, of course, and giving it to your designer to place into the code. You'll know if you have it in place if it's there when you place the cursor over the image.

Example:

You are posting photos from a recent search engine marketing conference. A good keyword phrase may be "search engine professionals."

Before:

Alt text: 00589-yter.jog

After:

Alt text: "Group of Search Engine Professionals at SEM Event"

A Word or Two About Dynamic Content

Dynamic pages are generated by a software program whenever someone requests your page URL. Search engines also call them up. Dynamic pages work by using template and database information. The IT department, site developer, or database team in your company usually controls them. These developers usually don't understand that there are SEO considerations for these dynamic pages. Basically, you'll need to influence and manage this process to ensure that three things get done:

- The pages have title tags
- All the titles are different on each of the dynamic pages
- The titles are written using the rules I have outlined in this chapter

Your IT or database person may need to create a new title field in the database, and it's very important that this is done. Working closely with your tech person will usually ensure a positive outcome. That's essentially it for dynamic content.

Does the Content Work? Analyzing the Results

Now that you have optimized your content, how will you know if it's working? This will take time to determine, of course, but within two to three months (sometimes much sooner), you should be seeing an impact—if it's working that is.

Check your keyword phrases in the search engines and see if you come up. Be sure to look in multiple search engines: I check Google, Yahoo!, and Bing monthly. Look at your link popularity. Your links should be increasing steadily.

How about your search traffic? Are you getting more leads/referrals from the web? Check your log files; look at your traffic through your analytics provider (Google Analytics). Finally, how many people who end up on your site are being converted to a sale? That's the most important statistic, of course. If the results aren't what you want, keep working to improve your site. Look at the suggestions in this chapter again, and reread other important chapters on keyword research and writing content. Talk to others and see what they think.

One way or another, with enough hard work, you'll get the rankings—and the conversions—that you want!

SEO Best Practices: A Review

Just for good measure, let's go through the most important areas you'll need to focus on to ensure you are optimizing correctly. Remember, your top competitors are doing the same things on their sites, so it won't be easy, but you can get your share.

- Provide unbelievably great content that people love
- Use your important keyword phrases in your content, keywords that describe exactly what the content is about and that line up with what people search for
- Place keywords in the important places: in titles, headings, links, metadata
- Write for people first, search engines second
- Don't forget to use your keywords in image and video tags (more on video in Chapter 10)
- Make every page count and make every page specific—unique, custom content, with its own meta title and page-specific keywords
- Try, try, try to get others to link to your content (your blog posts are the best way)

Good luck!

PART II

Content for the Web

CHAPTER 5

Website Content—Including Case Studies, E-Books, White Papers, and Articles

The web has been in the public consciousness for more than fifteen years now. And websites have been around just as long. But when the web started out, no one knew what a website was or what it should look like. Just imagine yourself sitting around in 1996 or thereabouts hearing about "the web" for the first time. For most of us, it was a slow introduction. At first, we were intrigued, but probably a little hesitant. I know I was. I mean, the idea of having your own "property" or "space" on the web where you could have a business, talk about your opinions, or sell things was totally new. How would people find you? How could you make money, exactly? What if no one showed up? How did the whole thing work? Well, those same questions are being asked today, so that part hasn't changed.

In 1996, I remember thinking, "Oh, that web thing would be good for doing a little research before I go to the library. It might be cool for looking at photos from friends." I definitely discounted the whole thing. Looking back, I think the reason for that was my lack of technical ability. I don't know about you, but as a marketer, I'm not a technically inclined person. And so I naturally thought, "A new thing for the computer . . . OK. Maybe I'll check it out sometime."

My, how things change! Fast-forward to 2012, and I have a much different opinion. I not only make my living off the web, but have been fortunate enough to contribute thought leadership within the web content space over the past few years. What was missing from my thinking back in the '90s was the idea that the web would be so influenced by writing and words and content. That was what clicked for me. Like many of you, I was a marketer (and writer) to the core, so when that "aha" moment happened, it was electric. I saw my future in two seconds.

So, I look back with fondness. But, of course, will always regret that I didn't get into it just a bit sooner. The good news for the rookies out there in today's world is that the web can be a truly democratic place. If you have an idea or topic that you want to share with others, you can get it online very quickly, putting together a simple WordPress or Joomla site that will have you on your way to building a community and market for your product or service, all in the same day.

When we refer to "website content," what exactly are we taking about? This can be a pretty broad category and may be interpreted many ways. In the interest of keeping things simple, website content in this chapter refers to *the pages that make up your website*. From the all-important home page to the less-used why us or resources pages, and everything in between, we'll spend the first half of the chapter on this area. We'll also cover landing pages, a specific type of web page. The second half of the chapter will focus on content that you use on your site for lead generation: e-books, white papers, case studies, and articles.

Which pages are most important from an SEO perspective? It really depends on the type of company you have—e-commerce, service provider, local company, or something else. Each type of site has unique requirements when it comes to optimization and the types of content you want to use. But, there are also "cornerstone" content items that practically all sites should use, and we'll get to those.

For SEO purposes, all your top-level pages are critical:

- Home page
- Products and services pages
- Solutions pages
- Company page
- Contact us
- Order page
- "How we work" page (or something to that effect)

Also important are pages where prospects can find *quick information*:

- Comparison to the competition
- Frequently asked questions
- Location page
- Pricing page
- Site map
- Search page/box

With the exception of the site map and search pages, these are the pages that you'll want to be sure to optimize for high-impact search rankings. But, in reality, practically *all* of your pages are important for SEO. Think about the long tail keyword strategy we discussed earlier. Pages you want to target for these could be article pages, which typically wouldn't be deemed that important. But, hey, if you generate some long tail leads from them, then they can be pretty important.

As I mentioned earlier, why not get fifty pages of your site ranked on page one of Google? That's a great goal to have. And it makes it important to have strong secondary pages, like your resource center, subpages for your products and services, maybe a community involvement page, pages about your corporate team or executives, etc. These are all important to consider.

Of course, you'll have landing pages, too. As some of the most important pages on your site, these need to appeal to your potential customers from a sales conversion point of view. They need to really speak to the customer. More on that later.

Think of Your Website in Terms of Content Modules

A really good way of seeing your website content is in terms of *modules*. These are individual areas on your site that are consistent from page to page and serve specific purposes, areas that address certain user needs. What you want to do is get away from the idea that your site is made up of only two things: copy and graphics. It's actually much, much more than that.

After all, you have many types of people coming to your site, all of whom have their own agendas about what they want to accomplish. You have folks who are just looking, you have the information seekers, you have companies that need to make a decision quickly. So, how do you address all of these needs within the confines of your website? By *modulizing the content*.

Remember how we said that you are in the publishing business now? That is an absolute truth. Those who embrace the role—really embrace it—are coming out way ahead. So, how would a magazine think about its content each month? How would it approach setting up each magazine issue? Well, we are all familiar with how a typical magazine is organized: you have your editorials, your reader commentaries, your feature stories, some advertising, and maybe news or industry updates. Take that same idea and apply it to your website, and you have something like this:

- Information module—main body copy
- Lead-generation module—e-book, white paper, or free trial offer
- News module—scrolling news section on the home page
- Opinion module—a preview of your blog on the home page
- Impulse buy module—perhaps a graphic banner that advertises your new product
- Human interaction module—live help/assistance feature

Think about the types of modules you will need. Every business and each type of industry has unique needs when it comes to its site modules.

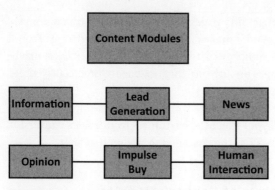

FIGURE 5-1   Website Content Modules

The Philosophy Behind Great Website Content

Great website copy acts as a *virtual salesperson* for your business. This principle is so true online that, in fact, there are thousands of successful companies all over the world that have no salespeople whatsoever. Many of them fired the sales team years ago and saved a lot of money in the process! Now, I am not recommending you do that, but it is a fact that warrants mentioning.

Web content is critical for any business that wants to succeed online. If you want to engage prospects, attain high search rankings, and grow your business, there is no better way. But what is the best philosophy to take? Why is web content so important? How do the best website owners out there perceive their online presence? Well, number one, the best website content folks out there work on their sites almost every day. They are constantly tweaking, optimizing, adding to, and improving their content. It becomes an extension of themselves.

Second, they make changing their sites easy by choosing user-friendly WordPress, Joomla, or Drupal CMS systems. If you're worried about this, don't stress out. You **do not** need to be a technical person or an HTML coder to be a great steward of website content.

In addition, successful website owners know that:

- Great website content engages like nothing else—it helps people and companies solve problems
- Great websites provide a comprehensive place for all your knowledge—your site should transfer everything from your employees' heads, put it on the web, and make it readily available to your prospects
- Great website content gets the search engines to take notice—see the discussion in the previous chapter
- Content positively influences social media efforts—people link to content **they've found on the web** on Facebook and Twitter

And you know what else? Your website content is a workhorse! Content you produced ten years ago can still bring people to your site. That's powerful communication. For now, let's get into a discussion on your website content and review the important individual pages.

Important Site Pages

The home page. It's where everything starts. The home page is like the *foundation of your house*: Without it, your house just isn't built quite right. If it's built wrong, the house could collapse in a storm and you would face an uncertain future. With it, your home is stable, secure, and strong. The same thing goes for your site. The best home pages I've ever seen do everything right: They look good, they have just enough content (200 to 350 words), they use a nice balance of design to content, and they make everything super easy.

The main products or services page would be next in line. If prospects don't know what you're selling, how are they going to buy? Be as detailed and specific as you can be on these pages. And for the purposes of SEO, this is a best practice: If you have twenty products, you should have twenty separate pages, along with a main products page.

Also important is a page about the people who run your business (usually called "About Us" or "Our Team"). This type of page is underrated and underutilized, for sure, but it's essential. Why? It puts a human face on your business. It gives it warmth and personality. Be sure to have some photos of real people there, the actual folks in your organization, not the popular stock photos of the happy corporate team! I think these stock photos really devalue a site. Of course, it's better than having no imagery at all, but see what you can do about getting professional photos taken.

It almost goes without saying, but your contact page is super important. I need to bring this up because of the opportunities businesses miss on this page. It still surprises me how many companies use just a web form on their contact page and nothing else. Remember, some of your prospects want to call you! You need to provide your phone number. Also important to include are all the other channels where they can reach you—Twitter, Facebook, Skype, etc. And think about providing mobile numbers, too. Make it easy for them!

And how about a "How We Work" page? This can be a great place to show your unique value proposition, a direct comparison to the competition, or what a client can expect when they do business with you. It helps visitors become more familiar with what it is that makes your company so interesting, and it sets expectations.

If you are an e-commerce site or are selling something directly on your site, then an ordering or payment page, integrated with a shopping cart, is also critical. We'll talk more about content for e-commerce at a later point.

Your Home Page

The number one problem we see with new clients' sites at my company? An absolutely beautiful home page with nice images, a good look and feel, contact information, social media profiles, and . . . *only three sentences* of copy (and an unoptimized title tag). They ask us, "Why can't I get ranked on the search engines?" My answer is: because you don't have enough content. The solution is easy—build out more pages. Optimize. Make your site content rich. What's interesting is that some of these clients have great off-line businesses, selling hundreds of thousands—or even millions—of dollars'-worth of products to customers around the world. Whether they just recently put up a website and aren't sure what they are doing or have always had a site and never saw a potential for online sales, these companies come in all shapes and sizes.

One of the clients that comes to mind is a manufacturer of piping equipment. The company has been around for more than fifty years and is number two or three in the industry. But having a website was just never that important. They had one, but the home page was exactly as I explained above: slapped together with a template and a few awkwardly constructed sentences. By revising the home page and the rest of the site, we were able to help the company expand into new online markets, much to our client's delight.

I think you get the point, and most of you know this: The home page represents a big opportunity. But are you really setting up the content correctly? Are you maximizing the space? And what type of free content are you offering? Are your newsletter, blog, and social media icons visible?

When we think about the content that should appear on the home page, we need to keep some basics in mind. First, the home page should be the most general or broad of all of your site pages, in terms of scope. You also should use your most important and broad keyword phrases here. You want your home page to be the highest-ranked page on the search engines. In terms of headings and subheadings, you want them to read almost like headlines—make them stand out, create interesting and thought-provoking sentences. I'm a big fan of creating two to three content sections or paragraphs on the page with two to three main headers, each of them using important keyword phrases.

And, as I've said before, make it easy to *scan* the content. Balance the page design with the page copy, another strategy that I always preach. And think about *tone and voice*—get those right, for sure.

I mentioned "free" content. What is this? It's anything you can offer to visitors that will get them to give you some contact information (of course, you can also offer it without having them submit their information). It's the cool e-book you're offering, *Top 10 Ways a Landscaper Can Add Value to Your Home* or *The Best Ideas in Leasing Office Space*. It's the free one-week trial of your software. Put it up in the top right corner on every page, and you'll convert like crazy. The same goes for your newsletter, blog, and social media icons. First rule: Have this type of content. Second rule: Make it easy to click on. Third rule: Give them something cool for subscribing.

Some of this seems pretty common sense, but you know what? Sixty to seventy percent of sites out there are missing these features. More to come on lead-generation content.

Finally, be sure you communicate what you do, front and center. There are still a lot of sites out there that use that hard-to-decipher corporate speak that confuses more than it communicates. You may be in the "enterprise-wide software as a service market" and you help companies "solve their most pressing IT problems," but you need to tell me more than that. What *type* of enterprise software? Which *types* of problems? And please tell me how you are different from the other dozen firms out there that provide the same thing.

Do this, and you will be hitting your home page content out of the park, every time, with every prospect.

Company Page

So who the heck are you anyway? Who is running the show? Your "Company" or "About Us" page is really important content to have. But why? In looking at websites all day long, like I do, it's startling to see how many people forget that. Though the web is just words and images, customers still like to know that there are *real people* behind the business. They want to know about how you got into business, what drives you, and that you care about your business and your customers. Perhaps you might put a picture of the management team on the page? As I've mentioned, you'll want to use this page to put a face on your business.

As with your other pages, make the copy on your company page familiar and warm; put a little heart, soul, and passion behind the words you use; and try to really connect with people on a human level. And remember, from Chapter 2, that tone and voice are important.

One other thing about this page—it can mean the difference between someone choosing you or choosing one of your competitors. Why? Well, if it comes down to two sites offering the same exact service for the same fee, some will naturally go with a company whose people they know a little bit about. This brings up another good point—a service business, like a law firm, accounting practice, or doctor's office, definitely needs to have one of these company pages. If you're in a "people business," make sure your website prospects know it.

FIGURE 5-2   Sample About Us Page

Products Pages

So, what are you selling? Do your customers know? Even more than *what* you are sell-ing, what are your customers going to get from buying? What are the benefits of your specific products?

From a copy point of view, there are a few things you should focus on. First, you'll want to do a quick analysis of what you are selling and then categorize it so your cus-tomers aren't confused. If you are new to this, you might find it helpful to draw a tree diagram, and then for each limb coming off the "tree," create a separate page for the product or product group.

The product page is where you want to use good keyword phrases and specific lan-guage, so you can answer your customers' questions before they ask. Assume your custom-ers don't know anything at all about your products and you need to teach them. Who, what, where, when, and how. Give them all the necessary information they need to help them make a buying decision, or at least a decision on narrowing down the competition.

You'll also want to use some good call to action copy on the page, asking (or recommending) that they take some action right now! Whether it's "Ready to order?" or "Call us now for more information!" or "Take a look at what our customers have to say!" Get them to *do something*.

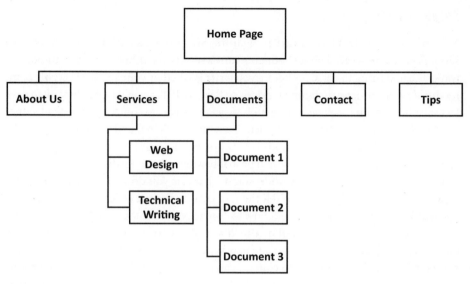

FIGURE 5-3 XML Site Tree Diagram

This is also a page where you need to have good balance between the images of your products and the copy that explains them. In scanning the web, you have probably seen more than a few sites that have great-looking images of their products, but absolutely no feature/benefit content to speak of. A picture of the product and a "click here to order" command just doesn't cut it anymore. Not with such intense competition online. You need to assume that your prospects don't know anything about your products and you need to educate them.

Product features: Copy about your products' features is not nearly as important as copy about your products' benefits, but features still need to be mentioned. Make sure you write copy that focuses on what your product does and looks like. Some technical specs may be good, too, but don't go overboard.

What many companies do, especially those that know very little about good copywriting, is write only about features. Although this is better than having no copy at all, it's still a long way from optimal. And here's the other thing about writing about features and benefits: People seem to have a hard time knowing the difference. They confuse them all the time or simply can't put into words how their product impacts a customer's life. So, how can you make it easier on yourself? *Ask your customers* how they use your products. They will tell you. When they do, turn their answers into some great, hard-hitting, conversion-friendly product content.

Services Pages

Most of the points mentioned earlier regarding the products page will also apply to a services page. But writing about your company's services is different in some important ways. The first thing to consider before you write is whether your service is highly commodified (think attorneys, staffing services, or florists). If it is, you'll typically want to have less specific copy on the page; your goal is to get prospects to contact you instead, either by e-mail or phone, so you can "sell them" in a more personal and persuasive way.

If your service is less commodified (think a dog-walking service or a saltwater aquarium building service), then you'll probably want to be more detailed in your copywriting, so people who may not understand what it is you do will get their questions answered upfront. It also helps to sell them or qualify them a little upfront. Of course, you'll also want copy that tells them how to contact you for inquiries, but if they found you, they are probably pretty well qualified already. Also, a noncommodified service has a better chance of being a relatively new type of service, so there may not be many competitors. Getting prospects to contact you right away won't be quite as important.

Local search. It's been all the rage in the past few years. For a service like a barbershop or pet groomer, you'll want to definitely use geographically specific keyword phrases like "*Springville* barber shops" or "*Missoula* pet grooming" in your service page copy. This is where most, if not all, your customers will be coming from, so you want to be sure you are popping up in search engines based on your location.

Order/Payment Page

What type of content do you think an order or payment page should have? Probably a very detailed explanation of how customers order or pay. Make the process clear and specific. Maybe list the steps they'll need to take. Include copy that makes them feel safe and secure. Many sites make the mistake of leaving customers feeling adrift here. Think about going online to make a purchase. You want to know, beyond a shadow of a doubt, that it's a secure transaction, and that this is a reputable company that won't cheat you.

You'll also want to write some content that speaks to your return or exchange policy. Again, answer the question before it is asked. If you don't have a return or exchange policy, think about establishing one. Most of all, make your order/payment page copy simple and easy to follow.

Frequently Asked Questions (FAQs) Page

It's great to see so many websites with a frequently asked questions page. This is always a good idea. One of the great benefits to having a website and an online business is that you can automate many parts of your business and eliminate overall costs. Think about it—if you have a very good, comprehensive FAQ section, do you need to spend money on a customer support function? Maybe not. Couple your FAQ page with a robust forum tool, and perhaps your users can help answer each other's questions. Not sure what questions to feature on this page? Again, ask your customers; they will tell you. Send a short survey to them or check out the competition. What type of FAQ section do they have?

In terms of the copywriting, you'll want to make it very specific and keyword rich. When people are surfing online, they usually have a question or two about what they are looking for. They may even put their search words in the form of a question. If you have that particular question on your FAQ page, worded the same way (or close), your site may come up on the first page for that query.

Finally, I would make the question and answer copy short and to the point. Remember, people are scanning. They want super-quick information.

Contact Us

You *do* have a way for prospects and customers to contact you, right? Hope so. The biggest problem I see with contact us pages is making the page too content-heavy or too content-light. Or it's too confusing. All you really need is a short, one-paragraph section on this page that shows your genuine interest in your customers' needs and then provides your detailed contact information: e-mail addresses and phone numbers, street address, city, state, zip. Maybe a map.

A word about phone numbers: Give your customers a way to call you! There are so many sites out there that don't give their customers this opportunity. Also, provide a street address. People want to know that there's some level of permanency to your company. A street address provides credibility.

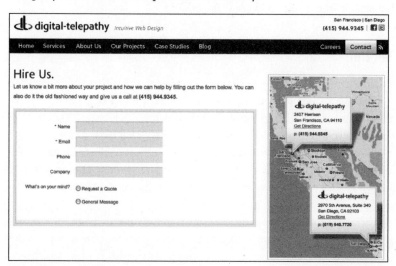

FIGURE 5-4   Sample Contact Us Page

Places to Expand Content

Now that you've learned a few things about search engine optimization (SEO), you know that adding more relevant content to your site is a really good thing to do. But how do you do that exactly? Which pages are the easy targets for expansion? How can you make it simple?

Let's cut to the chase: If you have the same exact site up, with the same pages and same content that you did a year or two ago, then you're in dire need of a content update. So, let's discuss it.

Products/Services

This is an easy area to expand. Many sites are a little light in this area to start with, so it can be a fairly straightforward fix. Again, think *specific products/services* and think *product/service groupings*. You could easily turn a simple and general products page into ten specific new pages in short order. Google will take notice of this and hopefully reward you with some higher rankings.

If your business is a day spa, for example, and your current services page has a quick general blurb about your massage therapy, facials, and mud baths, make each of these a separate subpage under the larger services page, and then write more specifically about each service, both in the language that entices your potential customer and in the keywords that you are using. You could go from ranking well for "spas in Concord, CA" to maintaining your ranking for that phrase and also adding new rankings for "massage therapy in the Bay Area," "facials in the Bay Area" and "mud baths in the Bay Area." And that equals one thing: POTENTIAL NEW CUSTOMERS!

Resources Section

There's lots of opportunity with a resources page. Acting as the ultimate information source for your prospects and customers, take a step back and ask yourself, "What could I provide to them that will help build the relationship?"

On our site (www.contentlaunch.com/resource-center), we have webinars (both recorded past events and upcoming ones), articles, PowerPoint decks from past event presentations I've done, an online marketing kit, an online content grader, a link to our blog, whitepapers, and videos—essentially, the keys to the content kingdom! What could you provide?

Note: Some sites include links of interest on their resources page, too, which is a great way of showing your commitment to partnering with other firms in your industry.

FIGURE 5-5   Sample Resource Center Page

Customer (Service) Friendly Content

As I've said before, one of the big missing elements on many websites is the human touch. Most people like dealing with other people, whether it's the chance to talk to someone on the phone, get a quick answer via instant message, or watch a video of your CEO on your site. And when your customers have issues, you want to give them a way to deal with the problem, right away. Don't wait until you hear about it on Twitter or in the news.

I like what Tim Frick said in his great book *Return on Engagement*:

> People like interacting with people. Build your strategy around customers being able to get in touch with an actual person as quickly as possible . . . how does one build effective communication into one's web-based support system? Here are a few ideas:
> - Make support content searchable both within your site and via the web
> - Create a searchable FAQ page for each product or service
> - Implement live chat support features
> - Include phone numbers on every support page
> - Create easy to use forms
>
> When devising a customer service and support strategy, consider the following questions:

- What information will site visitor's need?
- How can you get it in front of them as quickly as possible?
- Will search functions help them find the information they need?
- How much will it cost to offer support via phone or e-mail?[13]

Great advice, Tim! I have to agree with this customer-focused approach. It will help you take care of customers in the short term and keep them for the long term.

FIGURE 5-6   *Return on Engagement* by Tim Frick

Widgets

These "miniapps," little pieces of content magic, are shareable, and they can easily be embedded on your website and other places (blogs, social media profiles). You've probably seen them but didn't know what they were called. These are the local weather apps, news tickers, stock reports, blog feeds, and other small apps that you see on a lot of websites. They are a great way of building sponsored content on a smaller scale, for relatively low fees.

Although they do involve software development, there are widget engines that can help you build one from scratch. These include Widgetbox, Widsets, and Akami. Widgets are a great way to connect with a wider audience. If you have an idea for a cool widget that people would really respond to, consider it. It's just another type of content that can make a difference in your ability to compete effectively.

---

[13] Frick, Tim. 2010. *Return on Engagement*. Burlington, MA: Focal Press.

FIGURE 5-7   Widgetbox

Forums

A forum is a place where users, customers, or others can start conversations with each other and with you to get answers to their questions. This is usually managed by an outside service or set up with a plug-in, an added module that comes ready built and customizable for your site.

With this section, your customers write the content for you! You'll want to review all the postings and threads before they go up, but this is a great place to build out content and improve usability for your customers. It also does one other very important thing from a copywriting point of view: It keeps your visitors on the site much longer and increases your chances of having them jump to other pages on your site. The longer you can keep them on the site, the better.

Other Considerations

Consider the above recommendations as the most important areas to address first. Doing so will put you in good position to make additional changes to your site content. Let's discuss these other considerations now.

Adding to Short Existing Pages

If you want to add content fast and easily, look to your existing pages, as well. Adding a paragraph or two to your home page or about us page is a quick and relatively painless activity. Why? It's always easier to add to existing content than to create it from scratch. So, take a look at your site. Which pages could use a little beefing up? Write those first. That will at least get the ball rolling for developing other content for the site.

Segment Your Pages As Needed

On many large sites, especially those that have been around a long time, there is a need to categorize or group certain sections. For example, on the company or about us page, instead of putting all the information about the company on the same page, split it up. Create "Company Profile" as one page, "Latest News" as another, "Board of Directors," as still another, and "History" as the last.

You should also do this for other sections on your site that have lots of subcategories.

Don't Forget These Pages!

For some reason, many companies forget to populate a privacy policy and/or terms and conditions page. This is important to write from a legal perspective. It's also good to write one for your customers' peace of mind. It helps you build credibility with them. If you don't know the first thing about writing one, take a look at your competitors' websites. Don't steal theirs, but use it as a template for what you should do. Be sure to include copy that outlines what you will do with the information you are collecting, explains the customer's rights, notes that the site will be updated on a regular basis, and includes some language about how they can contact you if they have a question about their privacy rights. "Terms and conditions" explains what customers can expect if they buy from you.

E-Commerce Website Content

There are many types of websites that require unique content based on differences in the user experience. One of these is the e-commerce website. This type of site sells products directly on the site and usually includes hundreds, if not thousands, of different types of products. E-commerce sites heavily emphasize product images, videos, and descriptive text in order to motivate customers to buy. By engaging visitors and addressing their needs—no matter what they are—they can compete effectively and grow market share.

If you plan on operating an e-commerce site, how should you be thinking about your content?

- Provide choices and create a user-friendly experience
- Lead prospects through the sales process, one step at a time
- Focus on building a long-term relationship with the customer

- Use benefits-rich product descriptions
- Include "trigger" words and emotional appeal
- Write strong call to action statements that improve conversions
- Use zooming, multiple images, 360 views, and visual detail tools with products
- Think video—it sells the products like nothing else
- Know that third-party verification by TRUSTe or other certification provider is key
- Have products listed in several categories
- Include "top" products or "what's new" listings

FIGURE 5-8   Amazon

E-Commerce Product Descriptions

Product descriptions are critically important with e-commerce sites. In them, you want to fully explain what customers will get out of the product. Communicate how it will save them money or time or bring new efficiencies to their life or business. Describe in detail what the product can do, what it looks like, and how it works.

Remember, people want to read about it (through text) and see it (with photos/video). Use language that appeals to the senses and to people's aspirations. Be sure to use descriptive adjectives and the word *you* as much as possible; personalize the experience.

The Power of Customer Reviews

Like anything else in life, third-party validation plays a big role in e-commerce sales success. People naturally gravitate toward products that others enjoyed. As long as there have been businesses, word of mouth has been a proven way of driving sales. Customer endorsements carry powerful credibility that retailers can't duplicate in product descriptions. Reviews can be leveraged everywhere: in e-mail, catalogs, and newsletters, not only on the website.

Top vendors for seamless customer review applications include Bazaarvoice and PowerReviews. If you run an e-commerce store, be sure to see how these two resources can help you capture the power of customer reviews.

Other Important Content Elements for E-Commerce Sites

- Sell up and sell down: Increase margins with upselling and clear out inventory with downselling
- Cross-sell: Don't leave money on the table
- Don't keep your great deals a secret: Promote free shipping, sales, and other special offers with strategically placed banners
- Make it easy for customers to buy: Create a more targeted shopping experience with dynamic landing pages
- Provide secure transactions: How? Preferably with SSL/SET
- Disclose policies for customer privacy, returns, exchanges, and other customer concerns: Prominently display them on every page on the right or left side as well as in a link at the bottom of the page
- Offer many types of the product being sought, relevant brands, and/or an appropriate range of products
- Offer customer service by phone, preferably twenty-four hours a day: Whether your customer service is done offshore or domestically, the important thing is to have a resource displayed on your site prominently
- Let visitors know your site is widely reputable and credible: Apply for TRUSTe, PriceGrabber, Better Business Bureau Online programs

Landing Pages—Getting That Magic Conversion

Regardless of the tool you use to drive traffic to your site, landing page optimization should be an important step in your process. It all comes down to providing the content that searchers are looking for.

People get to your site in many different ways, and they can "land" on many different pages. In order to bring some control over this process and drive high rates of conversion, you can use a specific type of page: a "landing" page. These pages are set up in a unique way in order to drive a specific and directed action. Don't use your home page as a landing page; your home page's function is to act as a general overview of your company, not to provide specific offers like a software trial download or a free fifteen-page e-book.

The three key attributes of a landing page are: having a strong offer, limiting the page navigation, and including a persuasive call to action with a simple contact form. But how do you set these up to get the intended action? How do you improve your landing pages and test for best results?

Let's review a few tips on improving landing page performance and methods for analysis:

1. Keep in mind that the entry path to the landing page is almost always an ad (banner, text, or pay per click), e-mail, or a search listing.
2. Ensure that your landing page delivers on the promise your ads make. The content needs to deliver on expectations.
3. Review page titles, heading, and page copy to ensure you use keywords that align with user intent.
4. Make the action you want them to take obvious. Whether you want them to buy something, download a file, or get in touch with you, make sure you spell it out. Lead them by the hand.
5. Beware of too much information on the page; too much information means too many choices, and this usually equals confusion and low conversions.
6. Use *simple* contact forms. Collect only the information that's absolutely necessary: name, e-mail address, and phone number, perhaps. Once they convert, you will have the opportunity to gather more information.

FIGURE 5-9   Sample Landing Page

You also want to show your concern for your customers' privacy, include customer testimonials (videos are great) and ratings, and show awards that your products or services have received. If you are selling something through the landing page, provide a secure checkout.

Landing Pages: A/B and Multivariate Testing

With A/B testing, you set up two separate landing pages with identical content except for one variable. Then you attempt to drive an equal amount of traffic to each landing page and check the results. One by one, you can test different variables, including copy, type of offer, graphics, and form details; reviewing the results, you will be able to see which one performs better. Go with the version that yields the better performance.

Google Website Optimizer is a great way to do multivariate testing, a more advanced testing method. Sort of like performing multiple A/B tests on a single landing page, it tests several variables at the same time and helps you to determine the variation that works best.

The Page That *Everyone* Forgets About—The Thank You Page

Has there ever been a page more neglected, underappreciated, and underused than the thank you page? The answer is absolutely not; the thank you page gets no respect at all, and it's a real shame. Remember, if somebody bought something on your site, you just turned a *prospect into a customer*—you still have her attention, even though the transaction is complete. Almost all companies make this mistake, so if you are guilty of it, no worries—you're in the majority!

But, what type of content should you place on the thank you page? Hint: you need more than "Thank you for your order. We'll be in touch soon." What you want to do is think about how you can *further the relationship* with your new customer. How can you strengthen it, take it to the next level? You'll never have a better opportunity to do this, so you need to take advantage of it!

You can use this opportunity to educate new customers about your brand, share a free e-book with them, invite them to check out your blog or Facebook page, showcase upcoming events and promotions, share their friends' contact information, or **get them to join** *your club and buy more stuff*! Yeah, now that's the ticket!

Virgin Wines does a great job of this on its website. After someone has purchased a few bottles of wine, the company essentially asks, "Would you like half your money back right now?" If you join the "Discovery Club," you get eighty dollars back in your account, which you can use to buy more wine any time. You simply agree to have a case of fine wines come to your door every month. It's a great idea, and right on the thank you page is a great place to offer the program. Conversions for these types of offers can be through the roof.

Can you incorporate something like this on your product or service thank you page? The same idea goes for **registration confirmation pages**: Beef up the content and make them count!

FIGURE 5-10 Sample Thank You Page

User-Generated and Crowdsourced Content

If you have customers' product reviews or testimonials on your website, you already have some user-generated content. The web is becoming ever more participative, and whether it's your customers, subscribers, prospects, or partners, many of the people who are interested in what you do like to be a part of the process.

What has driven the user-generated content (UGC) movement? A demographic shift to younger age groups with higher technological skills, greater willingness to engage online, and less hesitation to reveal personal information online, together with the development of communities and collaborative projects. UGC can take the form of text, photo, video, or audio content. Two of the most popular types of UGC are comments on blogs and videos on YouTube. Wikipedia also represents a mass of user-generated content, and is probably the most successful and far-reaching user of UGC.

Why is it great for your purposes? Your users, communicating and sharing their ideas, help to keep your content fresh and interesting. User-generated content is unique and valuable to your overall site footprint, which helps the SEO effort and provides third-party viewpoint, which your new site visitors will typically trust more than the content you wrote. The one issue with UGC, however, is the occasional lack of accuracy and accountability that goes with it. Of course, you get to decide what ultimately goes up on your site, but sometimes the bad stuff sneaks through.

With crowdsourced content, you are outsourcing your content production to a group of people through an open call. Whether you lack the time, expertise, or resources to develop the content yourself, you'll find that there are many benefits to getting content from the outside. You can also use crowdsourcing to get customers to discuss ideas, provide feedback, and vote on things. In 2010, Starbucks launched My Starbucks Idea for this exact purpose. See how they use crowd sourced content at http:// mystarbucksidea.force.com/.

Microsites

Some of you may have heard the term "microsite." A microsite is a website that is developed to meet a set of objectives that are different from your standard site's goals. For example, if you have one product that makes up 80 percent of your business and has great branding, you may want to spin this product off and give it more dedicated web real estate with its own site. This gives the product more influence and more power, and you'll end up with more web traffic. Your microsite would have its own unique web address (URL), but share the visual design of your corporate site.

The microsite strategy is very popular with large, well-known product brands, most notably automotive manufacturers: BMW, Ford, Honda, Toyota, and others. Because they have so many vehicle lines and niche markets, they can use microsites to appeal to the specific vehicle aficionados, connecting with many more people than they would using just the corporate site.

Whether you want to generate more leads, improve your SEO, or just test out a microsite strategy, it's worth looking into.

Lead-Generation Content for Your Site

People love free stuff. When they can learn from the free stuff, that's even better. This, essentially, is what you are doing with lead generation content on your site. Whether it's a free e-book, white paper or something else, you will separate yourself from competitors very quickly if you have these items in place and visitors to your site find them valuable.

E-Books

One of the most popular types of content that my firm has developed over the years has been e-books. People everywhere simply love these easy-to-read yet substantive juggernauts of online publishing. And there may be nothing better for successful lead generation than a free e-book with high perceived value. Your company gives prospects a complimentary digital book on a subject that interests them, and they give you their e-mail address so you can keep in contact with them: it's one of the fundamental exchanges of information in the content age.

First distributed on websites, e-books can now be offered via any online content vehicle: through social media, blogs, via mobile marketing or e-mail marketing, whatever. Writing and marketing an e-book that is relevant to your business also does one other very powerful thing: It establishes you as an expert. And isn't that great, because even though an e-book may be made up of your ideas (which is the important part), you don't necessarily have to be the one who writes it. You can hire other people to do that for you.

Your website basically acts as a way to *advertise* your e-book. What's the difference between an e-book and a white paper? E-books are more basic, informal, conversational, and interesting enough so that people who may not be familiar with what you do understand it after they read the book.

What else should you know about writing effective e-books for lead generation?

1. Know your objectives: What is your goal in writing your e-book?
2. Keep it short and simple: Ten to fifteen pages works
3. Come up with a great title for your e-book
4. Write quality content or get someone else to do it for you
5. Wrap it up in a nice design: It's almost as important as the copy
6. Use it for B2B and B2C, though it's best for B2B firms

Last, but most important, promote the heck out of your e-book. Blog about it, tweet about it, post it on Facebook, share it with your LinkedIn groups. Send it out to your established network. Leave no stone unturned. We'll talk a lot more about social media in the chapters ahead.

FIGURE 5-11 *Fearless Software Outsourcing,* E-Book by Steve Mezak

White Papers

So, we have a handle on the powerful online content known as an e-book. But what's a *white paper*, and how can it be used effectively on a website? Research shows that white papers are among the best ways to get new leads. White papers are similar to e-books in their customer-outreach goals; if you are in the B2B area, you need to use white papers. Providing up-to-date research, offering value-added tips and advice, and assisting companies in making purchase decisions, white papers provide a high return on engagement for almost any company. **Prospects who are in the early stages of the sales cycle** are the ones who frequently register in order to download white papers. In fact, it's been shown that white papers can offer higher interest and better conversion than free trials, analyst reports, and even webinars. That's powerful content marketing in action. Plus, white papers show another interesting behavior pattern in corporate America: They are frequently passed around to many people in an organization.

What are some of the important things to remember as you develop white paper content?

1. Feature well-researched, substantive content that stays away from selling.
2. Begin with a discussion on the major issues or problems, and line them up with a need faced by the reader.
3. Provide some solid learning; try to teach prospects something they may not have known and show benefits that they may not have been aware of.
4. Place the white paper on your website in exchange for prospect contact information as a good first step, but make sure you leverage your white paper and get it in front of as many targeted prospects as possible. Try giving it away without collecting contact information.
5. Promote your white paper **via syndication networks**, which will distribute your white paper through a network of specialty, vertically oriented websites that are targeted based on your ideal lead.
6. Seek a vendor that can target both your industry and your perfect prospect.

Good luck! White papers are a key type of content for your company. Be sure you produce content you can be proud of.

Case Studies

Case studies or client success stories are always good to feature. An effective promotional tool and a way to showcase your company's talents, they are second only to white papers in promoting the benefits of a product or service. A case study is fairly simple and easy to put together. The most difficult part of the whole process may be securing client permission. The good thing here is that many of your clients enjoy the attention and awareness they generate as a result of being showcased, so there are definitely some fringe benefits for them. Essentially, a case study demonstrates how a specific challenge or issue was first identified, which solution you offered to resolve the issue, and how your client benefited. It also includes a summary of the final results. As far as length, think brief and succinct. A case study can be as short as three hundred to five hundred words.

There are three sections to a case study:

- Problem—tie it into something the prospect can identify with
- Implementation—focus on how the solution addresses a very specific issue
- Results—what happened? How was the problem resolved?

Be sure to support your case study with key stats and charts that illustrate the benefits of your product or service. Remember, decision makers will use case studies as a source of reference and may even ask you for an example of your success with a similar type of company before they agree to do business with you. Most companies will assume that if you can successfully handle a major challenge similar to what they are facing, you'll be just as successful with their problem.

Case studies work. Put them to work for your website's lead-generating machine. It's a type of content that many companies undervalue.

"Themed" Pages or Article Content

If you want to make your site more robust, more content rich, and more respected, then writing a series of substantive, keyword-rich articles is a no-brainer. In fact, creating *themed* pages, optimized for target keywords, is a core part of SEO. These article pages don't have to be long—three hundred fifty to five hundred words should do it. The main thing you need to ask yourself is this: What are the topics I should write about?

If you are an alternative health therapist, perhaps you write about "holistic healing," "the benefits of juicing fruits and vegetables," "massage therapy for relaxation," and others. The cool thing with these examples is that you are using the exact keyword phrase for the title of your article, so you simply link them off the home page. This way, you also get some interior anchor text linking benefit!

Think about it: You could have instant website copywriting and SEO breadth with a simple series of ten articles a month for six months. And to break a commonly held myth—people do read these! In fact, they sometimes read them word for word, print them out, refer back to them over and over, and share them with friends. Talk about powerful! If you write your themed content pages from a place of conviction, passion, and knowledge, all the better. Be sure to have a separate section on your site dedicated to articles and include links to them from the home page. Either the bottom footer or the left or right side can be good places for this.

Other Types of Website Content That May Help SEO

There are three other areas of content that you should think about including on your site for further optimization benefit. I saw this mentioned on the EConsultancy website as well as on web expert Dave Chaffey's site, and thought it was a nice addition to the chapter:

- **Archived e-newsletters:** Often newsletters are broadcast, but the content is not placed on the site. As well as the content in the newsletter, internal links to other places on the site can be helpful for optimization. Be sure to remove content with really old dates, though.
- **Glossary:** A glossary of terms will often appear in Google searches using the "define" syntax. This is particularly useful for informational or B2B sites.
- **Technical guides or briefings:** Sometimes content that is used to explain various concepts to customers in printed form, perhaps as PDFs, may be useful for generating visitors, particularly for exploiting the long tail of less common search terms. Of course, there are issues of maintaining this content.[14]

Build Content Through Licensing

To get some great links, you can take those cool e-books and white papers you've developed and license them to other sites. Essentially, this is building content that can be shared through a *citation-based licensing agreement*. How do you do it? Use a Creative Commons Attribution, which you can find at www.creativecommons.org. Each time someone uses your material, you get a link back to your site. You can also do this for photos, videos, graphics, charts, and raw data.

---

[14] Chaffey, Dave. "E-Marketing Essentials Briefing." DaveChaffey.com. Accessed 2/9/11. http://www.davechaffey.com/E-marketing-Essentials.

CASE STUDY: A Dramatic Website Content Makeover for Ethical Markets Media

Ethical Markets Media, LLC, is a media company that promotes a sustainable and green global economy with the goal of increasing its channel distributions via strategic online partnerships. Their website, ethicalmarkets.com, has more than thirty thousand partner links with 4,361 pages of content.

The content problem for Ethical Markets Media? Its forty years of legacy content was not being indexed by the search engine algorithms, leaving people who could benefit from this highly specialized information without critical pieces of research, including digital articles and reports, television interviews, and series and commentary on important news.

To increase the number of visitors to the website and to increase the visibility of the company's thought leadership content on the green economy—including pieces on socially responsible investing (SRI) best practices, transforming finance, and its Green Transition Scoreboard®—it partnered with Kore Access, a provider of online sustainability marketing services. Kore Access accomplished both goals using search engine optimization (SEO) strategies, along with a website strategy that reorganized content into user-friendly sections and thought leadership branding. Site redesign included:

1. Clearly defined areas of content, organized by category, on the homepage
2. Categories organized into original content versus aggregated content vetted by the editor, Hazel Henderson
3. A cleaner design that highlighted Ethical Markets Media videos, books, and banners to attract attention
4. Automated updating of the latest headlines to encourage users to sign up for daily alerts
5. A navigation bar with drop-down menus

The results were astounding. Between July 2010 and January 2011, unique page views per month increased from 6,700 to almost 11,000, and absolute unique visitors per month increased from 2,800 to almost 5,000. In the first month, Google Analytics data revealed that visitor traffic at www.ethicalmarkets.com was up 91.52 percent, and that the second-quarter traffic of unique visitors was up 86 percent. Visitors were spending, on average, 38.46 percent more time on the site and were visiting more pages per visit.

(continued)

CASE STUDY: *Continued*

In addition, the use of targeted keywords allowed portions of the Ethical Markets website to be placed on Google Sitelinks, an enhanced listing in Google's search results. After six months, based on Google Analytics data, traffic that had averaged 1,700 unique visits per month increased to 5,000 monthly unique visitors. Google worldwide search engines referred over 44 percent of traffic, up from an average of 30 percent. And the traffic is still growing exponentially.

But, it wasn't solely the search engines that noticed the website changes. Ethical Markets earned the endorsements of various business leaders for its online branding efforts of Green Transition Scoreboard®, a tool that tallies private investment in companies growing the green economy. One such business leader was Don Tapscott, author of *Macrowikinomics*. Other prominent and well-known leaders included Matthew Kiernan, author of *Investing in a Sustainable World*, Dennis Meadows, coauthor of *Limits to Growth*, and Ashok Khosla, chairman of Development Alternatives and pioneering social entrepreneur.

The lesson? Search engine optimization, applied the correct way and with a parallel emphasis on user experience, can have a dramatic impact.

CHAPTER 6

Press Releases and Media/Press Rooms

One of the challenges of being in business today is *getting the word out about what you do*. It can be expensive, time consuming, and lots of hard work, right? Add in all the competitive pressure and deadlines you need to hit with your own clients, and it is left on the backburner, just about every time.

But one fact is most certainly true: Those who can master the public relations game have the future growth of their business assured. You can "write your own check," as they say. And things are changing fast in the public relations game. In Clay Shirky's great book *Here Comes Everybody*, he points out that we are going through a communications revolution. No one really knows how it will turn out or what's going to happen, but it's going to be a good ride.

One of the great things about today's world is that we now have *lots of places* to tell our company stories. But we need to perform our due diligence; we need to approach it right. It's all about **listening, developing relationships with influencers, speaking authentically, and communicating in plain English.**

Getting the Word Out

Imagine for a second that *everyone* in the world knows about you. That's a lot of people, right? Probably about seven billion. Now imagine that just your target market knows about you. Still a lot of people. Let's say it's a million or so. Now, imagine that just 5 percent of that number knows about you. At fifty thousand people, it's still an incredibly high number!

And you know what? There are probably people everywhere, all over the place, around the globe that can use what you have to sell. ***You just need a way to get to them!*** Online press releases help you do just that. And in addition, they help you get **search engine rankings** and **offers for other business and promotional opportunities**.

What *is* a press release? A press release is a statement written and distributed with the purpose of initiating media coverage of a topic that your company wants to share with the world. News directors, editors, and reporters decide whether the story is interesting and newsworthy for their audience. Whether they cover the story or use the press release exactly as it's printed, you win. A story is *newsworthy* when the story has relevance for a large group of people, stands out, contains human interest, and comes from a trustworthy and well-known source. You may think that your company doesn't fall into this category, but the reality is that you don't need to have groundbreaking news to make it into the newspaper, radio, or television. You just need to have *interesting* news. And anything could be interesting to many people.

A press release gets the promotion and publicity ball rolling and a *captivated, influential* reader takes it from there. Think about it: You could be the next host of a local program featuring the subject of your passion, and you could be just one press release away from that happening. All you need to do is connect your content with the right person. The more exposure you get, the greater the likelihood that your content will connect.

Your news can be groundbreaking for the community in which you work and therefore might be covered in many small (or large) media outlets. Plus, all media outlets need "filler" stories to complement the big stories. Why is being a filler story a good thing? Because it's free publicity!

Become the News

Did you know that up to 75 percent of news stories come from press releases? It's true. Reporters and news outlets are *always* looking for a new story. Important or interesting press releases are like gold to these hungry media professionals.

Many news items are actually *planted* by companies themselves. If you're savvy and smart, you'll do the same thing, right? How can you exert some control and authority over the process? The first step is coming up with good stories or good tie-ins to what's already happening in the news. Most small businesses (and some larger ones) don't take full advantage of this powerful online content tool. And they really should, because press releases are an easy and inexpensive way to generate media coverage and help the SEO effort.

The Numbers Don't Lie

Almost thirty million people a month use Google and Yahoo! News to find relevant and local news content. Consider these statistics from PR Web and PEW research:

- Research has shown that editors take approximately seven seconds to read your headlines and first paragraph
- 98 percent of journalists go online daily
- 92 percent of journalists use the web for article research
- 81 percent go online to do searching
- 76 percent go online to find new sources, experts
- 73 percent use the web to find press releases
- On an average day, sixty-eight million American adults go online

- 30 percent of adults use a search engine to find information
- 27 percent use the web to get news

Use these numbers to your advantage and get your news out there!

A Little Bit of History

Press releases have long been used to get media exposure, but before the web, a press release was used solely for a newsworthy announcement. In fact, press releases are one of the holdover marketing tactics of the pre-Internet days that experienced a new lease on life in the world of the web. A standard tool in the public relations arsenal, they have been around for decades. (You can't say that about e-mail, blogs, pay-per-click ads, and some of the other new online communication tools.) What's interesting is that PR professionals weren't the first to see new potential of press releases in the digital age—the search engine and content marketing professionals were.

Yes, the web came along and changed what a press release could be. In fact, the whole process was turned upside down and expanded. Big time. With the web, a press release can be seen by people everywhere, not just journalists. In fact, it doesn't even need to be seen by media people to be successful. You could have a thousand prospects see it and get five hundred external links to your site from just one release!

Sites like Google News are always updating their search results with new press releases from sites like Marketwire, PR Newswire, and PRWeb. What does that mean for your company? *It means you can reach thousands of new prospects and partners within just a few days.*

Your Game Plan—Putting Together a Press Release SEO Strategy

If you have been writing press releases for a while, you may not need to read everything in this chapter. Writing them is half the battle. You may already know that press releases have incredible value and can be a great way to get some instant exposure. Press releases have always had a sort of panache, and are a great way to legitimize your business.

But let's assume you don't know much about press releases. How do you start? Well, the first thing to ask yourself is this: **Do you have a newsworthy item to talk about?** There are lots of things that can fall into this category:

- New business announcement
- A partnership
- New suite of products
- New service offering
- Winning an award
- Hiring a new executive

These are all great things to communicate. If you're not sure that your topic is a good one, put yourself in someone else's shoes and ask yourself whether they would want to read about this topic. If you can't come up with anything to write about, go out and *make* some news happen! Apply for that award, hire some people, develop a new product. Put yourself in a place where you can write about the good news.

What should your strategy be? Look at your content marketing plan for the year and set up a calendar for your press releases. I would plan to write one every month for a year. See how that goes. If you can't come up with twelve newsworthy items, then, like I indicated, maybe you need to start making some things happen in your business. If you're doing a lot of things right, you'll have thirty or more newsworthy topics for the year, and your challenge will be narrowing them down to the best ones.

Writing a Release

Copywriting for a search engine optimized press release is different from writing any other type of online content. As I mentioned earlier, there are certain traditions that press release writing holds and specific ways to write them that are very standard. The great thing about this is that it follows *a formula*. Once you write one, you can write dozens. If you've never written one before, the first one will take some time—and maybe a few revisions.

Here is the process:

1. **The first thing, of course, is *the headline*.** As you would think, this is very important. It's what pulls your reader in. It should have a little flash to it, maybe an eye-grabbing statistic or benefit. It should be fewer than eighty characters, if possible (you could use as many as 170 if you need to).

Some great press release before and after headlines[15]:

> Original Headline:
>
> Students Compete in Prestigious Scholarship Competition with Unlimited Award Potential, Renewable Energy Benefits
>
> Rewritten Headline:
>
> Unlimited Renewable Energy Industry Scholarship Offered
>
> ———
>
> Original Headline:
>
> Champions of Champions Elite Begins Coverage of Sportaccord Combat Games in Beijing
>
> Rewritten Headline:
>
> Beijing Olympics of Martial Arts Championship Broadcast Starts Aug 27
>
> ———

---

[15] SEO Press Releases. "Headline Examples and Rewrites." Accessed 2/14/11. http://www.seopressreleases.com/recent-searches/headline-power-online-press-releases/headline-examples-rewrites/.

Original Headline:

iPreserve Opens its First International Franchise in Mexico

Rewritten Headline:

Digitization and Imaging Franchise System Archives Mexican Documents

See the benefits of being succinct and direct?

2. **Next is the summary paragraph.** This is a small blurb, usually one to four sentences, that comes right after the headline and says a little bit more about what the release will cover (see Figure 6-1).

3. **Now comes the lead sentence.** Use this key spot to tell the most important information in thirty words or less.

4. **Use the first paragraph to tell the "who, what, when, and where."** Use the paragraph after this to discuss the *how* and the *why*. Expand upon the first paragraph and give additional information and quotes. Be sure to focus on making the release interesting to the reader.

5. **Remember the journalistic inverted pyramid style of writing** we talked about in Chapter 2. Use that.

6. **Use the end of the press release to summarize.** The summary could be as short as a sentence, but it needs to wrap up the story well and give the reader something to remember.

7. **In the last paragraph, known as the "boilerplate," provide brief but substantive information** about your company.

8. **Press releases should be 350 to 600 words**, with most falling in the 400 to 450 word range. Make the release brief and to the point. Think "lots of facts."

9. **Come up with two or three good quotes from executives, customers, or other important people** and use them in the press release, spaced out so they fall in the third and the fifth paragraphs, for example.

10. **Here is an important point: The tone should be objective and neutral.** This isn't a place to advertise or get too creative. Remember, there is a standard process that all press releases use.

11. **Don't use pronouns.** There should be no "you," "we," or "I" (unless it's a quote).

12. **Use two to three important keyword phrases two to three times**, spread out in the release; put important ones in the headline and first paragraph (be sure to do some keyword research for this). For the keyword phrases in the body of the release, you'll want to link the anchor text to pages on your site that are relevant and that use the same keyword phrases.

13. **Finally, include company contact information** for questions regarding the release.

Content Rich Author Jon Wuebben Speaking About Content Marketing at Online Marketing Summit

Jon Wuebben, founder and CEO of Telegent Media, will speak at the 2010 Online Marketing Summit, the premiere event for online marketing in San Diego on February 24th.

Fallbrook, CA (PRWEB) February 10, 2010   ▣ ShareThis ✉ Email ▣ PDF 🖨 Print

Jon Wuebben, founder and CEO of Telegent Media and Custom Copywriting.com, is set to speak at this year's Online Marketing Summit, the premiere educational event in Online Marketing. Mr. Wuebben, one of the leading experts in online content marketing and seo web copywriting, will sit on the interactive panel "Why Your Online Strategy always Starts with Content," which will include fellow content evangelist Joe Pulizzi of Junta 42 as well as other web content experts.

> **"** With so much competition on the blogs and in the social media space, you need to do everything you can to stand out. **"**

The Online Marketing Summit will be held at the Paradise Point Resort and Spa in sunny San Diego, CA on February 22 - 25, 2010. The event will offer engaging workshops, thought-leadership panels, and one-on-one labs on Search Engine Marketing, Website Strategy, Email Marketing, Web Analytics, Website Usability and Social Media. Attendees will collaborate, network, and learn how to execute on the best practices in Online Marketing. There are no exhibit floor or vendor sales pitch distractions. Final registrations are being taken now, upon availability.

What sets OMS apart from the typical conference or tradeshow is its strong focus on providing educational content without the fluff. Over 700 marketing professionals from around the country are expected to attend the event in San Diego.

During the Q & A Panel, Wuebben will be addressing many of the issues that content marketers are facing every day, like finding the time to produce content, ensuring the highest quality and putting together a comprehensive content strategy.

"Whether you are a large global company with many different websites or a local retailer with a simple blog, providing quality content is what it's all about. With so much competition on the blogs and in the social media space, you need to do everything you can to stand out," says Wuebben. "It's one of the messages I tried to drive home in my book, Content Rich: Writing Your Way to Wealth on the Web. It's great to see that readers all over the world have responded to that message."

About OMS
The Online Marketing Summit (OMS) is a not-for-profit organization with the simple mission to educate marketers on the emerging best practice of Online Marketing. The environment facilitates networking and collaboration amongst like-minded marketing peers and the application process ensures only peers serious about gaining a competitive advantage through education attend.

About Telegent Media
Telegent Media and its main division, CustomCopywriting.com, is one of the leading online content providers in the industry. Jon is the author of Content Rich: Writing Your Way to Wealth on the Web and speaks at business conferences and association meetings around the country. In summer, 2010, Telegent Media is launching Content Launch, the next evolution in their business-to-business content services lineup, which will provide custom text, audio and video content to companies worldwide.

Jon Wuebben publishes one of the leading content marketing blogs, Content Rich.

FIGURE 6-1   Sample Press Release

Other Tips and Suggestions

- Try to piggyback your press release topic off something that's already going on in the news. If your part of the country is having record heat and you happen to sell outdoor lotions, this may be a good opportunity to promote your new tanning spray. Pay attention to the news to see what's going on out there, and capitalize on it.

- If you are going to use a quote, statistic, or other fact that needs validation, be sure to get approval or permission. I have personally seen what happens when a source objects to the use of its material, and it always causes a major problem for the company.
- Be honest. This isn't the time to stretch the truth. If you do, you may have just told a lie to ten thousand people. If they catch you in a lie, it can't be good for your business. Credibility and integrity are way too important to risk.
- Don't use the passive voice in your release—make it active instead. Active voice brings people in and emphasizes the subject. People don't feel as close to a passive communication. What does this mean?

Example:

Passive: The house was purchased last month.

Active: Mark purchased the house last month.

Passive: The boxes were being stored in the attic by the movers.

Active: The movers stored the boxes in the attic.

- Don't use verbose, flowery, or unnecessary adjectives. Keep the language simple and concise. Also, don't ever use exclamation marks.
- Keep the press release short. Remember, you want the people reading it to click on a link within the release to visit your site. Don't put more information in the release than is needed. It's meant to pique their interest and leave them wanting more.
- Make your press release one or two pages, printed on standard letter-size paper, and double-spaced.
- Don't forget to review local radio and television shows. Talk radio and local morning programs could be perfect for your company.
- Also, start thinking about which charities in your local community you might get involved with. Find a way to be a part of their story; of course, you must do this in a sincere and genuine way.
- Find out which magazines, blogs, and other sources of news your customers read. Over time, you'll develop a customized database of media outlets that has relevance to your business. Every time you have a news story, press release, or pitch ready to go, you do two things: Send it out through an online wire service like PRWeb, and then do the off-line thing and let the media list know about it via e-mail, fax, or phone call. The two strategies working together will be your best bet.
- For the big papers, get your press release to the newsroom and, if possible, to the reporter who covers your field.

- For the smaller media outlets, get your press release to the one news editor that they probably have on staff. Note: It is definitely worth it to cultivate this relationship!
- Follow up; sometimes a follow-up phone call is a good idea, but don't be too pushy. Editors and reporters appreciate it if you are mindful of a potential deadline, so be sure to ask about that.
- Monitor your release by subscribing to a clipping service or by using www. google.com/alerts.

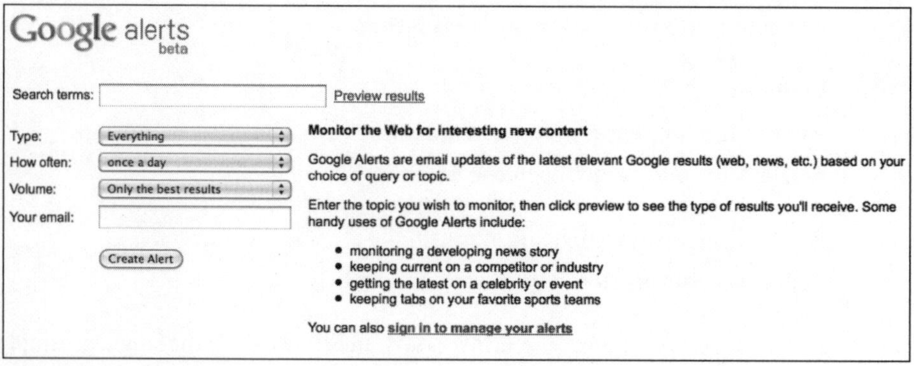

Google alerts
beta

Search terms: [   ]   Preview results

Type: [Everything   ▾]   **Monitor the Web for interesting new content**
How often: [once a day   ▾]   Google Alerts are email updates of the latest relevant Google results (web, news, etc.) based on your
Volume: [Only the best results ▾] choice of query or topic.
Your email: [   ]   Enter the topic you wish to monitor, then click preview to see the type of results you'll receive. Some
                                        handy uses of Google Alerts include:
       (Create Alert)
                                          • monitoring a developing news story
                                          • keeping current on a competitor or industry
                                          • getting the latest on a celebrity or event
                                          • keeping tabs on your favorite sports teams

                                        You can also sign in to manage your alerts

FIGURE 6-2   Google Alerts

Make Sure Your Press Release Copy Is Perfect— Avoid These Common Mistakes

What type of mistakes should you look out for in your press releases?

- Improper grammar
- Bad formatting, including strange characters that may show up in the release after it's distributed
- E-mail address issues (i.e., instead of using "john@accme.com," using "pr@ accme.com")
- Don't use all capitalized letters in your releases

Press Release Distribution

Now that you have your press release written, what's next? Two things: distributing it across the web through a wire service and pitching your story to a hand-selected group of journalists and other media folks. What's a **wire service**? A wire service is an agency that supplies news reports to news organizations: online media, blogs, newspapers, magazines, and radio and television broadcasters.

And what's a **pitch**? Unlike a full-blown press release, which assumes news-worthiness, a pitch is a *suggested story idea* that's submitted to individual journalists via phone or e-mail or in person. A pitch gives a reporter an idea for a story that he could write. If the journalist likes the idea, he writes a story for his media outlet and puts your name in lights. How is a pitch different than a press release? Pitches tend to be shorter and more informal. And most media people like them a whole lot more. The more personalized you make it the better—this shows the reporter that you've taken enough interest in him to get his name right, mention a past article, etc.

The key for you at this point is to know *what* you are pitching, what you have *to offer*, and *who* you are pitching it to.

Online Wire Services and Press Release Sites

Who are the major players in press release distribution? PRWeb, PR Newswire, Business Wire, and Marketwire in the United States. There are others in the international space. On an average day, thousands of press releases are sent out by these organizations. Personally, I have used PRWeb the most. They are affordable, efficient, and send your release to hundreds, if not thousands, of media sources. In addition, when you distribute your release through PRWeb, hundreds of other sites will republish your release via their RSS feed service, which means it will appear in more places and more people will read your news. It also means more links back to your site, which we know is great for SEO. PRWeb charges eighty-nine dollars for its basic-level service, and it goes up from there, depending on what your needs are.

Most of the other wire services also have a syndicated news feed through XML/RSS. In addition, they will regularly send out e-mail listings of press releases to thousands of media people, bloggers, writers, and others who have asked for certain releases in the industries they cover.

Both of these features can dramatically increase exposure for your press release, placing more eyes on your newsworthy story and more mouse clicks on your site.

To find out more about the wire services and to see which one you may want to use, I suggest checking out their sites. You could use one or several, depending on your preferences.

FIGURE 6-3   PRWeb

What Can Happen If You Do Releases Right

If you are able to put together a killer release that has great buzz and newsworthy flair, you could have a linking juggernaut on your hands. I've heard of a single release bringing in a dozen or more new clients for certain businesses. In addition, news organizations may read your release and decide to use it in a larger feature story. I once had a big business radio show call me to see if I wanted to be interviewed on the subject of content marketing after they read one of my releases. All kinds of unexpected things can happen.

The other cool thing is this: A release that you write and submit today could still be bringing in traffic two, three, or five years from now! Now that's some phenomenal free advertising.

Pitching Your Release to Writers in Your Industry

Many public relations and marketing firms provide an added service for press release distribution by sending your releases to key writers in your particular industry. This can give your releases added fire power, because the marketing firms will put their name behind your story and get it to other important people who may blog about it, contact you for more information, or just find creative ways to increase overall exposure. Of course, you can send releases out to the media yourself, but it takes some homework on your part. And not having a personal relationship with the writers and journalists could make it tough.

Remember, journalists are always looking for good things to write about. Their goal is to come up with an angle that they can use to create an entire series of news stories. The more interest they can generate, the brighter their star shines. Plus, it's super competitive out there in the news business. There are lots of reporters looking to outreport others. If you can feed this need, then it means more exposure—and more subsequent sales for your company.

Track the Page Views and Pickups

After you send your release through the wire service of your choice, be sure to keep track of how it's doing out there. Search for your headline on Google and Yahoo! See where it's being picked up. View your stats on the press release site and follow them closely. You'll probably see the most action right after the release is sent. Whatever ends up happening, there are always nice surprises that occur.

So, how many people end up seeing your release once it's sent out? Well, it changes all the time, but if you are B2B (business to business), you could get ten thousand to forty thousand page views in the first month. If your company focuses on B2C (business to consumer), it's more like seventy thousand to ninety thousand! Those are impressive numbers, right?

Handling the Attention After a Release Goes Out

Don't be surprised if you get some attention from your release or story. People are curious creatures. If you are doing something at your company that is interesting, your phone may start ringing off the hook. This is a very good thing! Make sure your release includes multiple ways to contact you. Watch your e-mail and be available by phone. Say yes to any and all interviews.

Here's the other thing: Prepare a longer statement (or more information) for when the media contact you. If someone wants to do a story, then it's *time to take this thing to the next level*, storyboarding it, coming up with all the other interesting facets of the story. Like a resume, a press release gets you the interview. The feature story gets you the massive exposure you are after.

The Social Media News Release

A social media release is a newer type of release that is designed to enable the content to be removed and used on blogs, wikis, and other social channels. These types of releases feature multiple embedded links (a YouTube video, Flickr slideshow, SlideShare presentation, etc.) and blocks of text similar to those found in traditional releases, including spokesperson quotes, boilerplate, and contact information. Social media releases also aim to replace the "corporate speak" and stilted writing that is found on many traditional press releases with more interesting, usable content.

A social media release also:

- Incorporates social media tools into the press release
- Includes rich media content such as videos, photos, and the release tagged with keywords
- Includes an audio link such as podcast or product announcement (connected to an RSS feed)
- Encourages visitor to share the release through Facebook, Technorati, StumbleUpon, Delicious
- Includes a "keyword cloud"
- Integrates Technorati tags and links to Delicious.
- Provides the reader with more options to get the word out

How did this type of release get started? Influential Silicon Valley journalist and blogger Tom Foremski's now-famous blog post[16] was the spark that led to the creation of the social media release. He suggested a reconstruction of the press release that would

---

[16] Foremski, Tom. 2006. "Die! Press Release! Die! Die!" Silicon Valley Watcher, February 27. Accessed 2/4/11. http://www.siliconvalleywatcher.com/mt/archives/2006/02/die_press_relea.php.

address the more social web. Todd Defren, of famed PR firm Shift Communications, created the template for the social media release shortly thereafter.

The social media press release has been around for more than four years now, and is still evolving as social media changes right before our eyes. Some PR folks stick with the classic news release as I've described it in this chapter, but many forward-thinking content marketers favor a direct or social way of distributing news, like the social media press release. Although this type of release is *not* the new standard in public relations, it *is* an option to look at for your company.

Here is a template for a social media release:

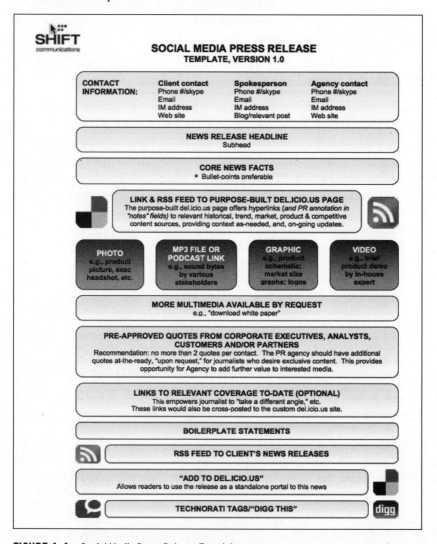

FIGURE 6-4   Social Media Press Release Template

Definitely look into trying out one of these types of releases with an upcoming press release for your company. It's worth a test!

A Forward-Thinking Wire Service: PitchEngine

In addition to the wire services mentioned earlier, you should also consider sending your release through PitchEngine. This firm represents a new type of media format and is very popular with bloggers and those on the cutting edge of the modern publishing platform.

PitchEngine enables users to create:

> *social and search optimized content that is consumer-facing—like digital flyers, press releases, real estate listings, and more. Last year, more than 100,000 pitches were shared by 30,000 organizations looking to get the word out to not just journalists, but to bloggers, consumers and other influencers. PitchEngine's "Co-op SEO" concept enables brands big and small to experience exceptional indexing in major search engines, while their social integration tools like Newsroom for Facebook, continue to push the boundaries of industry norms."*[17]

I personally recommend PitchEngine. I have used it for my company, and think its service is outstanding.

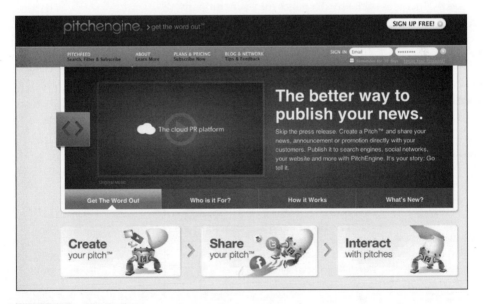

FIGURE 6-5　PitchEngine

---

[17] PitchEngine. "About Pitch." Accessed 2/11/11. http://www.pitchengine.com/about.php.

The Social Media "Newsroom"

Many companies are now developing social media "newsrooms" on their websites, with all their company information, visuals, videos, background materials, story ideas, and contact information easily accessible and searchable. Within a social media newsroom, you can place all of your multimedia assets in one online location. Placing this content on third-party sites means the potential conversation that your release generates could be happening there rather than on your corporate site. You want to be a part of the conversation as much as possible.

A newsroom like this allows you to host all of your social media releases, contact information, and links to social channels in one place. You also get to leverage the search engine optimization value of the news you release. Other important benefits of an online social media newsroom are that it:

- Offers a more modern version of the press kit
- Is cost effective
- Puts you in charge of your own PR
- Makes it easier for journalists and reporters to get quick information on your company
- Includes all press releases, high-resolution artwork, contact info, background, etc.
- Gives the media and others the ability to search for items
- Includes social media pages for your company
- Makes your releases and related items part of your site, not separate
- Offers subscription opportunity for updates

Here is great social media newsroom template:

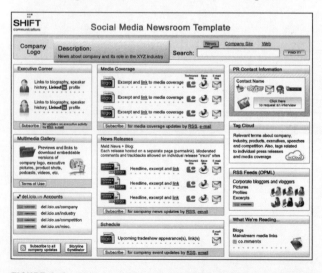

FIGURE 6-6   Shift Communications Social Media Newsroom Template

Summary

A press release is a type of content that can really work hard for your company. Done correctly, its positive influence can be multiplied many times over the course of just a few weeks. Unfortunately, many traditional and smaller companies out there still think the press release is something they submit to newspapers and that's it. They sit back and hope that their announcement will get press. Well, this mindset is at least twenty years old. In the new content age, the press release holds significant power.

What company news can you announce on a regular basis? How can you take your message and create a viral press event? Think about how you can maximize this content vehicle. It will pay off big time.

And don't forget to optimize your releases. Even some of the big companies miss this step. You want to be sure to get the search engine exposure you deserve.

Good Luck!

PART III

Content for Community and Mobile

CHAPTER 7

Content for Social Media

Social media. It's all around us, moving, shaping, and influencing everything we do—Facebook, Twitter, LinkedIn, YouTube, and all the rest of the social media platforms. It's pretty breathtaking to see what has happened in this space recently. In a few short years, social media has gone from "zero to a hundred" in rapid fashion, into a whole new paradigm of personal connection and communication.

There is no doubt that social networking or social "business," as it is now quickly moving into, has been the biggest thing to hit the business world since the Internet itself. It has been *that* massive of a change, plain and simple. Whether you are a business with a fan page on Facebook, a Twitter page, and a YouTube channel, or are simply reconnecting with old friends through social media, the phenomenon has affected practically all of us.

So, what is social media? Wikipedia says this:

> Social Media is media designed to be disseminated through social interaction, created using highly accessible and scalable publishing techniques. Social media uses Internet and web-based technologies to transform broadcast media monologues (one to many) into social media dialogues (many to many). It supports the democratization of knowledge and information, transforming people from content consumers into content producers.[18]

Andreas Kaplan and Michael Haenlein, two well-known social media gurus, define social media as "a group of Internet-based applications that build on the ideological and technological foundations of Web 2.0, and that allow the creation and exchange of user-generated content."[19]

---

[18] Wikipedia. "Social Media." Accessed 2/15/11. http://en.wikipedia.org/wiki/Social_media.
[19] Hermida. Alfred. 2010. "How to Teach Social Media in Journalism Schools." PBS MediaShift, August 30. Accessed 2/20/11. http://www.pbs.org/mediashift/2010/08/how-to-teach-social-media-in-journalism-schools242.html.

Social Media Optimization

I brought the concept of *social media optimization* up earlier in the book, but let's take a deeper dive. Again, for the sake of definition and understanding, let's start with the basics. What is it? Also from Wikipedia (and a pretty good definition):

> Social Media Optimization (SMO) or Social SEO is the methodization of social media activity with the intent of attracting unique visitors to website content. SMO is one of two online methods of website optimization; the other method is search engine optimization or SEO.
>
> There are two categories of SMO/Social SEO methods:
>
> (a) Social media features added to the content itself, including: RSS feeds, social news and sharing buttons, user rating and polling tools, and incorporating third-party community functionalities like images and videos
>
> (b) Promotional activities in social media aside from the content being promoted, including: blogging, commenting on other blogs, participating in discussion groups, and posting status updates on social networking profiles[20]

It basically comes down to putting your social media presence to work for your company, spending quality time with it every day, leveraging like crazy, and generally getting out there to gain maximum benefit. In many ways, your efforts start paying off exponentially when you do so. Why? People love to be a part of something big (and something social). With SMO, users are rewarded for both *consuming* and *distributing* content.

But let's take each of the important tenets of SMO individually. There are a few solid rules to live by with social media optimization:

1. **Create sharable content.** To optimize a site for social media, you need to make your content shareable and increase the *linkability* of the content. So, you get a blog set up, you start producing some great content, and you want people to link to it. And you also want them to "Like" it on Facebook and tweet about it on Twitter. You can also write e-books, white papers, and the like, all of which will encourage sharing.

2. **Make sharing and tagging easy.** Add buttons to your posts like "Tweet this" and "Add to Delicious." Make sure your posts include a list of relevant tags, suggest linking to your blog, and tag your pages on popular social bookmarking sites. Your people can post a short link to their profiles, embed a video, send out a tweet, or create a hashtag for a conversation. Whats a hashtag? It's a special tag embedded in a tweet that helps you search for tweets that have a common topic. For example, if you search on #CONTENTISCURRENCY, you'll get a list of tweets related to this book.

---

[20] Wikipedia. "Social Media Optimization." Accessed 2/20/11. http://en.wikipedia.org/wiki/Social_media_optimization.

3. **Proactively share content.** With this rule, you want to proactively share content in many different ways. Creating slides to post on SlideShare or documents to share on Scribd, tweeting about your content or offering embeddable versions of it, and using RSS feeds to syndicate it are all great ideas. Proactively sharing even includes posting your content to social networking profiles or creating profiles on video-sharing sites.

4. **Encourage the "mashup."** A "mashup" is material combined from multiple sources to create a new work. You need to let others use and share your content. Syndicating your content through RSS makes it easy for others to create mashups that can drive traffic or augment your content.

5. **Be a resource for others, whether or not you benefit directly.** It's the old "give what you get" thing. Paying it forward. Being cool toward one another. Not always thinking of only yourself or your company. Essentially, you want to add value to users, including links to sites that you think would be helpful for them. People will notice your efforts, especially in the social space.

6. **Build relationships with those who help the most.** If certain individuals are rising to a level of influence in your community and helping you (without asking for anything in return), you should promote their content or develop a rating system. E-mail or call them and build a true friendship. Chances are, they will be surprised or even shocked. And both of you will benefit, a whole lot.

7. **Participate and get involved—genuinely.** This could be the most important tenet of them all. Join the conversation. Be active. Show your concern. Social media is a two-way street. By getting involved, you create awareness. Your message spreads and your influence grows.

8. **Create compelling content.** Yes, content is king in social media too. No matter what your business is, whether it's sexy or boring, there is always content you can develop that will get people interested. Create a widget, write an award-winning white paper, have a webinar with three of your best clients, whatever it is, it's important to embrace the "publisher" part of the process with SMO.

9. **Develop an SMO strategy and make it a part of your business life.** You don't want to get into social media without a good plan. Define your objectives and set goals. Your outcome depends on it. Find ways to incorporate SMO tactics when you first start developing your content. Be consistent, get involved, and stick to your plan.[21]

In essence, SMO is the process by which you **make your content easily shareable across the social web**. It's helping people view your content through widgets, apps, and other social media entry points. The more transportable you can make your content, the better.

---

[21] Singer, Adam. "16 Rules for Social Media Optimization Revisited." *TopRank Online Marketing Blog.* Accessed 2/9/11. http://www.toprankblog.com/2009/08/social-media-optimization-redux/.

Why Social Media Optimization Matters

There's one big reason that social media optimization matters: **social networks are driving an increasing amount of traffic to an increasing number of websites**. In fact, many companies are seeing more traffic from social networks than they see from Google. If your content is interesting and easily shareable, you have social media power captured in a bottle. But SMO isn't just about growing your social media presence, it's tying into and *leveraging the social networks of others*. Therein lies the true beauty of it, in building a web of influence.

How do you make changes to optimize your website so it is more easily linked to within social media?

- Engaging in general SEO for your website, adding content, rewriting meta tags, etc. (See Chapter 4)
- Adding a blog and using the plug-in "Share This" to get people to distribute it for you
- Adding your social media icons to the top of every content piece
- Using the Facebook "Like" button on your content
- Using Google's +1 (their answer to Facebook's Like button and something that can also help with Google search rankings)

And what are we talking about when we say "social media content"? Writing for social media could take the form of blog posts, tweets on Twitter, videos that you share on Facebook or YouTube, and sites that you give a thumbs-up to on social bookmarking sites like StumbleUpon.

But knowing how to write and publish content for a social media world can be a challenge—and can be very time consuming. How do you do it and why is it important? We'll get to that very soon . . .

Social Media Is Expanding Like Crazy

It seems like with every blog I frequent, the topics covered have morphed into a social media cornucopia of delights. The topic used to just be "social media," but now it's divided and multiplied into a number of subtopics within the larger umbrella. From video marketing and distribution to social media tools, and from social media training and advertising to integrating social media and traditional media, the list is endless. Despite all of this activity and buzz, there are many thousands of companies out there, large and small, that are still resisting it—or confused about it.

Why? Because resisting an idea, for many, is *human nature 101*. Even for some of those who like to be out in front. And I surmise it's more of an issue in the United States, where it seems we are always wondering, "How can we turn this great idea into quick cash?" Oh yeah, that *ROI thing*. Well, maybe social media will finally help place "building a community" and "establishing a brand" above ROI (where they should be), once and for all. Whether we are talking about Twitter, Facebook, LinkedIn, your blog—they're all excellent ways of connecting with your customers and offering them something useful. Embrace these platforms now and they will love you back. With each passing week, this notion seems to be more and more clear.

And you know what? There *are* companies—many of them—that are even making money from their involvement in social media. We'll get to that in a bit.

What can you get out of your social media involvement? How about a speaking slot at a big industry event? How about an important introduction to an industry partner in Europe? How about a book deal? There are a thousand or more great things that can happen as a result of your involvement. Think about it more as a return on *engagement*.

And consider this: If you aren't convinced of social media's ability to capture "eyeballs" and cold hard cash, you'll be interested to know that **Dell Computers generated $3 million in sales in 2010 with links from its various Twitter accounts**.[22] Wow. I think that's really impressive. There are a thousand or more similar stories of ROI with social media. So, to all the B2B naysayers out there—stop already! You're wrong. Get on board.

Gathering in Groups

One thing is clear: All social media sites have a "groups" feature that helps gather like minds together. This can help you cut to the chase and find out who *your people* are, right away. On Facebook, this feature is naturally called "Groups." On Twitter, it's called "Lists." Of course, as with any social interaction, you can't just join the group and expect things to happen, you have to *actively participate*.

You also have the ability to create "Events" on the social media sites. This can be a powerful feature as well. Why? It's fundamental to the human experience: Everyone loves being invited to an event. Whether it's web seminars, live in-person events, or another type of gathering, creating a series of popular events through social media is a great strategy to employ.

So, lets focus on three major areas:

1. How your company benefits from social media content
2. Types of social media content
3. Finding time to create social media content

By reviewing these three areas and understanding how the information can apply to your business, you can make the very most of social media and stay out in front of your competitors. In terms of getting your feet wet, you may want to contribute first by joining existing social discussions about other content. See what people are talking about and what types of content are the most popular.

So, let's get right into it . . .

---

[22] Miller, Claire Cain. 2009. "Dell Says It Has Earned $3 Million from Twitter." *The New York Times* blog, June 12. http://bits.blogs.nytimes.com/2009/06/12/dell-has-earned-3-million-from-twitter/.

How Your Company Benefits from Social Media Content

How exactly does your company benefit by using social media? With Facebook, Twitter, YouTube, your blog, and other venues, you can:

- Build new relationships
- Provide thought leadership
- Respond to customers
- Improve search engine rankings
- Drive and augment media exposure
- Implement promotions and contests
- Impact sales, ultimately

But let's be fair, it isn't just the ROI issue that stops companies from jumping in with social media. In fact, there are a number of other issues that various surveys cite, including lack of knowledge, executive resistance, not having the time to do it, etc. The bottom line: **Social media is about influence, connection, and brand.** When considering getting into the social media space, it's important to ask a few key questions: Who is your audience? Who will you connect with? What's your strategy? These are all things that you want to think about and plan for. If you haven't done it yet, get yourself a calendar and start mapping out what you want to do.

The great thing about social media is that we are able to do things that we've never done before, more efficiently, at a higher level. Through these platforms we can facilitate new relationships, new conversations, positive influence, and close customer interaction . . . all at a faster rate than ever before. Why? One big reason lies in that definition I started off with: *Social media uses technologies to transform broadcast media monologues (one to many) into social media dialogues (many to many).*

It's the "many to many" dynamic that really changes the game. When your content is shared, it has tremendous power. Unbelievable power. If you're old enough to remember what life was like before the Internet, you'll recall that all of this social connection stuff used to happen at conferences, in the workplace, or through a social service group or association. Whew, that was a lot of work! Although it's still important to attend live events, thankfully, we have the super-efficient web to help out now.

How times have changed, and for the better! Social media is taking us to exciting places.

Types of Social Media Content

So, we know now that social media is any online media that allows users to interact with one another. We also know that there are many different types of social media. But what are they? What does the landscape look like? Here is a list of the unique forms of social media and the sites that are the most important for getting your content out there.

- **Social networking—Facebook, Twitter, LinkedIn, Google +1**
  Social networking sites allow users to add clients, prospects, and partners and to send messages and share content using either the "one-to-many" or "many-to-many" format. Typically, people on social networking sites get together in communities of like-minded interest.
- **Video Sharing—YouTube, Vimeo, TubeMogul**
  Sites like YouTube have revolutionized online video, allowing users to share video content either privately or publicly. More on video content in Chapter 11.
- **Blogging platforms—WordPress, TypePad, Blogger, etc.**
  Most people have interacted with blogs for many years now, and we'll get into blog content in the next chapter. But for definition purposes, blogs are online journals where companies or individuals discuss anything they want to—reviews of products, opinions on industry news, interviews, etc., and can share this with their blog subscribers. There are many easy-to-use blogging platforms, including WordPress, TypePad, and Blogger, that host blogs for free.
- **Wikis—Wikipedia**
  A wiki refers to content created online by multiple users working on the same content, but at different times and from different places.
- **Photo sharing—Flickr, Photobucket**
  Photo-sharing sites allow people to upload photos to share with anyone they like.
- **Presentation sharing—SlideShare, Scribd**
  Have a PowerPoint deck that you want to share with lots of people? No problem. Using a site like SlideShare, you can upload as many presentations as you like and even get some SEO benefit by doing so. Have a manuscript you want people to review? Check out Scribd.
- **Social bookmarking—StumbleUpon, Digg, Delicious**
  Social bookmarking applications allow users to share their favorite online content with one another while creating online bookmarks. The bookmarks are on a website, so other people can see your bookmarks and ideally be exposed to sites they wouldn't otherwise encounter. Some social bookmarking sites, like StumbleUpon, use a voting system that allows users to indicate which bookmarks they found interesting.

Making an Impact with Social Media Content

Obviously, in this time of social media growth, there are hundreds of sites to choose from when you ponder where you want to focus your efforts. Selecting the right social

media channels for your company or individual tastes is based on your specific preferences, goals, and long-term content strategy. If you are a business, you naturally want
to go where your target market, customers, and partners are.

A good place to start is by setting up profiles and learning the basics of these
sites:

- Facebook
- Twitter
- LinkedIn
- YouTube
- SlideShare
- Flickr

These sites are, in my opinion, where you can get the most traction and they are,
as you will see, the most popular of all the social sites. There is a learning curve, but
hopefully the information in this chapter will fast-track your process.

Using Link Bait in Social Media

"Link bait" is a term used to describe viral, linkable content designed to attract thousands of links; it is recognized as one of the most effective ways to build links—and
relevance for a site. Essentially, it means putting together really good content that has
solid, value-added information in it. So, link baiting is really building *link-friendly
content*. It's also a great way to approach social media content, because it gets people
interested and gets them engaged.

The traditional way of getting links, circa 2003, involved contacting other relevant
websites, e-mailing the webmasters and asking for a link. You'd contact people you
know—vendors, partners, customers, and suppliers and you would "reciprocate" links.
You would carefully explain in your e-mails that linking to you would be worthwhile
for their visitors and beneficial to them as well . . . and you'd spend hundreds of hours
doing it. This process was all fine and dandy, but the companies that really made an
impact were the ones that were producing solid content that others naturally wanted to
link to. How did they do it? They would put together a thirty-page e-book on a popular
topic in their industry and publish it on their blog. Others would see it, want to link
to it immediately, and just like that . . . they were off to the races.

There is no doubt about it: Developing high-quality, very popular, link-friendly
content is the way to go in the social media world. With "link bait," you can do this.
First, as all the experts will tell you, you need a good "hook" for your blog posts,
tweets or Facebook status updates. A hook is the angle, or the way of grabbing the
reader's attention. You do it by capitalizing on something that's really important to
most people—new information, security, money, respect, gossip, new ideas, a secret,
etc. . . . and give it a little sizzle.

Types of Hooks

- Providing something important—The Resource Hook
- Tying in to what's relevant—The News Hook
- Going against the grain—The Contrary Hook
- Taking the offensive position—The Attack Hook
- Making people laugh—The Humor Hook[23]

Providing Something Important—The Resource Hook

- Develop a comprehensive list of blogs in your niche; link to them, and chances are they will link to you.
- Create a useful tool related to your niche that people like.
- Write how-to posts: How to do _____. Make it substantive and link-friendly!
- Create a compilation of news stories on a theme that you analyze and create a post for.
- List related resources. For example, if you run a hotel, discuss all the places to visit in the surrounding area.

Tying in to What's Relevant—The News Hook

- Find out who reports the news to the news reporting agencies—and then jump on it.
- Call someone or something out—if you can expose a fraud or flaw in a news story and report on it, the content could be very link-friendly. You could have thousands of links very quickly.
- Give your opinion on a popular news story.
- Don't rehash what someone else already reported—give any reporting your own slant.

Going Against the Grain—The Contrary Hook

- Put any contrarian tendencies to use! Be the one guy who finds something to not like about a story, a product, or a service, and then defend your position.
- Write posts that explain "Why <insert prominent blogger or company name here> is WRONG about . . ."
- Find something that's really popular and then tear it apart—but do it the right way, not with vindictiveness. People will notice.

Taking the Offensive Position—The Attack Hook

- Point out why a particular product or service is doing more harm than good.

---

[23] Performancing. 2008. "The Art of Linkbaiting." Accessed 2/25/11. http://performancing.com/the_art_of_linkbaiting/.

- Go after the government (regarding almost anything—it is a great target).
- Stand up for an underrepresented or disadvantaged group.
- Choose a topic that has a fair degree of truth on both sides, and then write away!
- Make your content informed, smart, and very controversial.

You have to be careful with this one—you don't want to write the wrong thing about the wrong person. It's a good idea to go after a company or product rather than an individual. However, if you're gutsy, have some proof for what you are claiming, and really want to gain some instant traffic, using this hook can give you instant credibility and build your reputation like wildfire. Most people love controversy, and when you use an attack hook, you stir it up.

Making People Laugh—The Humor Hook

- Photoshop a funny picture or cartoon for the subject you are writing about and post it.
- Post a list that takes a humorous slant: "Top 20 Ways I'm Going to Work from Bed This Week."
- Post an idea: "You know you're a _____ when . . ."
- Play off another funny bit that you came across: jokes, funny stories, etc. People love to laugh.

On that last point, we all could use some comic relief from the craziness of life on the web, right? Or life in general. If you have a natural way of lightening things up through your personality, you may be able to write that way too. Give it a shot with your next blog post. You'll create some link-friendly content in the process.

Other Ways to Link Bait

Of course, there are so many other ways to get visitors engaged by your content. Think of the ways you respond positively to something you see online. Sometimes it's a cool contest with a great prize, other times it's an interesting interview with an industry guru. Let's discuss these other methods of link baiting.

Contests

Another thing you can do to build link-friendly social media content is to run a contest or sweepstakes on your Twitter or Facebook page. It doesn't have to be expensive—you could give away your services, actually. This way, it will only cost you in labor. And if this labor is your labor, then it doesn't really cost a thing for you financially (dollars out of your pocket). In the past, my company has given away ten free pages of web content to a group of new prospects, which proved to be very effective, every time. This has been an especially good tactic at trade shows as a giveaway at our booth, a book signing and yes, as a special online social media event. People absolutely *love* contests ñ and the prospect of winning something. If you can tap into a magical marketing technique and grow your business at the same time, well then thatís a pretty good idea, right?

What could your company give away? If youíre an Accountant, perhaps a free tax return preparation service? If youíre a Management Consultant, maybe you could give away three hours of consulting time. Whatever it is, make it something of value that people will want. Of course, you could make it fun and easy too. For example, if you run a winery, you could hold a contest to name the new Cabernet vintage for your vineyard. Run a restaurant? Have your customers submit names for a new award-winning dish. People love this type of contest. They may not get a big financial benefit, but when they see the name they submitted end up on the wine bottle or on the restaurant menu, itís a pretty cool feeling to know you were the one to name it!

Once you decide what your contest is, promote it and blog about it like crazy . . . on every social media channel at your disposal.

Interviews

To build some high-quality link bait, you could interview prominent people in your industry. How about that for an idea? You know that the people you interview will link to you, right? Absolutely they will. I have interviewed business book authors, CEOís from web development firms, some of my partners, and a few others. In fact, Iíve never had anyone turn down an interview request. Most people love to be asked and they also love to share their wisdom and insights.

Think about it: Most of the prominent people in any field have fairly large egos. Play off that and get some great traffic as a result! They will blog about it and promote it through their social media profiles. And if they have 50,000 followers on Twitter, this could be massive exposure for your Twitter profile. Try this on your YouTube channel next week.

Product or Service Reviews

There are a thousand products or services that your target market would love to read about. What are they? Think about what your customers like. What do they use in their lives? You may even want to survey them to find out. The great thing about reviews is that they are easy to write and give you instant content. Plus, youíll get people who want to link to them, especially if itís a review for a popular product or service.

The secret, of course, with all of these link bait approaches is that you need to have peopleóyour clients and prospectsósee what you write. Itís all useless unless itís seen and acted upon. And if you are brand new on the scene, that can be a challenge. So, how do you do it? For starters, link to your clients and prospects in your post, send e-mails to them, call them, etc. Add them as friends on Facebook, follow them on Twitter . . . whatever it takes! If you can get at least one prominent blogger in your niche to take notice, the rest will most likely follow. Remember, the offers, specials, and rewards content can be one of the most powerful types of content. For example, the 1-800-FLOWERS.com Facebook page24 shows a discount code only when you click the îLikeî button. More to come on incentivized content in just a few pages. . . .

Sharing Knowledge

What about gracing others with your supreme intellect by giving away your own business knowledge? Your personal experience with clients and your expertise in your field will definitely be of interest to others in your social community. From "how to" or review videos to writing cornerstone content for your blog, providing your knowledge to others establishes you as a clear authority, motivating people to get in on the conversation and be a part of your online social media world.

Getting involved with social media is fantastic for developing an audience of new customers, partners, and others—including the media!

Using Lists

And then there are lists. Top ten whatever. Top hundred whatever—think David Letterman here, but even better. Not just funny, but interesting and thought provoking. There is something about lists that people love. Maybe it mimics the way we think. Our brains are probably wired like that. Maybe it's because we are drawn to order and like categorizing things. Whatever it is, lists encourage debate and give people solid hooks to remember the points you are making.

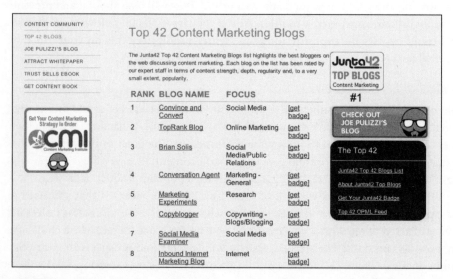

FIGURE 7-1   Using Lists

Debate a Popular Figure

For you adventurous types, you can light the social media world on fire by debating another popular member of your community or taking the contrarian view on a particular topic. Think about it: Some of the best arguments and debates of all time got massive exposure. From the marketing campaign driven "Coke versus Pepsi" ads from the 1980's to the more serious ongoing global warming issue, disagreeing with conventional wisdom can become very powerful social media content.

Whatever type of social media content you decide to produce, be sure to make it about *your audience* in one way or another.

Profiles of Important Social Media Sites

If there is one thing we all know it's that online social networking takes time. It takes us away from other business activities and can easily turn into an obsessive pursuit. So, how do we make it work for us? Which sites should we focus on first? Let's dive right in.

Facebook: As Powerful as Google

Facebook has probably changed the game more than any other social media giant. Everything I mentioned in the first couple pages of this chapter applies to Facebook more than any other social media site. As a force in both commerce and culture, it will be around for a long, long time. As a business, if you're not already involved, you want to get engaged with Facebook immediately. It could very likely be one of the best things you ever did.

Although this book is not a comprehensive social media guide, it is a *social media content guide* and there are basics that all companies should follow if they want to maximize their efforts with Facebook. The first thing, of course, is to set up a company page (not profile) through Facebook Pages.

But where do you take it from there? Well, you'll want to **populate your page with information about your company**. Be sure to use your important keywords while you do this, because the search engines do crawl these pages. Then you want to focus on **Applications**. You can create as many as ten additional tabs, which can contain lots of cool content. A few you definitely want are:

- **NetworkedBlogs**—allows you to post your RSS feeds directly to your wall
- **Twitter Tab**—posts your Twitter updates to its own tab
- **Extended Info**—adds an additional box that supports HTML/FBML, images, video, and music to the left sidebar of your page
- **Fan Appz and Promotions**—helps you with contests, sweepstakes, and give-aways, an absolute must for building your following

FIGURE 7-2   Facebook Company Page Example

Offers, specials, and rewards content can be one of the most powerful types of content. For example, the 1-800-FLOWERS.com Facebook page[24] shows a discount code only when you click the "Like" button. More to come on **incentivized content** in just a few pages. . . .

The Power Behind the Facebook "Like" Button

As you'll learn with your Facebook fan page, you have access to what's called a "Like" button. Essentially, it is a way to show your affirmative belief in something, whether it's a brand, event, video, or whatever. And the "Like" feature taps into the magic power of popularity and the influence of groups. There's a lot of power behind the Like button, and Facebook knows it.

How will the Like button help with your advertising and promotions? Facebook allows advertisers to retransmit users Likes as sponsored messages. For example, if you

---

[24] 1-800-FLOWERS.com Facebook page. Accessed 2/19/11. http://www.facebook.com/1800flowers?v=app_4949752878.

see the movie "The Social Network" (which I loved), and decide to Like it, Columbia Pictures can republish your Like as an ad on your friends' pages.

Think about how much an endorsement from a friend means to you. Whether it's the Hawaiian hotel your best friend recommended last summer or the restaurant your sister thought you would like last weekend, our friends' opinions are very meaningful. And you know what? Every time someone in your Facebook network passes your content on to someone else, the person who shared it is giving it an implicit seal of approval. Not only is this supremely effective, it gives you the best chance of converting that person into a new business relationship when the time is right. It really doesn't matter *where* your content is published, it's *who endorses it* that makes all the difference. And this has been true since the dawn of human relationships.

So why is the Like button so effective? Because we *like to give approval*. It's part of having a meaningful connection. We also use it because *it fosters a social experience*; it's shared. Let's face it: You're more likely to remain on a site if you see that ten of your friends have "Liked" it. The Like button works well because *it's easy*. We know that there is no commitment to clicking it. We're in, we're out, and no one gets hurt. It sends the positive energy out and the positive energy comes back to us. Good stuff.

Recently, Levi's implemented Facebook Likes across its site and saw a great deal of success with it.[25] In fact, after doing so, Levi's determined that Facebook became its number one site for referring traffic. Wow, that's significant, especially when you've been through SEO, blogging, and all the other online marketing tactics and strategies like that brand has.

Other tools are the "Like Box," which allows you to become a Facebook fan without leaving the web page and "Live Stream," which is often used while broadcasting events. Facebook Ads can also serve you well, driving people to your page. Be sure to check them out.

FIGURE 7-3   Facebook Like Button

Twitter: The Rise of a New Type of Web Content

What is Twitter? It is the ultimate in microblogging. It is one of the fastest-growing web phenomena in the history of the web itself. Twitter is a web service that lets users send short messages up to 140 characters in length to a group of people. Launched in

---

[25] Owyang, Jeremiah. 2010. "Social Commerce Breakdown: How Levi's and Facebook Prompt Your Friends to Improve Your Buying Experience." *Web Strategy*, April 30. http://www.web-strategist.com/blog/2010/04/30/social-commerce-.

2006, Twitter was designed to keep friends and colleagues informed about each other's daily activities.

Twitter is increasingly used by businesses to tell customers and prospects what's new. In addition, politicians and celebrities use it to keep constituents and fans informed. Twitter messages are not sent indiscriminately; they are distributed only to those who have elected to become your followers. Messages can also be sent via instant messaging, the Twitter website, or a third-party Twitter application. A Twitter message is called a "tweet," and an ongoing stream of Twitter messages is a "Twitter feed."

So, how is Twitter inspiring a whole new type of content and communication style? One way to approach this question is by considering *body language*. Researchers say it makes up 70 percent of communication. The way people say things, their facial expressions, their gestures, all are critical to the communication, and need to be understood for the exchange to be meaningful. Of course, in the online world—with e-mail, instant messaging, social media sites, and the like, where we don't see people in front of us—there is no way we can duplicate this body language information, right? Not true. Think about it: Because we have the opportunity to so "expose" ourselves online, in many different formats and unique ways, including—here is the kicker—via *online video*, we are able to communicate very similarly to the way we communicate in person. It's true that we can't precisely replicate the back-and-forth, interactive nature of being in the same room with another person, though with **two-way video** coming on strong, maybe even that will be impacted.

In this day and age, we all have less time. We all need to do more with less. But we all still have a deep need to communicate with each other. Could the Twitter dynamic—that of short, substantive, real-time interaction, paired with the burgeoning two-way video technology—be the template for future content and future communication? Well,

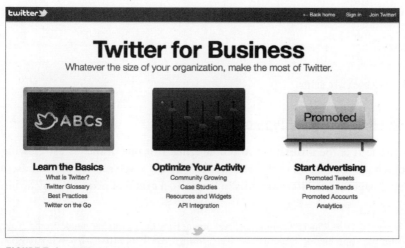

FIGURE 7-4   Twitter

it's happening now. Despite some occasional bandwidth issues, it works well. It's simple. It's cheap. And it aligns with our need for quick, meaningful communication. True, not all tweets are substantive. But we are getting really good at filtering this stuff out. So, what is Twitter? It's a great way to communicate and market using content. How do we use Twitter? Often, and with purpose.

Here is the deal: Future content, quite a bit of it anyway, will be "micro" in nature; it'll be tailored to a specific little group, will address their needs or wants, and will be delivered in short bursts. More and more content will be customized, clear, and with a call to action, a call to action that addresses something you want or need right now. The reason it will have more impact? Because the quicker you can address what someone wants right now, the quicker he will respond, and this is especially critical for you when there are competitors offering the same thing.

Case in point: If there is a Starbucks and a Peet's Coffee location, and both are nearby when you suddenly want a Carmel Machiatto, the one that delivers the virtual coupon first will get your business, right? Yep. (They have your geolocation because you've opted in.)

Using Incentives for Influence

People love free stuff. So, as I mentioned briefly a few pages back, it's no surprise that social media content such as giveaways, contests, and sweepstakes are really effective at building your Twitter followers and Facebook friends list. How do you do it? Invite people to follow or friend you. They provide their name and e-mail address in exchange for a chance to win something of value. Whether you are giving away a free service or free product, a sweepstakes is an easy way to increase your fan base. Selecting the Like button on Facebook requires a very low level of commitment, and when people see that they can win something cool if they Like you, the chances are high that they will participate.

A contest is a good way to both increase and engage your fan base. Requiring thought or skill, a contest is more than simply a giveaway like a sweepstakes. For example, entrants may compete to come up with the new name for your clothing line or protein bar. A contest gives them a voice and shows that you care about them.

You could engage your fans by hosting a "Fan of the Week" contest. Fans simply post a picture of themselves using your product, and winners get to see their photos on your Facebook page. It's so simple, and can be very effective. You could give your fans an opportunity to compete with others to name your new product or service. You could have them put together a video advertisement for your company. Whoever comes up with the best video ad wins the contest. There are all types of things you could do.

Thousands of companies use Facebook this way. With Twitter, you can also reward fans for retweeting events and specials.

What could your company give away or do to grow and engage your fans? Try a sweepstakes or a contest and see what happens.

Finding Time for Social Media Content

So, all this social media content stuff is great, but how do you start it and how do you get it all done? Well, you are not alone in wondering that. In fact, this is the number one question I'm asked when I go out and speak about social media. Well, you'll be happy to know that your social media content development process is all taken care of—or at least a plan to set up your own process, that is . . .

1. First, understand who your audience is. Who are the stakeholders? And what do they want to know about?
2. What are the top industry issues? What type of content is popular? You'll want to see what other companies are involved with in the social media space for your industry.
3. Who are the important bloggers in your industry, and what are they saying about these issues? This is important to know. These are folks that you will either partner with, compete with, debate with, or all of the above. Research this by going to Technorati, Delicious, and Google Blogsearch.
4. Where are the top bloggers and influencers in the social media space? Which groups do they belong to on Facebook? Who are the guys in your industry with five thousand or more followers on Twitter? And what about LinkedIn? You want to analyze what they are discussing and find out how you can fit in.
5. Join the conversation in these places. Comment on blogs and social networks in a nonpromotional way. Become part of the community. Make your thoughts known!
6. Determine who will create the content. If you are more than a one-person show, get more than one person involved. Assign a schedule and make the person (or team) responsible.
7. Put together a content strategy/schedule and then start creating content!

Creating great content for your social network starts with a good plan. Get to know the community and the types of content they like before spending your time and energy on content development. Once you know the important personalities and what content "plays" well, you can do anything you want—create a great list, get an informative interview, tell a client success story. None of this, of course, comes easy. As with any type of content marketing, you have to come from an authentic place and keep at it.

Mine Social Media for Keyword Research

Another thing you can do with social media is get information on what people are talking about. What's hot? What's trending? How can you find an angle or a way into the conversation? What you'll want to do is research how social media authors in your space are tagging their content. You can use tools like Omgili, Boardreader, IceRocket, and others as well.

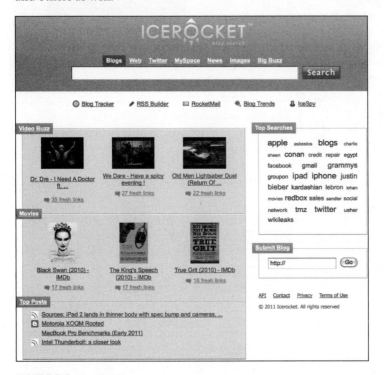

FIGURE 7-5   IceRocket

With StumbleUpon, you can search by criteria and review the "filter by tag" list. All of this gives you great ammunition for developing a video or e-book or other piece of content that incorporates the keywords and is tagged in the same way. This is one great way to shorten your path to social media success. If you write about something that you think is important, but no one else does, then you could have done a lot of work for nothing. If you use these social media tools, that won't happen. You get a handle on what's popular using these very simple tools.

But how do you organize all the research? I think the advice provided in a great book called *Audience, Relevance, and Search* says it best: "Using an economical social media analysis tool such as Alterian SM2, you can export data about social media posts to excel and use any text analyzer tool, such as testSTAT, to see the relationships between words and keywords that are associated with a keyword phrase that you entered. This will help you craft your long-tail keywords. Think of SM2 as a social media warehouse."[26] This is a phenomenal idea.

---

[26] Mathewson, James. 2010. *Audience, Relevance, and Search*. Upper Saddle River, NJ: IBM Press.

⊙ALTERIAN
SM2 Social Media Console

> Analyze & actively engage in social media conversations

SM2 Social Media Console offers a dynamic approach to scaling social media engagement across an organization. It allows users to easily capture, analyze and actively engage in social media conversations while coordinating outreach across multiple business divisions. The application's interactive workflow process allows users to respond and prioritize conversations by importance.

Key features include:

- Engagement
- Listening Grid
- Interactive Workflow
- Real-Time Coordination
- Activity & Conversation History
- Twitter Integration

Simplify Customer Engagement

Businesses realize that participating in social media conversations is crucial in enhancing brand loyalty, addressing customer service issues, analyzing marketing campaigns and generating sales leads. SM2 Social Media Console allows users to not only listen to what consumers are saying about their brand, but provides them with the ability to actively join within the conversation. By working collaboratively across multiple business divisions, organizations are able to effectively manage their social media strategies and marketing efforts.

User Benefits

SM2 Social Media Console simplifies the process of integrating and engaging social media across an enterprise by:

- Respond and actively engage in social media conversations directly from the platform
- Interactive workflow process for easy assignment, prioritization, response and reviews
- Respond with individualized accounts for personalization
- Work collaboratively across departments
- Monitor competitive conversations for prospective opportunities
- View the audit trail of interactions, responses and notes of specific posts

FIGURE 7-6   Alterian SM2

Social Aggregators

Your time is precious. With social media, you need to find shortcuts. The key here is leverage—you publish your blog post, and it automatically gets published on your Twitter, Facebook, and LinkedIn pages at the same time. You can do this very easily with HootSuite (http://hootsuite.com/).

Why is Hootsuite so great? It helps save you time and spares you the frustration that so many companies complain about with social media. Essentially, it enables you to manage multiple social networks through one venue. And if you have more than one content contributor, you can easily manage multiple users. You can also track statistics.

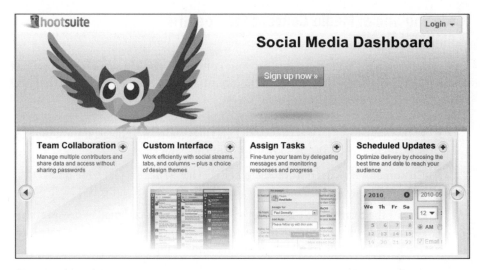

FIGURE 7-7   HootSuite

You can also gain some leverage by checking out other tools like TweetDeck. Use KnowEm to set up social profiles, rather than doing so manually. And then be sure to check out cool account management tools like Facebook Connect, OpenID, and Google Friend Connect. You can use a single login for all your social sites, so you don't need to stress about all of those user IDs and passwords!

FIGURE 7-8   TweetDeck

Creating Social Media Content for Specific Company Needs

The social media content you create for your company can help serve more than just the marketing department and to gain the attention of new audiences and garner new sales. Content can also be developed to serve:

- **Human resources**—you can recruit and prescreen candidates, improving new hire quality while reducing recruitment time and cost

- **Customer service**—resolve customer service issues in real time and reduce costs; Best Buy and Dell use it for this purpose, and so can you

- **Sales**—the buying cycle has forever changed with social media: prospects are researching like crazy, putting together lists of possible vendors; generate leads and build credibility with social media content for sales purposes

- **Product development**—your customers and prospects want to tell you what they think; with high value and low cost of use, social media can serve as the new focus group

Final Notes

Do your research. No matter what type of content you are developing, the first step to crafting it is to get a feel for the background. And don't just look at two or three sources for your content project; review ten or more. It's good to get perspective.

Write an attention-getting headline. Your headline is probably the most important factor for determining how popular your social media content becomes. Look at the concept of status updates on Facebook. Make your headlines, updates, tweets, or other content enticing enough for people to want to know more.

Follow with a great opening. The hardest part of anything is starting it, right? Well, the most important part of social media content (right in line with the headline) is how you begin the blog post, article, video, or whatever. You've got to keep them interested! If not, they will click away from you within three seconds.

Be conversational. The key word in social media is *social*. You need to interact! Boring, tired content will not bring you or your readers into the conversation. If they were there right in front of you, how would you talk to them? Develop content like that.

Never give up. Social media marketing requires a long-term commitment. Produce great content, learn from your mistakes, and tweak your approach until it starts working. Remember, social media is not about making money; it's about relationships and building community.

CASE STUDY: A Facebook Page for NOLA Photo Fun

NOLA Photo Fun, a New Orleans–based service similar to Snapfish, was struggling to attract users. Because many people living in New Orleans are Saints fans, it made sense for NOLA Photo Fun to connect with Saints fans on an emotional level and give support during their struggle to retain a piece of New Orleans culture. The company partnered with HERO|farm, a creative guild that provides website design, social media marketing, and more to local companies. The approach HERO|farm took with NOLA Photo Fun was to use social media to ingrain their cause into the psyche of the consumer, forming a connection that was valuable to them while promoting feelings of loyalty and enthusiasm.

NOLA Photo Fun was positioned as the "preserver of New Orleans memories"; HERO|farm also wanted to associate the photo-sharing company with defending the city's heritage. They did this by creating the "Who Dat Nation" Preservation Project, to allow Saint fans the opportunity to immortalize their fandom through NOLA Photo Fun's online services. To do this, HERO|farm developed a Facebook page for the project, using an endearing logo that symbolized the Superdome. To reward the group's fans (the "Who Dats"), a fan photo challenge was issued to see who had the most black and gold in their veins. This contest was promoted through Facebook interactions such as status updates, comments, and tagging members, as well as with web banners on NOLA.com and local news station WDSU's website.

In two short months, the project gained 1,921 fans and had 1,330 interactions. Consequently, in that time NOLA Photo Fun's website had 2,787 unique visits and 5,081 page views, with more than three hundred new-user profiles created in two weeks—the biggest single jump in the company's history. The campaign was even documented in an article by the New Orleans newspaper, the *Times-Picayune*.

Shaun Walker from HERO|farm said, "It doesn't matter what it is—life, business, advertising—if you connect with a person in some meaningful way, you form a connection with them for life." Amen, Shaun, amen.

Summary

Social media content can make a big difference for your company. I know not everyone out there is convinced of its importance, but I suggest you give it a shot.

Remember, the best way to start integrating social media with existing web content is to audit your use of text, audio, images, and video. What are you currently doing?

How can you transition it to the social media space? Analyze your clients' communications, and figure out ways that social media could help continue and improve upon those conversations.

Social media is amazing for so many reasons, but what it really comes down to is *improved communication*. With social media content, you are addressing three issues simultaneously: shifting conversations to a different medium, allowing for easier updating of content, and reaching a wider audience. And what a phenomenal opportunity to do it!

When you know your customers, understand what's important to them, and give them the content that addresses the things they care about, you will not only enjoy a beneficial social media presence, but you will dominate your space and be well positioned to take advantage of future online marketing developments.

CHAPTER 8

Blogging to Connect with Prospects and Customers

Weblogs, more commonly known as "blogs," have been with us for well over twelve years now. In that time, millions of blogs have populated the web, providing a new means of communication, a connection that can truly be interactive and enriching. In fact, before blogging came around, there was nothing quite like it.

So blogging has truly been revolutionary, impacting both business and culture in unbelievable ways. Through its influence, regular, everyday consumers and citizens have been given a voice and a new way to interact. Many blogs are company or organization blogs, and these are the types of blogs we'll focus on in this chapter.

Used to communicate and interact with clients, customers, and the general public, the blogs of corporations, nonprofits, governments, and small businesses provide a channel of open dialogue with stakeholders and help to break down the walls that have traditionally been in place between those who *produce* the goods and services and those who *consume* them or are *interested* in them.

Consider that Technorati, a search engine for searching blogs, has indexed 133 million blogs since 2002, yet only around seventy-six thousand blogs are considered "important." This means that less than .06% of the blogs out there are really making an impact and being read.[27] If you want your company to be a part of this esteemed group, you have to consistently develop *great* blog content—that's the bottom line. So, I'm going to teach you how to do that.

This is not a "Blogging 101" guide. But it *is* a blog *content guide*, and focuses on optimizing, writing, and marketing the content on your blog, for maximum influence. How can you develop a blog that resonates with your audience and becomes the "go to" blog in your industry? How do you become an important resource for your readers? Let's find out.

---

[27] Singer, Adam. "16 Rules for Social Media Optimization Revisited." *TopRank Online Marketing Blog.* Accessed 2/9/11. http://www.toprankblog.com/2009/08/social-media-optimization-redux/.

Blog Titles—It All Starts Here

The title is everything, right? A great start to your posts ensures you've captured people's attention and have truly *engaged* them. But it's not easy. It's much simpler to be a "me too" blogger and copy someone else than to come from a totally creative place. And let's face it: Not everyone can do it. But I believe that good blogging can be learned.

Before we consider titles for your blog posts, let's back up a bit. The first step is to come up with a solid topic. You then use your subject idea to naturally lead into a good title. Need help? Look at the best blogs out there to see what they do. Check out newspapers or magazines to see how they do it.

Brian Clark from Copyblogger had some great examples of blog headline ideas from a post he wrote a few years ago:

1. **Who Else Wants [blank]?** Starting a headline with "Who Else Wants . . ." is a classic social proof strategy that implies an already existing consensus desire. While overused in the Internet marketing arena, it still works like gangbusters for other subject matter.

- Who Else Wants a Great WordPress Theme?
- Who Else Wants a Higher-Paying Job?
- Who Else Wants More Fun and Less Stress When on Vacation?

2. **The Secret of [blank].** This one is used quite a bit, but that's because it works. Share insider knowledge and translate it into a benefit for the reader.

- The Secret of Successful Podcasting
- The Secret of Protecting Your Assets in Litigation
- The Secret of Getting Your Home Loan Approved

3. **Here Is a Method That Is Helping [blank] to [blank].** Simply identify your target audience and the benefit you can provide them, and fill in the blanks.

- Here Is a Method That Is Helping Homeowners Save Hundreds on Insurance
- Here Is a Method That Is Helping Children Learn to Read Sooner
- Here Is a Method That Is Helping Bloggers Write Better Post Titles

4. **Little Known Ways to [blank].** A more intriguing (and less common) way of accomplishing the same thing as "The Secret of . . ." headline.

- Little Known Ways to Save on Your Heating Bill
- Little Known Ways to Hack Google's Gmail
- Little Known Ways to Lose Weight Quickly and Safely

5. **Get Rid of [problem] Once and for All.** A classic formula that identifies either a painful problem or an unfulfilled desire that the reader wants to remedy.

- Get Rid of Your Unproductive Work Habits Once and for All
- Get Rid of That Carpet Stain Once and for All
- Get Rid of That Lame Mullet Hairdo Once and for All

6. **Here's a Quick Way to [solve a problem].** People love quick and easy when it comes to solving a nagging problem.

- Here's a Quick Way to Get Over a Cold
- Here's a Quick Way to Potty Train Junior
- Here's a Quick Way to Backup Your Hard Drive

7. **Now You Can Have [something desirable] [great circumstance].** The is the classic "have your cake and eat it too" headline—and who doesn't like that?

- Now You Can Quit Your Job and Make Even More Money
- Now You Can Meet Sexy Singles Online Without Spending a Dime
- Now You Can Own a Cool Mac and Still Run Windows

8. **[Do something] like [world-class example].** Gatorade milked this one fully with the "Be Like Mike" campaign featuring Michael Jordan in the early 1990s.

- Speak Spanish Like a Diplomat
- Party Like Paris Hilton
- Blog Like an A-Lister

9. **Have a [or] Build a [blank] You Can Be Proud Of.** Appeal to vanity, dissatisfaction, or shame. Enough said.

- Build a Body You Can Be Proud Of
- Have a Smile You Can Be Proud Of
- Build a Blog Network You Can Be Proud Of

10. **What Everybody Ought to Know About [blank].** Big curiosity draw with this type of headline, and it acts almost as a challenge to the reader to go ahead and see if they are missing something.

- What Everybody Ought to Know About ASP
- What Everybody Ought to Know About Adjustable Rate Mortgages
- What Everybody Ought to Know About Writing Great Headlines[28]

Start with a Great Opening

Master copywriters through the years have preached that there is nothing more critical to printed communication than the headline and the opening paragraph. There's got to be substance. There needs to be steak to go along with that sizzle. You have to stand out, it's just that simple. So, how do you capture your blog readers' imagination and pull them into your content?

---

[28] Clark, Brian. "10 Sure-Fire Headline Formulas That Work." *Copyblogger.* Accessed 2/5/11. http://www.copyblogger.com/10-sure-fire-headline-formulas-that-work/.

1. **Be inquisitive by asking a thought-provoking-question.** There is something I do with my Jack Russell terrier, Barney, that will get him to tilt his cute little head in wonder every single time. What is it? *I ask him a question.* It doesn't matter what type of question it is, as long as I have that questioning tone as I say it. People are the same way. They get curious. They *want* to answer you. Opening your post with a question gets the reader thinking, right away. Also keep in mind the "who, what, why, when, and where" so you can target the right audience with the right message.

2. **Share a really good story.** As I mentioned earlier in the book, everybody loves a good story. Whether you make people think, laugh, or remember the past, your little story will make it seem like the beginning of a really good piece of fiction. And it will get them to read the rest of the post.

3. **Engage the imagination, fire up the soul.** Finding a way to get into your readers' subconscious right from the get-go can be very powerful. As children, we are easily led into our imaginations, conjuring up all types of inventive images, ideas, and make-believe places. Engaging the imagination is a powerful opening technique. You could say, "Imagine if . . ." or "Do you recall, way back when . . ."

4. **Use an analogy or metaphor.** Used in popular songs by the greatest composers of our times, including Paul McCartney, John Lennon, Paul Simon, Brian Wilson, and others, analogies and metaphors are some of the most powerful language tools we have for communicating a thought in a single sentence. These techniques can conjure up mental imagery, allowing readers to see themselves in the story and, for your blogging purposes, engage them so they're drawn to post a comment.

5. **Mention something "hot" from the news.** Starting off with an interesting fact from the news media is also a great idea. The best public relations firms in the world will tell you that finding a way to tie into current news is almost always a winning strategy. People want to know what your opinion is or how your product or service could be involved.

Blogging Content—Best Practices

So, now that we know how to start the content production, what are the tried and true "rules" of blog content, in general? How can you really start building a mass following with your blog? Remember, the hardest part of the entire blog development process is the first six to twelve months. Getting established can be very tough. But once you have three to four thousand subscribers or more, it gets a whole lot easier. So, here we go . . . best practices:

1. **Have a conversational tone.** Think of the blogs you like to read. They are all really easy to digest, yet are substantive, have a set format, and are informal. The most

engaging blogs communicate in a casual and conversational tone. By being personal and candid, you will make readers feel almost like they are sitting down with you for a chat. And if you do it right, you will keep them coming back for more. That should interest a few advertisers, if your goal is monetizing your blog, right?

If you are the straightlaced corporate type and find it hard to be casual in your writing, do what you can to write in a relaxed voice. We all have it. The best advice is to simply be yourself. Share your interests and opinions, and it will be much easier to be conversational.

2. **Be personal; write about what you know.** Whatever business you are in, you are probably an expert. So, write about this expertise! Telling your audience the backstory of your business or a behind-the-scenes story will really generate interest. Revealing setbacks, successes, or anything else in this vein can involve readers. If you want to discuss new products and services, make these topics more appealing by sharing personal insights like the funny things that happened along the way or a story of a customer and how she used your product. A more personal story like that will be read and commented on every time.

3. **Blog three to four times a week, at minimum.** This is the one that separates the great bloggers from all the rest. They never stop. They embrace the fact that they are publishers of information. They take their blogging practice seriously. Once you have established a couple thousand subscribers, offer new insights regularly to keep them coming back, day in, day out.

4. **Use common sense; don't just shoot off your mouth.** Remember, you are still running a business here. You can't just shoot off at the mouth about whatever you want to on your blog. Respect the confidentiality of your organization and employees. Though you may express disagreements or concerns, do not make personal attacks or be too negative. Although the actual blogging process can be very therapeutic for some business bloggers, you don't want to cross the line and reveal proprietary information. Use common sense and don't offend or incriminate anyone.

5. **Make sure the spelling and grammar is correct.** In the casual blogging culture, sometimes we can get *too* casual and actually lazy. Remember, what you blog about and how you write your posts reflects on your company. Maintain professionalism and shape the impression you want others to have of you. In the blogging world, your readers may actually comment about your careless spelling. It has been known to happen. Don't let it!

6. **Keep your posts short and sweet.** As I mentioned earlier in the book, we *scan* on the web rather than reading word for word. You need to be respectful of people's time. Tell your story or make your case quickly. Remember, some of your readers just want to get to the end so they can post a comment! Help them in that effort. Publishing

short posts more frequently is better than writing long, essay-length posts every couple of weeks.

And why are marketers like Seth Godin so respected in the blogosphere? Number one, because he is smart, a real thought leader. But, right up there is the fact that he is succinct with his blog posts. However, just because it's brief doesn't mean it shouldn't be substantive. It needs to be quality, absolutely.

7. **Link often and use keywords.** Think SEO. Always think SEO. It's like online oxygen, baby! The best bloggers of all time build credibility by linking out. Likewise, many others will link in to your blog. Linking to other blogs in your space is just a great idea. It helps you build community and relationships, if nothing else.

Also, do your keyword research and use them in your posts. Doing this well will get the search engines to love your blog. Your rankings will increase, more people will come, and you'll have more subscribers in no time. Perfect!

8. **Balance your content with great imagery and formatting.** A photo tells a thousand words, right? Any blog post without an image simply looks stale. Spice it up and add some contrast to your posts. How do you do it? Simply go to Creative Commons or get a photo from Flickr. It works for the most revered bloggers, so it can work for you too.

In terms of formatting, make your piece look nice on the page. Check it three times before you hit "publish." Also, think about breaking up the copy with bulleted lists. It provides a nice structure for the post.

9. **Show your passion for your subject.** Do you have passion for your business or subject matter? If so, you have a rare gift that should be shared. It can make a huge difference, just ask Gary Vaynerchuk from Wine Library TV. He is very wealthy and probably very happy because of his passion, plain and simple. Passion and enthusiasm are attractive to everybody, but few people truly have and are willing to share them.

10. **Use research in your posts.** Using some research, even if it's just one small thing, can give added credibility and a nice sense of balance to your posts. And this is an easy step because there is research everywhere. What are the industry associations that you belong to? They'll have some solid research you can use. Or, you can just search for it online. I think the best bloggers out there are the ones who incorporate some data or others' researched opinions into their posts.

11. **End your post with a question, an invitation to have your readers respond.** Yep, this is the best way to end it. Initiate and encourage some interaction. You'll find your responses will go up quite a bit when you ask, "So what do you think?" or "Was there anything I missed?"

Finding Your Own Voice

As I said before, copying others is the path of least resistance. It's so easy, and it's so boring. And it's sort of a waste of time, if you think about it. And coming up with an original message for your business is the essence of branding. Did Starbucks just come into the market copying Folgers? Not quite. They changed the game forever. Talk about *great* branding—and amazing originality.

Look, I realize it's really hard to be unique and stand alone, especially when there are so many blogs out there, but it's important to try. Think of it like this: Everyone has a unique personality and almost everyone has opinions. Whatever yours are, make sure your distinctive voice translates to your blog. In blogging, originality should be the rule you live by. Though companies do it all the time, blogging is *not* about finding stuff online, copying the information, editing it a bit, and then posting it to your blog.

What have you learned from your experiences? How do you think things should really be done? Shake up the establishment and be a leader with your blog. Thinking of something new and coming from a creative place is a skill that takes time to develop, but once you have it, it becomes easy. A blog is the place online where you express yourself after all. You may not do it on your brochures. You certainly won't do it on a client proposal, but on your blog, you are journaling about whatever you want.

Managing a Large Blog with Multiple Contributors

Are you with a large company that has multiple blog authors contributing to the success of the blog? If so, you know how cumbersome it can be to manage it on an ongoing basis. Because there are lots of moving parts, the process can be really slow. But not if you are efficient. Not if all the pieces are working together in synergy. What you want is an "assembly line" or "group think" mentality with your company blog. You need to embrace the idea of shared responsibility to get the job done well.

So, what are some guidelines to make this process easier?

1. **Set your objectives for the blog.** Just like a magazine, every good blog needs a production schedule. But before you create one, you need to set your goals for your blog. Do you want to provide opinion-based articles? Updates on company news? Educational content? Whatever you plan on doing, get it all established up front. It's a key part of the planning process and, ultimately, the success of your blog.

2. **Do your keyword research—use important phrases for blog posts.** A good keyword strategy is key to successful SEO. Think about your potential readers. How can you target and segment them?

- Target different types of readers: Unique groups tend to use different phrases when describing their needs. Ensure your keyword list is reflective of this.

- Target key industry sectors and types of services—also include phrases relevant to your company's product and service offerings.
- Target gaps in your website SEO strategy—don't use the same keyword phrases that your site ranks for.

3. **Create an editorial calendar.** Again, you are a *publisher* now. You need to fully think like one, too. So, once your keyword lists are set, develop a full-year editorial calendar so you have good variety, a schedule that you can follow, and a plan for how you will use the keywords.

Whether you cover a unique customer group or a different market sector with each post, it doesn't really matter, as long as you are speaking to all your blog readers at some point. You don't want to bore your readers. The need to stay fresh is important. And if there is a hot topic or breaking news in your industry, definitely hop on that and get some publicity out of it.

4. **Recruit key team members as your featured bloggers.** Get out there and recruit the best writers and thought leaders in your company. Hint: It isn't always the CEO. Sharing the workload is essential with a big company blog. You don't want burnout. Changing up the writers also creates good variety in the writing from post to post, week to week.

5. **Assign someone the final editing task.** The assigned editor will need to check:
- The content for clarity, voice, relevance, and interest
- Keyword use and placement for optimization
- Title tags and meta descriptions to ensure they use keywords
- That the post has an image and is using the alt meta tag that includes keywords
- That there are links that connect to other content

6. **Analyze and share metrics, review comments.** You need to know that your blog is working, that all the time you are investing is paying off. So, take a look at the metrics and let the team know what's going on. Be sure to respond to reader comments, as well. It's best to be very timely with this step.

Creating Link-Friendly Blog Content

If blog content is "king," then *linked* blog content is the empire. Writing posts for your blogs—even if it's easy to scan, benefits-rich, and coming from an original place—can only get you so far. Over the years, as my company has written blog posts for a myriad of businesses, we've really seen it all: poor design, great design; bad content, great content; poor attempts at conversion, and conversion machines; nonlinked content and, yes, link-friendly blog content.

At the end of the day, you have to do a lot of things right in order to have your blog content found on the web and popular with visitors. For SEO, blog posts that have link-friendly content, or content that naturally attracts links, are the most important blogs by far. How do we know? Because Google tells us it is: Google's Webmaster Guidelines says:

> Give visitors the information they're looking for—Provide high-quality content on your pages. This is the single most important thing to do. If your pages contain useful information, their content will attract many visitors and entice webmasters to link to your site. In creating a helpful, information-rich site, write pages that clearly and accurately describe your topic. Think about the words users would type to find your pages and include those words on your site.
>
> . . . Make sure that other sites link to yours—Links help our crawlers find your site and can give your site greater visibility in our search results. When returning results for a search, Google combines PageRank (our view of a page's importance) with sophisticated text-matching techniques to display pages that are both important and relevant to each search.[29]

Link-Building Experts Speak . . .

It's important to also know what the most noted link experts in the search marketing space have said with regard to link-friendly blog content. Eric Ward, one of the guys who practically invented the concept of link building and who promoted the importance of links as early as 1995, says, "The visible text within the link (aka anchor text) can help the search engines make a forecast as to what content lies at the end of that link if clicked. If that happens often enough, and if the originating sites are of high quality, then the engine can use that signal as part of the ranking process."[30]

And Jim Boykin, one of the most successful link operators on the web, says, "The best backlinks in the world (and often easiest to get) are those that came because of great content."[31]

These guys *live* links—they eat, sleep, and dream in links, and what they say is always relevant to the discussion. Lee Odden, of Top Rank Online Marketing blog, said, "Whether you drive traffic to the site from offline marketing programs, paid search

---

[29] Google. "Webmaster Guidelines." Accessed 2/1/11. http://www.google.com/support/webmasters/bin/answer.py?answer=35769.
[30] Estrin, Michael. 2008. "5 Experts Demystify SEO Link Building" at IMedia Connection, September 5. http://www.imediaconnection.com/content/20448.asp.
[31] Boykin, Jim. 2008. "The Achilles Heel of Free and Natural Links" *Jim Boykin's Blog*, May 23. http://www.webuildpages.com/jim/the-achilles-heel-of-free-and-natural-links/.

advertising, or social media promotions, you still have to deliver the goods once visitors get to the website."[32] What are the "goods" that Lee is referring to? CONTENT.

Blog Link Bait

In the previous chapter on social media content, I brought up the concept of link baiting. Again, link bait is viral, linkable content designed to attract thousands of links and is recognized as one of the most effective ways to build links and relevance for a blog.

The best way of doing this is actually writing solid blog posts with great content. The links will come. Of course, you have to promote your blog, too.

Earlier we discussed the types of "hooks" you could use with your content:

- Tying in to what's relevant—The News Hook
- Going against the grain—The Contrary Hook
- Taking the offensive position—The Attack Hook
- Providing something important—The Resource Hook
- Making people laugh—The Humor Hook

I also brought up other ways to get others to link to you with contests, interviews, and product or service reviews. All of these will provide you with lots of great, linkable blog content. One thing to keep in mind is that you want to vary your anchor text every now and then. Target your keyword phrase, but then use it in your anchor text in different ways. If the phrase is "steel oil drum," use it in this way a couple of times, but also use it as "steel oil drums" and "oil drums made of steel." The reason for this is that people search for many different variations of your keyword phrase—it isn't always what you think it will be—and also because Google's algorithm looks at this factor.

Guest Writing on Other Blogs

What's another great way to build link-friendly content that most people forget about? Write for another complementary blog as a guest. Others in your industry are always looking for blog writers. With the demand for fresh, exciting, link-friendly content always out there, you will be welcomed with open arms when you ask to write for another blog. What you want to be sure to do is provide a keyword-rich, anchor text link to your site in your guest blog post.

Chances are you will get your link benefit in the bylined section of the post, but occasionally it may be appropriate to link to something on your site in the main post itself. When you put your link in the byline, make sure you consider the needs of the

---

[32] Odden, Lee. "Tips on Content Centered Link Building." *TopRank Online Marketing Blog.* Accessed 2/12/11. http://www.toprankblog.com/2008/05/tips-on-content-centered-link-building/.

readers and link to something on your site that they will find valuable, not just your blog's main URL. Do you have some important content that always stays on your blog home page and acts as a "101" or cornerstone content? Link to this page.

CASE STUDY: Big Impact Blogging at Born to Sell

Born to Sell, established in 2009, is a financial services website for income-oriented investors. It offers subscription-based research tools focusing on the "covered call" investment strategy. The company's business is 100 percent web based. As such, it needed to attract a large number of potential customers to the site. The firm didn't want to buy the traffic with PPC ads because there were many well-funded businesses and online brokers who bid five dollars or more for keywords that would have proven too expensive for Born to Sell. Given its conversion rates and lifetime value of its customers, Born to Sell could not afford PPC expenses like this.

Next, the company looked to SEO. But there was a problem: Because it was a subscription business, much of its proprietary content was not indexable by the search engines (because that content lives in a password-protected part of the site, accessible to members only). So, it had to create enough public content in places the search robots could crawl, so that the company could organically rank in the search engine results pages.

The solution was to create two content-heavy sets of public pages: (1) a tutorial, and (2) a blog. The tutorial was twenty-five pages long, and the company posted to the blog frequently. In both cases, every page was optimized for a different keyword phrase that Born to Sell wanted to rank for. It used the keyword phrases in all the right places on the pages so that the search engines would find it.

Next, it focused on off-page SEO by getting external links to each page with relevant anchor text. For example, company employees would write guest blog entries for other people's blogs in exchange for a link back to one of Born to Sell's tutorial or blog pages, with appropriate anchor text in the backlink. And, of course, the company had a Twitter and Facebook presence, which helped to promote new blog articles as they were published.

After five months of writing guest blogs, article marketing, social bookmarking, and forum posting, Born to Sell showed some great results: Its site now ranks in the top three organic search results for eleven of its chosen key phrases ("covered call screener," "covered call tutorial," and others), and it ranks on page one of the organic results for another thirty-nine of its key phrases. As Born to Sell adds more external backlinks each month, its rankings continue to rise. These organic search results now bring Born to Sell more than three thousand targeted, first-time visitors each month, which is all "free" traffic. Wow, what a great success story!

Seth Godin Might Have Said It Best . . .

How to write a blog post. Do it like this: JoelonSoftware.com.

An appropriate illustration,
A useful topic, easily broadened to be useful to a large number of readers,
Simple language with no useless jargon,
Not too long,
Focusing on something that people have previously taken for granted,
That initially creates emotional resistance,
Then causes a light bulb to go off
and finally,
Causes the reader to look at the world differently all day long.[33]

---

[33] Godin, Seth. 2006. "How to Write a Blog Post." *Seth's Blog*, November 21. http://sethgodin.typepad.com/seths_blog/2006/11/how_to_write_a_.html.

CHAPTER 9

The Relationship-Building Power of E-Mail Content, Auto-Responders, Newsletters, and More

"E-mail is the most used lead-generation tactic by businesses today, with 88 percent of marketers using it regularly—more than PR, trade shows, direct mail, print, search marketing, sponsorships, and other forms of media."

—Forrester Research

Forrester also says that e-mail is the single most trusted information source online and it's expected to grow to a $2 billion industry by 2014. Exact Target, a well-known e-mail marketing service provider, chimed in with this: Fifty percent of consumers make purchases as a direct result of e-mail, which also *drives more conversions* than any other channel. So, e-mail is one of the most important activities you can engage in.[34]

When you are in business, *connecting* with people is the first step. You do that through your website, a blog post, a well written e-book or white paper, perhaps your social media profiles. The next step, naturally, is to *build the relationship*. You do that best, in the digital realm, through personalized e-mails: autoresponders at first, perhaps, and then your regular newsletter for the long term. Of course, your blog and your social media content will help build relationships, too, but e-mail communication is the most personal, the most customizable, and the most intimate. E-mail has certainly been around a long time and even now, it is a very important part—some say in the top three—of the content marketing mix. The other reasons, of course, are that they are cheap to send and easy to measure.

---

[34] Stewart, Morgan. 2009. "Is Email Marketing Endangered?" Exact Target, http://www.exacttarget.com/uploadedFiles/Resources/Whitepapers/ExactTarget_EmailUtilization.pdf.

Whether you are e-mailing a newsletter, a sales promotion, a survey, an event invitation, or just a note to say hello, your connection through e-mail is special because you have secured a place in a coveted spot: *the e-mail inbox of your prospects and customers*. Staying in front of them is key. After all, every one of us gets inundated with ads, announcements, *stuff*—lots of stuff coming at us at all times. It's information overload. But if you can get that recency and frequency working for you, your prospects and customers will never forget about you. And when it comes time to make a decision and buy, they'll go to you instead of your competitors. It's an absolute truth in business: **E-mail subscribers and social media followers are among your company's best assets.**

Like your website, your e-mail communication is a job that's never done. Because you are nurturing relationships over time, you need to write e-mails on a regular basis. Unlike your website, though, your e-mails will involve customer relationship management (CRM) needs, database maintenance, and customer life cycle considerations.

And as with your blog, you want your e-mails to become an *information resource* for your subscribers. You want them to anticipate and look forward to receiving your messages each time. Think about it: The best e-mail marketers and brands out there have created this environment with their subscribers. Consider Starbucks. Personally, I look forward to getting the e-mails I receive from them because I'm in the Starbucks loyal customer club. Sometimes I even get a coupon for a free drink! And I, for one, think that is pretty cool. See how this whole powerful e-mail content thing works?

The personalization aspect is huge, of course. Unlike with traditional media, or even your website, it's a heck of a lot easier to customize with e-mail. It's a best practice to use what's called "dynamic insertion" in your e-mails to personalize for the subscriber's name as well as specific interests, location, and more. We all like to see our name in print and we all like that people consider what we like. It's that simple.

As I've mentioned in other chapters, what follows in the coming pages is *not* a comprehensive guide to e-mail marketing. It is, however, the best advice you'll find on e-mail copywriting and content generation and using e-mail in the greater content marketing game.

As you read the rest of the chapter, consider these key points:

- E-mail content is very dependent on *impressions*
- Readers begin forming their opinions *from the subject line*
- Every step along the way can either cement that impression or change it
- You want your subscribers to connect with your e-mail in a positive way every time
- The individual elements of your e-mail can artfully combine to create a significant impression
- Writing conversationally makes e-mails easier to read and creates more conversions

What are the four items that will claim the biggest portion of your content marketing budget? Search (SEO), social networking, blogging, and, yes, **e-mail marketing**.[35]

So, let's get into it.

E-Mail As a Content Marketing Medium

I'll take this moment to ask you to reflect for a minute. What are the challenges you face with e-mail marketing? Here are some of the most common ones we see:

1. **Establishing your company/brand.** The fact that someone signed up for your newsletter or for e-mail updates is great, but it's just the first step. Your move is the next one. So, what will you do? It's like the old adage, *Be careful what you wish for.* Now that you have subscribers' contact information and they have said, "Yes, I want to know more; I want to be connected with your company," you have some company awareness and brand building to do. The real work—and there is a lot of it—is just beginning.

2. **Being relevant.** This is a big one. The reason, of course, is that everyone is unique. No matter how many "buckets" you put your subscribers into, they still have individual needs and expectations. Your messages need to stay relevant. Otherwise, subscribers will unsubscribe or tune out. Segmentation and targeting can get you pretty far, but keeping a place of importance in the minds of your subscribers will remain a constant challenge.

3. **Determining the right number of e-mails to send.** Should you send weekly? (Probably not.) Should you send quarterly? (Probably not.) Should you send monthly? (Bing, bing, bing, bing!) In many studies and in my experience, sending something monthly is probably the best course of action. And to this I would add "at a minimum." Of course, there are those *event-triggered* and *behaviorally targeted* e-mails to consider, and these are different. If a customer or prospect is requesting something in addition to your newsletter, then you need to fulfill that request. We'll get into that in a bit.

4. **Dealing with a declining subscriber base.** Your subscribers are most engaged in the beginning, when they first subscribe. But like anything else, interest levels decline with time. This is something that all e-mail content marketers deal with. We could all use ideas on how to keep subscribers interested. So, we'll get into that.

Simply put, e-mail is one of the most brilliant ways of communicating that human-kind has ever devised. As we've said, it's fast, efficient, cheap, and fairly easy once you get the hang of it. And that's all beautiful. But how do we *best use* e-mail content? What's the process?

---

[35] Odden, Lee. "SEO Tops Digital Marketing Tactics for 2011." *TopRank Online Marketing Blog.* Accessed 2/4/11. http://www.toprankblog.com/2010/07/seo-tops-digital-marketing-2011/.

Define Your Goals/Audience

Ask yourself: What do I want to accomplish with my e-mails? What do I want the people receiving my e-mails to do, exactly? Are you selling something? Are you notifying people of upcoming events? Do you want to share your recent blog posts? Are you building a relation-ship? **Yes. Most definitely.** And that's what I want to stress more than anything else.

If you're old enough, you remember receiving *handwritten* letters, pre-1997 or so. Whether you wrote a letter to a friend or family member, what was your objective in writing a letter to someone you knew? Well, one of the goals was to *nurture* the rela-tionship, right? Think of your e-mail content in the same way. Your very first e-mail should maybe sound like this: "Hi, my name is Dave from XYZ Company! Here is what we do, how we can help you, and a few bits of great advice I think you'll appreciate," and every e-mail after that is further developing that initial message and growing that relationship over time. So, you'll want to produce e-mail content that reflects this approach. Remember, you'll be communicating with people over and over again, for many months and many years hopefully, even after they buy something from you.

Then you want to consider your *goals* for the various e-mails you'll send out. Maybe you are sending a monthly newsletter to your database. Perhaps you are send-ing a totally customized e-mail to your top twenty customers. You could be soliciting a donation, announcing a sale, getting new leads to visit your site—there are a thousand different goals with e-mail content. What are yours?

There's also your audience to consider. Keep in mind *who* you are sending these e-mails to as you write the content. Many companies don't actively do that. The people on the list are usually an afterthought. It's easy to think this way when so many e-mail campaigns are sent out to the entire "house" list, and everyone receives the same e-mail. Doing this can serve you well, but more and more, it's best to think about your customers in **groups and in different stages** in the relationship or "life cycle" you have with them. Many are just finding out about you. Some are ready to make a decision on something. Others just want to keep up with you and get the latest news. Segmenting your e-mails to each of their specific needs can be very powerful.

Start thinking about these important elements of your e-mail content:

- What types of e-mails will you send (promotional, newsletters, transactional, etc.), and what specific content will you provide?
- How frequently will you send your e-mails?
- How can you provide real value to your e-mail subscribers?
- Will you partner with an e-mail service provider to help with your campaigns, or will you keep it in-house?

The Benefits of Using E-Mail to Connect

We've mentioned some of the most obvious benefits already. But I understand that *return on investment* and ensuring you are engaging in *worthwhile business activities* are important. Whether you are running your own small business or are the head of marketing for a Fortune 100 company, you need to always be prepared to make the business case for future investment and identify potential benefits that you may not be taking advantage of. Here are some excellent reasons to invest in solid e-mail content:

1. **The cost to run an e-mail marketing program is low.** We've covered this one, but it's important enough to list here as one of the top benefits. Before e-mail existed, companies spent thousands and even millions of dollars on phone campaigns and in traditional mail lead-generation programs. E-mail changed all of that.

2. **E-mail encourages impulse activity and immediate action.** Think about it: Why do we check e-mail so many times throughout the day? Because we perceive it as important. We need to take action. Right now. When we get e-mails, we tend to click on the included links to other places in your online content empire—your blog, website, or social media profiles, for example. So, no doubt about it: E-mail increases the chances of a quick, spur-of-the-moment response. It's like direct-response mail, but even more powerful.

3. **It's great for relationship development.** There is simply nothing like it: Sending e-mail content, over a period of many weeks and months, is a great way to connect with people. Using it wisely, you can systematically, authentically educate people on the way you want them to perceive your company. And you won't do this simply by sending out a rehash of your blog posts each month. You'll truly engage them, asking them questions through polls and surveys, offering them coupons for great discounts, and more. You'll get them to *love* your company—one e-mail at a time. And they will feel like the relationship they have with you is indispensable.

4. **It is easily integrated into your total content marketing program.** This may be the most powerful benefit of them all. E-mail is very "sticky" and acts as a great *connector* for other types of content your company is offering. You can combine e-mail with social messaging, mobile marketing, your webinar offerings, or anything else, really—to impact open and response rates and improve engagement levels across the board.

So, with that, I think we have a good basis for getting into the heart of this e-mail content activity. Let's take it step by step . . .

Establishing Your Voice

It all starts right here, with the "voice" of your e-mail content. Ask yourself: How do I want my e-mail content to sound when read? Quirky and fun? Upbeat and positive? Serious and professional? Whatever it is, it should be a reflection of your brand, not some made-up character. The voice of your e-mails is the *persona* of your brand. Who exactly is "talking" to your subscribers through those printed words? Have a product or service that is essentially a commodity or a little on the boring side? Then your e-mail copy voice is even more important.

Of course, if you don't have a memorable, interesting brand, then go back to the drawing board of Marketing 101 and establish a strong brand identity before you send even one e-mail to anyone. Your e-mail voice can set you apart from the competition and do something else that is critical: help separate you from all the other "noise" in your subscribers' e-mail inbox.

The Subject Line

This is where the content rubber hits the content road. And this is where most of the mistakes happen—right at the beginning. I think we all know what bad subject lines look like; we've seen enough junk e-mail to last ten lifetimes. They have the worst subject lines every devised.

But how do you write your subject line so it will have maximum impact and won't be labeled as a "spam" e-mail? The first thing to consider is including your company name or brand. This provides instant credibility and the spam filters will look kindly on this, especially if you use this type of format in *all* your e-mail campaigns. Next, use a title describing the content, perhaps "September Newsletter" or "Invitation to Next Meeting." You can also make use of a benefit or call to action. That's right; you want to include something that will trigger interest immediately, especially if it's an offer.

Also, don't make the subject line too long. Forty to fifty characters should do it. You want people to get what the e-mail is about very quickly, at a glance. Note: The first two or three words of the subject line are the *most* important, so be sure to get that right.

Here are some good examples of good and not so good subject lines:

Best Open Rates (60%-87%)	Worst Open Rates (1%-14%)
1. [COMPANYNAME] Sales & Marketing Newsletter	1. Last Minute Gift - We Have The Answer
2. Eye on the [COMPANYNAME] Update (Oct 31 - Nov 4)	2. Valentines - Shop Early & Save 10%
3. [COMPANYNAME] Staff Shirts & Photos	3. Give a Gift Certificate this Holiday
4. [COMPANYNAME] May 2005 News Bulletin!	4. Valentine's Day Salon and Spa Specials!
5. [COMPANYNAME] Newsletter - February 2006	5. Gift Certificates - Easy & Elegant Giving - Let Them Choose
6. [COMPANYNAME] Newsletter - January 2006 [*|FNAME|* *|LNAME|*]	6. Need More Advertising Value From Your Marketing Partner?
7. [COMPANYNAME] and [COMPANYNAME] Invites You!	7. [COMPANYNAME] Pioneers in Banana Technology
8. Happy Holidays from [COMPANYNAME]	8. [COMPANYNAME] Moves You Home for the Holidays
9. ATTENTION [COMPANYNAME] Staff!	9. Renewal
10. ATTENTION [COMPANYNAME] West Staff!!	10. Technology Company Works with [COMPANYNAME] on Bananas Efforts
11. Invitation from [COMPANYNAME]	11. [COMPANYNAME] Update - A Summary of Security and Emergency Preparedness News
12. [COMPANYNAME] Jan/Feb 2006 Newsletter	12. Now Offering Banana Services!
13. Website news - Issue 3	13. It's still summer in Tahoe!
14. Upcoming Events at [COMPANYNAME]	14. [COMPANYNAME] endorses [COMPANYNAME] as successor
15. [COMPANYNAME] Councils: Letter of Interest	15. [COMPANYNAME] Holiday Sales Event
16. [COMPANYNAME] Coffee Exchange - Post-Katrina Update	16. The Future of International Trade
17. We're Throwing a Party	17. [COMPANYNAME] for your next dream home.
18. October 2005 Newsletter	18. True automation of your Banana Research
19. [COMPANYNAME]: 02.10.06	19. [COMPANYNAME] Resort - Spring into May Savings
20. [COMPANYNAME] Racing Newsletter	20. You Asked For More...

* Study only included campaigns sent to at least 100 recipients.

FIGURE 9-1   Mail Chimp E-Mail Subject Line Survey Results © MailChimp, http://mailchimp.com/

How do you get your subscribers' attention? Try one of these approaches:

- Teaser: "Find out what your fellow club members thought . . ."
- Question: "What are the Top 10 Nonverbal Communication Techniques?"
- Announcing an event: "If everyone is going to be there, maybe you should be, too"
- Direct approach, communicating an offer or benefit: "Act now or you will miss out!"
- Personalization: Using your subscriber's name in the subject line can sometimes pay off

Best Practices in E-Mail Content Development

Next is the e-mail body. If you have written business letters before, this may come easily to you. If you haven't, there will be a learning curve. It may take multiple attempts.

How to write the actual e-mail copy? It depends on what specifically you are e-mailing about, but there are certain elements that all e-mails have in common. At a basic level, make sure the message has a beginning, a middle, and an end. Like we discussed in an earlier chapter, use the "AIDA" format—awareness, interest, desire, action. Making the message about the recipient and keeping it interactive are important. Many companies are even experimenting with sending video through their e-mails. We'll talk about that more in a later chapter. Bottom line: Be sure to give the content some sense of urgency. Whatever you are communicating, you want the recipient to take some type of action: e-mail you back, click on an embedded link, check out your Facebook page and "Like" your company, etc.

Finally, make sure it's clear, concise, and not too "salesy," unless, of course, you are offering a sale, discount, or something else. You can and should send e-mails like this; just keep them to less than 15 percent of the total e-mails you send. Be sure to make the copy personalized, too, as we've mentioned: use the subscriber's name. So what else?

1. **Keep it conversational.** I'll keep beating the drum on this one: An informal style is always best. Why? Because it's easier to read, for one. And second, it breeds a *sense of friendship and familiarity*. So, get very used to using the word *you*.

2. **Create a flow.** The "From" address leads to the subject line, which leads to your main headline, and then into the rest of the e-mail. You may repeat the main messages and have a call to action toward the end. Keeping your recipients reading, and leading naturally into the next part of the e-mail, is part art, part formula. Just make sure you remember to practice this. Other things you can use to help your e-mails flow well:

- Headings within the e-mail: develop scan-friendly, punchy, and persuasive headings
- Communicate one idea/article per paragraph
- Use the inverted pyramid style, with a short summary of the entire message at the start of the copy
- Use bulleted lists to summarize features or benefits

3. **Never forget about the benefit story.** Set it in your mind now: Your mission is to *improve your subscriber's lives.* It could be in a small way or a big way, but it has to be there. If you are Apple, you are helping them connect to other people through music, phones, and computers. If you are a local deli, you are feeding people delicious sandwiches and inviting them to experience a pleasurable dining environment. Connect, connect, connect. And stay relevant.

4. **Keep your e-mails short and to the point.** Like everything else on the web and on our mobile devices, we want "brief." Paragraphs should be shorter than they would be in print: three to four short sentences, at the most. The one exception to keeping e-mails short is the monthly newsletter you'll send. I think those can (and should) be longer.

5. **Use the power of third-party validation.** Back up your message with facts and numbers. Build testimonial elements into your e-mails, including customer quotes, number of customers, client names, and independent reviews and awards.

6. **Consider the copy–design balance.** Like I've said before, lean on format and imagery to emphasize your offer and key messages. How to do it with e-mails? Use boldface and italics with copy. Include appropriate, easy-to-load images that help communicate. Leave some white space. Mimic the style you have on your website, blog, and social media profiles. Give all your online venues a consistent look and feel.

One other important note: E-mail messages come in two ways: HTML and plain text. The HTML types can contain images, while the text ones cannot. Give your recipients a choice of which type they want to receive.

Event-Triggered and Behaviorally Targeted E-Mail (Autoresponders)

These types of e-mails are automated, and are sent to prospects or subscribers when they do something specific or request something on your site, blog, or social media profile. These are separate from your main "campaign" e-mails, like newsletters, blasts, and sale announcements, because they are initiated by your prospects and subscribers. So, you need to set up a system to handle these requests.

Sometimes, the requests are very high priority. If the prospect is ready to buy *right now*, for example, you need to fulfill that request with precision and total efficiency. So if the person wants to buy, or has proven through his comments or actions (requesting information) that he has the potential for buying something soon, a sequence of two or three e-mails over a couple weeks may be the best idea. Staying in front of him will potentially encourage him to buy sooner.

Many of the e-mails that reply to specific user requests are *autoresponders*. This is how many people in the marketing community identify them, and the automated nature of the message is one of the best parts of the whole process. You set them up, load them in your software program, and let them do their work.

In addition, the prospect's inquiry gives you *permission* to follow up with her. And because you can prewrite and preprogram autoresponders, your job is much easier. You decide how many e-mails to send, what you will say, and how often you will send the messages. Smart autoresponder e-mails are like automated salespeople working for you, in the background, all the time. So, it's easy to see why this activity can increase your connections—and your sales. In fact, in my experience, sending multiple follow-up e-mail messages to prospects over time can impact the sales numbers up to 300 percent.

At our company, we use industry leader **AWeber** for this function. There are many other e-mail service providers that offer this function as well. AWeber is great, but I recommend you look at a few.

FIGURE 9-2   AWeber

What are the various types of autoresponder e-mails triggered by prospect requests? These include:

1. **Customer acquisition**
   - Welcome e-mail when prospect first registers
   - Series of autoresponder e-mails to establish awareness and start relationship building
   - Potential purchase offer following subscription to newsletter

2. **Customer conversion**
   - Abandoned shopping cart e-mails
   - Message when prospect registered, but did not purchase after set interval
   - E-mail when prospect clicked e-mail link on specific product or category, but didn't buy
   - Autoresponse when registered customer browsed category on site, but did not buy
   - Autoresponse when registered customer searched for product on site, but did not buy
3. **Customer retention and growth**
   - Anniversary e-mails—of registration or first purchase
   - Customer-birthday e-mails
   - Reactivation e-mails (either with indication of predicted inactivity or when inactive)
   - Prerenewal e-mails for annual subscription services[36]

What are your options for targeted messages? By their nature, behavioral e-mails are targeted according to *context*, but you may want to add relevant targeting if it will increase response rates. For example:

- Specific product or category the prospect expressed interest in
- Male or female
- Value of previous purchases

Essentially, you are writing different messages for each target group and setting up autoresponses depending on the type of group it is. When you find ways to group them, you can communicate a similar message and be more effective and efficient in the process.

You then want to test and refine your event-triggered e-mail program. Important elements of tests to check include:

- Timing—the interval after an event
- Subject line and main headline testing
- Offer and proposition testing, including number of offers and simplicity of offers
- Copy, especially the presence or absence of recognition of previous activity
- Creative layout

---

[36] Chaffey, Dave. 2010. "*E-mail Marketing Best Practice Guide.*" Econsultancy, http://econsultancy.com/us/reports/email-marketing-best-practice-guide.

Integrating Social Media

There are hundreds of millions of active users on social networks like Facebook, including many of your prospects and customers. So, how can you leverage this passion for online social and community interaction with your e-mail content? You do it by using "share to social" features, available with many of the outside e-mail service providers. This gives you the ability to include social links in your e-mails, so recipients can easily post your e-mails to their social network profile page, where friends can see the message, make comments, and even post the e-mail on their own profile pages.

FIGURE 9-3　Share to Social Sample Page

The really important key here is that share to social features allow your e-mail messages to move beyond your own e-mail list and your subscriber base. It essentially sends it out to the masses without you doing a thing! If your e-mails are used this way, your content is transformed from "push" marketing into a powerful "pull" campaign.

If you haven't used "share to social" features in your e-mails yet, try it out in your next campaign. It could be one of the most effective things you've ever done.

E-Mail Newsletters—A Few More Important Details

We know that e-mail newsletters are popular communication vehicles that you send to your subscribers on a regular basis. They feature valuable, timely information that can improve people's lives in small and big ways. And we know that you can easily draw people back to your website, social media profiles, or blog through your newsletter.

But maybe you didn't know this: Researchers at Nielsen Norman Group say that "newsletters can create much more of a bond between users and a company than a website can."[37] In fact, as many as 69 percent of the participants in the study said they

---

[37] Nielsen Norman Group. 2006. "*E-Mail Newsletter Usability.*" http://www.nngroup.com/reports/newsletters/.

looked forward to receiving at least one newsletter. I think that's a pretty amazing statistic. If you don't have a newsletter program started yet, with a newsletter sign-up on your website, you have to get one set up. Today! Think about it: You have a golden opportunity to "throw a personalized paper" right on the doorstep of every prospect and customer you have in your database, whenever you want. More than that, you have the ability to place that morning "paper" right on people's office desks.

So, what are some of the special points about writing newsletter copy?

- You want to include *many different types of content* in the body of the newsletter: articles, surveys, promotions, research findings, simple case studies, and, of course, links to multiple landing pages on your site.
- The way your newsletter *looks* is really important. Work closely with your graphic designer or e-mail service provider/vendor to ensure it looks perfect before it goes out. You don't want to look amateurish.
- Make it easy for your newsletter subscribers to forward to a friend or share on their social media profiles. Leverage the viral aspect of e-mail.

Different Customer Groups Need Different E-Mails

If you run a car dealership, do you think a guy who just bought a car from you should get the same e-mail as the woman who is simply curious about the models you offer? What about the lifelong department store customer who has been shopping at the same place for thirty years: Should you write the same e-mail to this person that you would to someone who just filled out the catalog request form? The answers here are obvious, and I think you get the point. The problem is that very few companies think about their e-mail content in this way. Tailor your messages to specific customer groups. The loyal customer should get more offers (and better offers) than the infrequent one.

Another good idea is to ask a few simple questions to those who are signing up to receive your e-mail newsletter for the first time. When you do this, you'll get a good understanding of some basic psychographics. Allow them to select their areas of interest. Subscribers could indicate their job titles or functions. They could check what types of e-mail communications they want, whether it's upcoming sales, newsletters, or other. They could also tell you what products or services they are interested in ahead of time. Once you know this information, you are set to write a specific e-mail customized especially for them. And if you don't want to ask for this information in the first contact form they fill out, ask for it in the second or third e-mail you send. This can sometimes work more effectively. Test it and see.

Choosing an E-Mail Service Provider

If you are an e-mail content marketing rookie, this may be new for you. Whatever you do, don't send e-mails out through Outlook or another type of e-mail account. There is way too much you'd have to do to manage that process to make it worthwhile. And you'll be missing the automation and analytics piece. An e-mail service provider or vendor will automate the entire process for you, providing sample templates, list selection functionality, the time you send the e-mails out, and, maybe most important, providing you with the detailed analytics of who opened the e-mail, when, and what they did when they read it. Did they click on a certain link? You'll know.

There are many reputable e-mail service providers in the industry. The names you hear most often are Constant Contact, Vertical Response, and Exact Target. They all have their pluses and minuses, and certain ones will appeal to certain types of marketers. If you are just getting into e-mail content marketing, take a few for a spin, and see what you like. Sign up for free trials and evaluate them.

Common Mistakes with E-Mails

There are quite a few mistakes you can make when it comes to e-mail content. Many of them we have mentioned already, but let's take a minute to point out a few of the more common ones, so we ensure e-mail marketing success:

- Bad e-mail addresses, unmaintained database, or sending to the wrong people. This is probably the number one most common problem. The wrong group gets the wrong message.
- Forgetting the call to action. Your recipients must have a way to get in touch with you. Make it obvious: use a button or a link—or use both.
- Not including your phone number and, if you are a local business, your physical address, so people who want to contact you in other ways can do so. Remember, not everyone likes using e-mail.
- Making people fill out a long contact form on your landing pages. Remember, you only have their attention for a few seconds. Make it easy.
- Not placing the most important content of the e-mail "above the fold"—in other words, in the section of the computer screen they can read without scrolling.
- Making it difficult to unsubscribe. This is one of my personal pet peeves. What's up with the maze of instructions to stop getting the e-mail? One click, and you're done: That's how it needs to be.
- Not asking your recipients to add your company to their contact list or list of safe vendors. Be sure your e-mail can get to them.

Life Cycle Stage	Communication Goals and Strategies
Awareness	Goal: Reinforce awareness of need. Strategy: Automated series of e-mails offering educational materials and best practices.
Evaluation	Goal: Identify decision criteria strategy. Strategy: Series of e-mails offering case studies and testimonials along with product/service data sheets.
Choice	Goal: Identify prospects, perceived risks and alleviate them. Strategy: Send pricing comparisons, feature comparisons, product capabilities, etc.
Purchase	Goal: Instill early sense of value in purchase decision. Strategy: e-mail product accolades, success stories, and key contact references.

FIGURE 9-4   E-Mail Life Cycle Chart

Getting Inside Their Head

In closing, I'd like to reference a great book that I read many years ago: "Influence: The Psychology of Persuasion" by Robert Cialdini.[38] In the book, he identifies six powerful elements that I think we can all use to ensure a greater impact and return on investment with our e-mail content:

- **Reciprocity.** Provide valuable, exclusive content, and your subscribers will feel the need to "pay you back" at some point in the future.
- **Commitment and consistency.** You'll get their commitment when they click on a link in your e-mail. If they have made the commitment, they'll be more likely to behave consistently and remain loyal to your brand. Get them to commit further by developing messages that are consistent with their values, priorities and interests.
- **Consensus.** We all know that people trust the opinions of their friends and family over the things you are saying. Use reviews, case studies and testimonials to get them to believe—and buy. Use recommendations or endorsements from others who are like your customers and who like your company, the true brand evangelists to get more of these types of converts.
- **Liking.** If they like your company, they will be more likely to buy from your company. And, they are more likely to buy if they know that you like them. Find a genuine compliment and/or commonality, and tell them!
- **Authority.** As an expert or trusted brand, you are a known authority, so leverage it with your e-mails. If you have expertise in a certain area, don't say you're an expert, show it, using case studies, award mentions and special industry

---

[38] Cialdini, Robert. Influence: The Psychology of Persuasion. William Morrow & Company, 1993.

designations in your signature block. To build a relationship with prospects and remind them of your authority, send them articles, blog posts and white papers that you have authored.

- **Scarcity.** People don't want to miss out. They don't want to see an opportunity pass them by or lose what they already have. So show them what they could miss if they don't get in on the offer. Tell them about a dwindling amount of product or time for an offer, if it honestly exists.

FIGURE 9-5   *Influence: The Psychology of Persuasion,* by Robert Cialdini

So, let's switch gears now and jump into one of the most dynamic, fastest-growing content types: video.

CHAPTER 10

Video Content

Everywhere we go, everything we do, we are surrounded by it. It's there when we surf the Internet; it's there when we socialize. It's there when we are logging into our e-mail accounts and when we are paying bills. It waits for us and wants to show us something, teach us something, give us an opportunity to comment. It's **online video content**, and its day in the Internet sun has finally come.

Yes, web video is taking over the digital experience, and I don't think any of us are surprised by it. In fact, I think we're quite delighted. After all, we had television to guide the way. We all have a love affair with that medium. Why not with the web equivalent?

Video makes the web experience more enriching, more substantive, more entertaining, and yes, a more compelling proposition for companies everywhere that are building lots of brand awareness and selling lots of goods and services using its power. And you know what else? Video is indexed by search engines. In fact, a Forrester Research report indicated that **your video content is fifty times more likely to appear on the first page of the search results than your website is!** The reasons for this?

1. Not many companies use optimized video content, so there isn't as much competition.
2. People are drawn to video, so if they find what they are looking for on Google, they will keep serving it up.
3. Google owns YouTube. Enough said.[39]

Studies show that online video improves e-mail click-through rates, sales conversions, and search engine rankings, so it's easy to see why companies everywhere are budgeting more ad dollars into this content channel.

---

[1] Elliott, Nate. 2009. "The Easiest Way to a First-Page Ranking on Google." *Nate Elliott's Blog* on Forrester Blogs, January 8. http://blogs.forrester.com/interactive_marketing/2009/01/the-easiest-way.html.

Powerful Statistics

So the mother of all online video is YouTube of course. It was the site that put web video into the mainstream and started an explosion of video uploads around the world. It engaged the creative mind and attracted marketers around the globe. So, how powerful of a force are we talking about?

    YouTube data:[40]

- More than 13 million hours of video were uploaded during 2010 and 48 hours of video are uploaded every minute, resulting in nearly 8 years of content uploaded every day
- Over 3 billion videos are viewed a day
- Users upload the equivalent of 240,000 full-length films every week
- More video is uploaded to YouTube in one month than the 3 major US networks created in 60 years
- 70% of YouTube traffic comes from outside the US
- YouTube is localized in 25 countries across 43 languages
- YouTube's demographic is broad: 18–54 years old
- YouTube mobile gets over 320M views a day (up 3× year/year), representing 10% of our daily views
- Nearly 17 million people have connected their YouTube account to at least one social service (Facebook, Twitter, Orkut, etc)
- 150 years of YouTube video are watched every day on Facebook and every minute more than 500 tweets contrain YouTube links

Two other key stats:[41]

- Sixty-seven percent of Internet usage is video based
- Seventy percent of Internet users go online to watch videos

FIGURE 10-1   YouTube

---

[40] YouTube Statistics. Accessed 8/8/11. http://www.youtube.com/t/press_statistics

[41] Beale, Ryan. "Why B2B Marketers Should Consider Adding Video Content on YouTube." RBeale. com Accessed 2/10/11. http://rbeale.com/internet-marketing/why-b2b-marketers-should-consider-adding-video-content-on-youtube/

The way I'd like you to think about your businesses video content is this: **You now have the chance to have your own online television "station" or "show."** That's right, you now have the opportunity on the web to have your very own branded, fully functioning, around-the-clock, information-providing video network. YouTube, Vimeo, TubeMogul, and others have given us this rare opportunity.

So, how will you use video to connect with your target market? What will you say? Will you fill it up with a bunch of commercials for your products and services? Absolutely not. Just like you wouldn't fill up your traditional television channel with commercials. Will you produce amateur-crafted, poorly edited material? No, not even close. It's fairly simple to shoot and edit quality web video now.

What you should do is put together a *robust schedule of programming*: "how-to" videos, opinion pieces, shoots from industry events and happenings, interviews with important industry figures, etc. Think about it: there is *so* much you can do with video that your prospects and clients would find interesting. You could even go the entertainment route and put together some comic pieces. It's worked for companies like Blendtec. Plus, online videos stay online forever. Produce a really good video, and it could still be getting views five years from now.

For my company's YouTube channel and website, I host a series called "Web Content Weekly," where I update companies everywhere on the latest and greatest in the web and mobile content and content marketing arenas. It's pretty cool, and I love doing it. Of course, I've been known to be quite the ham when a camera is around, so this doesn't hurt! Note that I'm not pitching our services in the series. If my viewers want to e-mail us or talk, they know how to get a hold of me.

So, there are two things you need to do as soon as possible: Go purchase a Kodak Zi8 video camera and then start carrying it around with you at all times. You never know when you'll need to video something for your business.

In a digital world, words are simply *not enough* anymore. You have to be doing *everything you can* to grow your brand and your business. Content marketing is about doing *lots* of things right: your website, blog, mobile presence, social media activities, and yes, video as well.

Before YouTube came along, video was a mess. There was no standardization, it was expensive to produce, and it was difficult to distribute effectively. But everything has changed now. And bandwidth continues to improve, so no worries there.

By showing your prospects the value of your content—using video as a "gateway" for this experience—you'll build rapport and influence way before you ever do business with them. If you aren't using video, and feel that it can fit with your content, you should get in the game as soon as you can. Video opens up a new marketing channel for your business, targeting those in your market who are engaged *first* by video content. Whether it's the more visually inclined, the younger generation, or folks with smart phones, people are watching videos, and some of them prefer it as *the method* to get to know you. In fact, people everywhere are watching more and more web videos with each passing day!

Let's face it: TV commercials are a shrinking medium. Talk about a waste of money! As a marketer for almost twenty years, I'm shocked that so many companies still spend their precious marketing dollars this way. It's crazy. Like television, web video provides the magic of moving images, the hypnotic quality that we all have experienced. But unlike television, online video content engages viewers and allows them to comment on it. Your potential customers are asking you for one thing and one thing only: **Show me the value.** When you've done that, they will consider doing business with you. You show value by building a relationship, not by splashing images of your products all over the screen. There's a very good reason that Google purchased YouTube in 2006. Google saw the future, and the future, my friends, is *right now.*

It's show time!

Trends in the Web Video Space

Continuing with my effort to help you maximize your time with online marketing activities, I thought it would be important to share the top trends in the web video space. If you are looking for guidelines on what you should be doing with web video, use this list as a starting point.

1. **Interactive video will become the standard for advertising.** The march of technology continues and, as a result, interactivity is coming to web video campaigns. Interactive video advertising gives viewers the opportunity to click and engage within the video player itself; they can get more information, download coupons, and more. Companies like Innovid provide a great platform for creating interactive online video campaigns, and YouTube annotations give brands the opportunity to create their own branded interactive experience

FIGURE 10-2   Innovid

2. **Augmented reality and 3D will let consumers explore products from home.** We all love to touch and feel the products we buy. On the web, that is pretty difficult. But, with new 3D manipulation of images and augmented reality, companies can now let users see their products from all angles.

Earlier this year, Olympus launched an augmented reality campaign[42] to showcase its PEN camera, using a paper marker that could be downloaded and printed out. When held up to a webcam, the marker was turned into a 3D camera. Pretty cool.

3. **Video analytics and targeting continue to improve.** If you're using video, you want to know how many viewers you have, where they are located, how old they are, whether they are male or female, what websites they like, which videos they are watching, and more. These analytic capabilities are now available and will continue to improve.

You'll also be able to target your ads with much more precision. On YouTube, you can target campaigns to specific viewer demographics, specific tags or categories, and even to specific videos.

4. **Ad formats will become standardized.** Although it's high-tech video "mumbo jumbo" to most of us, there are big changes coming in terms of video standardization through what's called VAST (Video Ad Serving Template) and VPAID (Video Player-Ad API definition). This standardization of formats and technologies enables advertisers to easily reach larger audiences across multiple sites. Video demand and ad budgets will thereby increase. With these standards in place, you'll be able to get your video ads out to more places.

5. **Mobile video advertising will get huge.** Like everything else, video is going mobile in a big way, and video advertising in this channel will be highly interactive and scalable. The infrastructure to support video advertising at scale, including proper third-party ad serving, measurement, and yield optimization will finally become the real deal.

Getting Your "Studio" Set Up—The Basics

If you are like most people out there and are totally new to the "video thing," it's important to understand the basics. Within the video production environment, there are five important, sequential steps: planning and storyboarding, shooting the video, editing the video, distributing the video, and marketing the video. All are important steps, and all of them need to be done well in order to be successful with this content channel.

---

[42] Boches, Edward. 2010. "A Demonstration of Olympus PEN Augmented Reality Camera on Vimeo." *Edward Boches's Posterous* blog, July 21. http://edwardboches.posterous.com/a-demonstration-of-olympus-pen-augmented-reali.

Got a mobile phone or webcam? If so, you have the makings of a video studio already. How about five hundred dollars and a little bit of time? Well, then you, my friend, could be a total pro in web video business. What will that small investment purchase? A video camera and Final Cut Pro video editing software. Both of these can be purchased for less than five hundred dollars out the door and, together, they will become the basis for your web video empire. Note: There is a learning curve with Final Cut, but it will be well worth the time you invest to master it. We've been using an older "Flip" video camera (no longer available) and Final Cut for my business videos for the past few years, and it's what I always recommend to others. Be aware, you could also use Mac's iMovie software for your video editing, which comes standard on most Apple computers. It's super easy to use, but doesn't have as many features as Final Cut. Final Cut Pro works only on the Mac, which is really the platform you should use to do any video or other creative work. If you are operating in a PC environment, you want to use Windows Movie Maker (free on most PCs) or Adobe Premiere Express.

FIGURE 10-3   [Kodak Zi8]

FIGURE 10-4   Final Cut Pro

Some other things you'll want to get are a **tripod**, for shooting stabilization, and an **external hard drive**, for your large video files. I got a great, portable, collapsible tripod at Target for fifteen dollars. And you can get a nice 500GB hard drive for these large video files (recommended) for less than a hundred dollars.

For shooting those informational or web show videos at home or at your office, make sure you have a basic set configured or a decent background. Lighting needs to be right, as well. Find out more about video set and production ideas on www.reelseo. com.

FIGURE 10-5   ReelSEO

If you are shooting on location, you won't need anything extra. Just make sure you are recording where this isn't too much background noise and the lighting is decent.

Putting Together a Video Content Plan—Strategy

Video is a cornerstone of content marketing, because your prospects and customers can *both see and hear your message* and they can be *moved and called to action* in ways that other forms of online content can't achieve. With sight, sound, and emotion all rolled into one, the medium is incredibly engaging.

Your video content strategy should include:

- **Your objectives**—Are you supplementing your other online content? Going after a new audience? Giving your sales team some material to use? Will this be an ongoing video series or a trial video ad campaign? Make your goals measurable.
- **Your message**—This includes the information and value you will provide, the feeling you want to convey, and your communication style
- **The "talent"**—This is probably you—or someone in your company who will be the official spokesperson. Don't worry, you don't have to be the best-looking person in the world. The key here is coming across *genuinely*. Being real and

having an air of approachability is a must. Don't worry about not being polished. That can actually work in your favor.

- **Consideration for the editing process**—This is one step you may want to outsource. It can be tough to get it right. Video editing is part art, part science. You want to deliver your message the way you are seeing it in your head, with a professional look and feel.
- **Distribution/marketing**—How will you get your videos to your target market? Will you set up your own free YouTube channel or get involved with paid video advertising? Perhaps you'll do both.
- **Archiving and curation**—How long should your videos be in circulation? Are they time sensitive, with a certain "shelf life"? You'll want to have a central repository where you store your archive of videos, both for ongoing marketing campaigns and for your own purposes.

Capturing Your Story in Moving Images

What is a story? It is a way of telling a tale. Every good story has a beginning, a middle, and an end. In Hollywood, the sequence would be defined like this: the story is set up, the characters are introduced, some drama commences, it builds to a climax, and then, finally, a resolution comes. Every good story has a plot, a setting, and a good cast of characters.

You, of course, don't have to be this elaborate with your web videos. It can be this simple: Your company faced a problem or challenge and you overcame it. How you did it becomes the story. Likewise, you could tell a story about your product or service and how it was used effectively; your customer faced a challenge and, with your help, overcame it. There are a thousand stories you could tell.

Think about how you want your company to be perceived on your web videos. How do you want to come across? What's your story? Do you have something to say that no one else is saying? Who will be the video host or spokesperson? These are all important questions.

Here is what it comes down to: Your company has a story to tell. *Every* company has a story to tell. I don't care if it's a hundred-year-old family-operated Fortune 100 company or a small, hometown accounting firm. What are your values? What do you believe in? What's the human side of your business? Think about this: If you never had to worry about making money, why would you be doing this activity? Hopefully, it's because you have a strong passion and love for it. If so, this can *easily* translate to the screen. People swarm to this like blue sky to sun.

In business, people deal with other people. We are all curious. We all want to be treated well. It's basic. Video can communicate and deliver on these elements like nothing else. Whatever your story is, I bet there are people out there who want to hear it. If you have a natural warmth and likeable personality, that can only help. Including others in your company story can also work really well. Customers, vendors, partners, and employees: They can all serve as your supporting actors.

Your goal? To be memorable.

Storyboarding and Scripting

So you have an idea. But what are you going to say? The first thing to keep in mind is this: Scripting what you will say is not a requirement. In fact, speaking naturally in front of the camera is always best. This is not easy for everyone to do, of course, but with practice, it becomes much easier. What worked well for me in past videos was to simply act like the camera wasn't even on. Pretending like I'm telling a story at a dinner table with friends can really help when I'm shooting a new video episode. What you *do* want to do is have an outline of points you want to cover in the video. Whether you're shooting a thirty-minute program or a quick five-minute industry update, an outline really helps organize your thoughts.

Take the process one step further, and storyboarding and scripting come into play. So what is a storyboard? It is a graphic organizer (like a series of illustrations or images) displayed in sequence for the purpose of visualizing how your video will play when complete. Scripting is the act of writing out your lines.

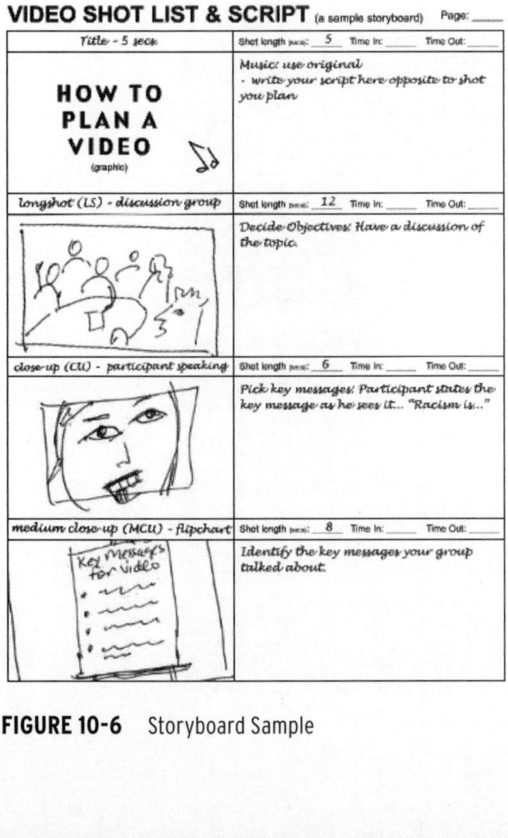

FIGURE 10-6 Storyboard Sample

There are content writing techniques that are great for video—stories and anecdotes, metaphors and analogies, mirroring, and mind eye's projection. All of these techniques can be used to tap into the emotional connection and the power of the subconscious, the same way that a good movie or television show does.

For shorter form videos (five minutes or less), a certain "structure" or approach also works well: attention, empathy, solution, and action. It's more challenging to engage viewers with longer-form video, so you may want to consider borrowing a three-act structure, where you give the audience three separate chunks of easily digestible content. These structures are used in movies and infomercials to great effect.

Keep in mind; you *don't have to be* in the video every time. You could simply narrate or do a voiceover. These are called presentation-style videos, and for these, you are off camera on purpose. The visual is what's important. This allows you to use your script directly and still present with a conversational tone of voice. The key here is to *not* sound like you're reading. That's really important.

You can also use a simple, free teleprompter software (www.cueprompter.com), and turn your laptop into a homemade teleprompter! With this cool tool, your web browser works like a teleprompter and no extra software is needed. I have done this to great effect in past videos. And I didn't have to learn any of my lines ahead of time. Hey, if President Obama can do it, so can we!

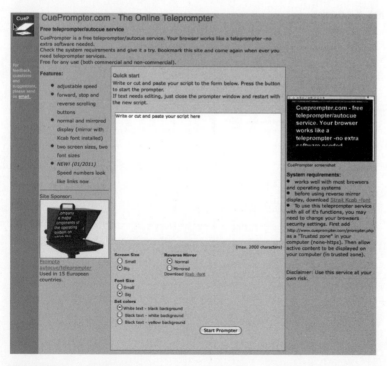

FIGURE 10-7   CuePrompter

Production: Shooting the Video Content

To start with, let's keep in mind the appropriate length for your videos. Think three to six minutes. Remember, attention spans online are short. You want to get in, get out, and let your viewer move on to other things. Of course, there are some exceptions, but as a general rule, you want to think simple. It will make it easier on you, too, from an editing, storing, and distributing point of view.

When it comes to production you need to know that people—your viewers—want to see what you look like. So video can be an easy way to get closer to your audience and help them experience your brand in a personal way. Plus, your facial expressions, mannerisms, and body language can communicate a great deal and support your message. Here is the other thing: Don't worry about being perfect. You don't need to get it all in a single take. It's usually better to string together a series of clips than to use one stream of unedited video footage.

Bring the visuals and charts, too! Remember, you'll have better viewer impact if you present concepts as pictures rather than words. The key is to identify the main concept in every sentence of your script and pair it with a relevant and engaging visual element. This also helps keep the viewer's mind engaged. Being boring may be the worst sin of all in video.

Just remember the importance of changing visual perspective often, whether you are in the video or not. Switching around what appears on the screen, using transitions, and/or using new camera angles can really pay off with increased viewership.

Here are some other important production tips:

- Get familiar with your equipment and do some tests.
- Use a tripod for camera stabilization.
- Frame the shot correctly—close-ups get zoomed in, surrounding area shots get zoomed out.
- Don't forget lighting—make sure you have enough of it. If you can't seem to get it right, just ensure the light source is in front of the subject.
- Be aware of shadows—they can *kill* your video. Don't stand with the sun at your back for outside shots and don't shoot in front of a sunlit window for inside shots.
- Remove as much noise as possible. Perfect quiet is what you are after.
- Make sure the audio sounds good—after you shoot, be sure to watch it on playback to see if it turned out the way you wanted, both in how it sounds *and* how it looks.
- Use a lavalier or shotgun mic, depending on your audio needs (check battery levels).
- To get the absolute best-quality video, use a "light kit" with at least two lights, and three if you can afford them: a key light, a fill light, and a back light. If you

are shooting outside, use a graduated neutral density filter, which is used to bring a bright part of a scene into the dynamic range of film or sensor.

Postproduction: Editing the Video Content

After you're done shooting the video, you're only halfway there. Now comes the editing. Hopefully, you were able to get some of the video done in one or two takes, so you don't need to edit out a bunch of stuff. Essentially, what you are doing with the editing process is putting the video together, each scene and each frame, piece by piece, to tell your story in the most effective way possible. This is the time when you'll break out your iMovie, Final Cut, or Adobe Premiere software and put it to work for you.

As I mentioned before, it takes time to learn video editing, but luckily for you, it's gotten much easier in recent years, especially with Apple's iMovie. But, of course, because it's a free tool, you don't have all the bells and whistles that you get with higher-end software like Final Cut or Adobe Premiere Express. Whichever software you use, your script and storyboards will serve as a solid structure for building your rough cut of the video.

Of course, you'll also be able to add in appropriate graphics, music (royalty-free only), sound effects, and other cool elements that will give your video that extra special touch. For music, you may be better off creating your own "loop" on Apple's GarageBand program or talking to a local independent musician in your area who wants a little exposure. If you want to really dive into audio editing, be sure to check out Audacity, a free cross-platform tool that is used by many companies. For photo editing, you can learn Photoshop, but it has a steep learning curve. Try using Image Tricks, iZoom, or iPhoto (Mac program) instead. Picasa from Google is also good for simple photo editing.

The editing step will take longer than you think, so be sure to budget the appropriate time for your project.

Compression

An important step in the editing process is applying **compression** to your videos, otherwise known as "outputting" your video into the appropriate format. Compression is done to make your files the right size so they will play back the right way and look good. This is a trial and error type of thing, and will take practice to get right. Final Cut, iMovie, and Adobe Premiere all perform compression functions for you, and have an "automatic upload to YouTube" function, which is nice.

The key with the compression step is to understand the size and format requirements for the site(s) where your video will be played or watched online. For example, these are YouTube's recommended upload specs: smaller than 2GB in size, in an acceptable file format, and less than fifteen minutes in length.

Here's a list of some well-known formats that YouTube supports:

- WebM files—Vp8 video codec and Vorbis audio codecs
- .MPEG4, 3GPP, and MOV files—typically supporting h264, mpeg4 video codecs, and AAC audio codec
- .AVI—many cameras output this format; typically the video codec is MJPEG and audio is PCM
- .MPEGPS—typically supporting MPEG2 video codec and MP2 audio
- .WMV
- .FLV—Adobe-FLV1 video codec, MP3 audio[43]

A good general rule: It's best to keep the original source video file size, codec, and format.

Optimizing Video for the Web and Mobile

Here is the step that most companies miss with their online video content. It seems they get so excited about their cool new videos that they forget that, in order for people to *search and find them*, SEO needs to be considered as well. Not to worry, we have you covered.

Like your text content, video must be search engine optimized to include a searchable title, keyword-rich description, and appropriate tags. Sharing optimization is important too: You'll want to use annotations to tell viewers how to share your videos and place share options next to embedded video, including options for sharing on Facebook, Twitter, YouTube, and other sites. YouTube captioning is important too.

Here are the important SEO items to consider for your videos:

1. **Create a relevant, keyword-rich title and description for your video.** This is the most important step, by far. Video titles can produce lots of great traffic. Be sure to use the appropriate keywords in your title, too, so it shows up on the search engines when people are searching for your topic. Include as many accurate "tags" as you can. For example, if you are loading a video on designing a website, you would tag it with "how to design a website," "designing sites for the web," "website design 101," and so on.

Here is the other thing: It needs to be a compelling, enticing title. Your video title functions in the same way that a headline for a blog post does: It gets people to check it out.

---

[43] YouTube. "Supported YouTube File Formats." Accessed 2/17/11. http://www.google.com/support/youtube/bin/answer.py?hl=en&answer=55744.

2. **Include your URL in your video.** During the editing process, you can add a text box to your video. It's a good idea to use your website address here, so viewers know how to find you.

3. **Provide a transcript of the video.** Speech recognition by the search engines is not a reality yet. In the meantime, we can use video *transcripts* to get us where we need to be. Using YouTube, you can place captions on your videos, which acts as the video transcript (getting attached to the video's timeline). This allows people to find specific portions of your videos by phrase, and the captions can be searched and indexed by the engines, meaning your video content itself counts toward ranking. YouTube does captions automatically, but be sure to review it to correct any mistakes in the text.

You can also check out a company called SpeakerText, which provides video transcripts as well, but maximizes SEO potential with a service they call "QuoteLinks."

FIGURE 10-8   SpeakerText

4. **Be sure to brand your video.** Include your company logo prominently somewhere on the screen or on the set in the background, so viewers can see it.

5. **Always provide an HTML link for your videos.** When you post the video to your YouTube channel, you should write a short description of your video. Be sure to start with the link you want to drive your viewers to.

6. **Place your video on all of your content channels.** Your video will be populated on your YouTube channel, for sure, but don't forget all the other places: your website or blog, your social media profiles, etc. Embed the video wherever it seems appropriate. And here's the other important thing: *allow others to embed and share your videos on their own sites!*

Distributing Video Content and Maximizing the Marketing Effort

1. **Create a YouTube channel.** This is where it all starts. YouTube is the nine-hundred-pound gorilla of online video. So, be sure to create a branded URL (i.e., www.youtube.com/yourcompanyname). Creating a channel is easy; just be sure that it reflects your corporate branding and messaging. And, be sure to add a link back to your site or blog at the beginning of the channel description.

Here is a good example of a customized YouTube channel:

FIGURE 10-9 NASA YouTube Channel

Note: Also check out Vimeo, Blip.tv, Viddler, and Metacafe. The bottom line is that there's no need to host your own video player on your site. You don't want the heavy bandwidth on your own server.

2. **Add your video to your blog or website.** Once you've uploaded your videos to YouTube, it's simple to add them to your blog or web pages. All you do is copy and paste the YouTube "embed" code from your videos. To get people to follow you on your YouTube channel, add the YouTube icon to your website and link it to your channel URL. Post links to your social media platforms as well.

3. **Use mass syndication service TubeMogul.** TubeMogul provides a free service that assists in distributing your videos to the top video and social networking sites. You can also distribute to custom sites and encode and create RSS feeds to syndicate your video anywhere you like. TubeMogul includes a cool analytics tool, too, which helps you see real-time viewership, audience engagement, geographic tracking, and stream quality. Using TubeMogul will help you compete more effectively for sure!

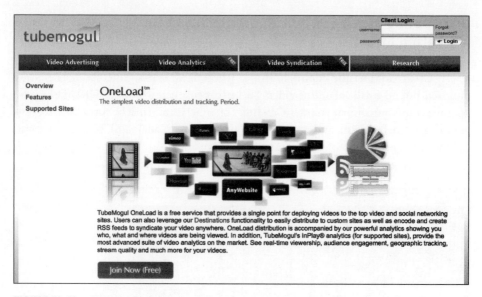

FIGURE 10-10   TubeMogul

4. **Add videos to industry publication websites.** Some industry publications let advertisers upload videos and then include them in their RSS feeds. If you are advertising, this is a great idea to exploit.

5. **Consider all your options.** You can also send your video out with a press release, link back to your video blog posts when leaving comments on other blogs, add video URLs to e-newsletters and other marketing collateral, and encourage people who follow you to add your videos to their blog posts.

Creating a Mass of Video Content

I know what you are thinking: Oh my, what am I possibly going to talk about in my videos? What type of content can I put together with my limited time? Never fear, there is no need to stress, there are plenty of things you can do with video that will prove to be very compelling for your viewers. And some of them are surprisingly simple to execute. Here are a few:

1. **Repurpose content you already have.** Now that you've made it this far through the book, you know that you already have (or will have soon) lots of content you can leverage for video. Simply take this content, update it, and release it in video format. For example, take the key points from a white paper you wrote last year, add the latest industry stats, and create a short video.

You could also use your blog posts to create visual slides that discuss important points about a certain topic. Narrate them with a slick voiceover, and your video is ready for prime time

2. **Create video versions of testimonials and case studies.** There's only one thing better than getting client testimonials and case studies: client *video* testimonials and case studies. Whether you capture the interview on audio or video, the personally delivered testimonial can be incredibly powerful. My company asked a handful of clients if they would create a testimonial video for us. And you know what? Eight of them did so—on their own, without our help! All you have to do is ask, right?

3. **Edit and repurpose webinars and podcasts.** Ever done a webinar or podcast? An hour-long webinar or podcast can be broken up into several shorter videos that cover specific topics. To create some additional value, you can provide an update or answer common customer questions.

4. **Interview partners and industry leaders at tradeshows/events.** Don't miss this easy opportunity. Easily done with a small video camera, you can make these videos low budget "reports from the field," so there's no need for heavy editing. Simply record video conversations with customers, partners, and industry leaders. Doing this successfully provides rock solid video content that others will surely want to watch.

5. **Make how-to videos.** Teaching will always be an in-demand skill. By educating prospects and customers about a certain topic, you get them truly engaged. And if your product or service can help solve the issue at hand, even better!

6. **Do product or service demos.** Online videos that demonstrate the value of your product or service are a no-brainer. Of course, you don't want to *lead* with these types of videos, but they are clearly important ones to have in your video library. They're especially valuable to those customers who have already purchased something from you and want to learn more about how to use it.

7. **Solicit user-generated videos.** Get others to create videos for you! How? Have them do product or service review videos for your company. Promise them you'll put them up on your YouTube channel. You can also hold a *viral video contest.* How would this work? Simple. You tell people that you want to put together a video ad for your business. The customer who puts together the best video ad wins and gets to see his video used for your business. The caveat? The video needs to showcase *how the customer uses your product or service.* This one is a real winner. Just be sure to have some type of prize that will entice prospects to get involved, perhaps an Amazon gift card.

8. **Answer your customers' questions.** Do the classic Q & A session. Ask your viewers some key questions that will spark conversation about the things they are looking for when it comes to your products and services. Use the video to answer their most important questions.

Using an Outside Vendor for Video Production

You've read every word in this chapter and you are thinking one thing: "Great, this all sounds wonderful, but there is absolutely no way that I have the time or desire to do this stuff." I understand. The time crunch and information overload are among the problems we all face in business today. I get it. We all need to stick to our strengths. Some of us are simply not cut out for video. Clearly, it's important that you have some role in your video content, especially if you are the CEO of your company. Despite what you may think, people *do* want to hear from you. And you *can* help sell your company—you really can.

The solution? You can easily outsource all the production, editing, distribution, marketing, and management functions. The important thing is that you *appear* in the videos. As I mentioned earlier, you don't even have to "learn your lines." You can use teleprompter software for that one. So, yes, you can use a vendor. Which companies are the most reputable? Well, it really depends on what part of the country you live in, but there are some great video services out there. Send me an email and we can get you taken care of.

CASE STUDY: Salesforce.com's Video Bonanza

Customer relations management giant Salesforce.com has been investing heavily in video content. The company posted a video called "What Is Cloud Computing?" last year that was viewed more than two hundred thousand times in twelve months.[1]

Salesforce was so pleased with this result that it partnered with YouTube, and now has roughly a thousand pieces of video content getting well over seven thousand views a day. Salesforce has equated this to forty-seven "hyper-efficient reps" working the phones daily.

[1] SlideShare. "Video Creation for B2B Marketers." Accessed 2/5/11. http://www.slideshare.net/Salesforce/video-creation-for-b2b-marketers.

CASE STUDY: Web Videos Working Like Magic for BizChair.com

BizChair.com is an online retailer of office chairs, as well as furniture for offices, schools, home offices, medical facilities, and restaurants. The site was founded in 2001 by Sean Belnick as one of the first online-only office chair and furniture retailers. BizChair.com's clientele includes the Pentagon, Fox's *American Idol*, Microsoft, and Google, as well as small businesses, churches, organizations, and individuals. For several years, BizChair.com held the first slot in the organic Google rankings for the keyword phrase "office chairs." Despite aggressive market competition, it remains prominently ranked.

In the past few years, BizChair.com's customer service department received numerous requests for additional office chair product images, information, and user instructions. But its customer service representatives had limited resources to help customers out. They would explain product instructions over the phone to customers or answer questions via e-mail, but they found that customers still wanted additional images and information. The company needed a solution to help educate their customers about their products. It also needed to cut down on the time its employees were spending answering product questions, so that the representatives could focus more time on orders. With this in mind, the marketing team set out to find a viable solution.

The remedy? ***Develop e-commerce product videos for the website.*** Creating and implementing e-commerce videos offered BizChair.com several benefits. First, it made the company an early adopter of a new e-commerce solution, which put it a step ahead of its competition. Second, BizChair.com knew that e-commerce video strategies had been proven to increase search engine results page (SERP) rankings, site traffic, and conversions. Third, video offered customers a quality way to see and familiarize themselves with the product outside of static product images.

After much research into the ROI on e-commerce videos, BizChair.com opted to partner with Invodo, an e-commerce video company, to create product videos. Invodo offered a full-service video package, including video content creation and a proprietary video platform. After Invodo presented a final copy of the edited video, BizChair.com simply uploaded the product video to its site. Invodo created video sitemaps and meta-information for all the videos, so they could rank prominently in the search engines for their targeted key terms. Instead of having videos hosted through other domains, BizChair.com used Invodo's player, so the videos were sourced from BizChair.com's own domain. This improved the SEO value of the video assets. The company is now in the process of implementing a second set of product videos with unique content for Facebook and YouTube.

(continued)

CASE STUDY: *Continued*

How did BizChair.com benefit? The video initiative resulted in high-quality product videos that fully demonstrated the product in the same manner that a sales associate would in a store. This has greatly improved the online shopping experience for customers. BizChair.com has seen a big increase in product views, time on site, and overall conversions.

The lesson? Web videos, done right, can turn your website into a cash machine!

A Final Word on Web Videos

Here's my challenge to you: *If you are new at video, make the commitment that you will record a video in the next month.* Don't postpone it. Just dive in and get started. The longer you wait, the more you'll regret it, trust me.

Your web videos should function like any other online content you develop. Make it high-quality. Maximize the social context of your videos. You want to grow an audience of devoted fans who will tune in for every video, every episode—and then pass it on to other companies or their friends to check out. Your web videos need to be interesting, relevant, and "sticky" if you want to achieve any type of viral activity. And be sure to use video to connect in a genuine, meaningful way that follows your larger content strategy.

Good luck!

CHAPTER 11

Audio Content—Podcasts, Webinars, and More

So far, we have covered a wide range of online content—website copy, lead-generation content, press releases, social media, blogging, e-mails, and videos. There is only one other type of content that has been with us since close to the "beginning" that we have yet to cover—*audio content*.

First, it was web seminars, known as webinars, in the late 1990s, and then podcasting shortly thereafter. Podcasts exploded on to the scene in the early 2000s, when Apple's iPod came on the market. In recent years, the podcast has fallen a bit in popularity, but is still used to great success by thousands of companies. Of course, audio content has a great deal in common with video content. Although video content is much more powerful and popular, there are many advantages to using audio content, both from a branding and a lead-generation standpoint. Plus, audio content is something people can consume while they are doing other things, like driving, working out, or multitasking at the office. Video requires more of our attention.

Ever since Thomas Edison shocked the world with the first phonograph, we have been spellbound by recorded sound. For decades, through radio and records, audio was one of the key technologies of the modern world. But then television entered the picture. Next came the computer age. Audio technology took a backseat. Then along came the web, and the recorded word gained a new lease on life. Why? It was inexpensive and easy to deliver. One thing has remained true from the very beginning: Captured sound has always been a powerful medium for connecting with others. Like video, it has a bit of magic to it. A popular podcast series can, in fact, turn your typical, "bland," corporate CEO into a mini-celebrity in short order.

So, with audio content on the web, we are talking about two things: podcasts and webinars.

A **podcast** is a prerecorded audio program that's posted to a website and is made available for download so people can listen to it on personal computers or mobile devices.

A **webinar**, a contraction of web seminar (and sometimes called a "teleseminar"), is a web/phone audio event that features one-way communication from a speaker(s) to an audience, but can be made collaborative by including polling and question and answer sessions. A **webcast** is a one-way audio event from the speaker to the audience with limited audience interaction.

Webinars are popular in the B2B space because they are very helpful for companies that are in the research phase of vendor selection. The more information companies have to make a decision, the better. A content-rich webinar on a specific topic that is relevant to the needed product or service can go a long way in finding the right partner.

Podcasting

So, you want to be the next web radio star? A well-produced podcast series may get you there. The most successful business podcasts have literally hundreds of thousands of regular listeners. Can you say *potential new customers*?

Podcasting, of course, takes its name from Apple's popular "iPod" merged with the word "broadcasting." What distinguishes a podcast is that people can subscribe, and when new podcasts are released, the audio file is automatically delivered, or fed, to a subscriber's computer or mobile device. Usually, the podcast features an audio show with new episodes that come daily or weekly. Most people listen to their podcasts through iTunes or on their iPod. From advice on business accounting to website design to offshore outsourcing, podcasts are used by companies to spread the word about their brands and showcase the passion they have for their subject. Similar to a talk radio show, a podcast can also take the format of an interview. A typical podcast will run anywhere from ten to thirty minutes.

For small business people out there, know that your *voice* can be a very effective marketing tool. Essentially, your listeners are hearing the voice of *your business*, so you have a great opportunity to build trust and awareness. Think about it: You're telling your audience what *you* want them to hear. That's huge.

And here's the other thing: Some people dislike reading, but will gladly listen to an audio clip. Capitalize on this with your podcast. For certain people, comprehension levels can increase if information is spoken by someone else, rather than read by themselves.

Podcasting is a simple, inexpensive method of syndicating your audio files online. And because you have the warmth and intimacy of a talk radio program, a podcast seems more personal. It's a great way to build a connection with new audiences.

Creating a Simple Podcast

How do you create a podcast? Well, you can do it all yourself or you can use a service provider like PodOmatic, Hipcast, or Palegroove Studios. Blog Talk Radio and Podbean are also good solutions. If you want to save some money and you have the time, doing it yourself it pretty straightforward.

FIGURE 11-1   PodOmatic

1. **First, you'll need to use software to record your own audio file.** Apple's Garage-Band program is a great resource for this. Another good free option is Audacity, which you can download at http://audacity.sourceforge.net/. If you use Audacity, you'll also want to download the MP3 Encoder, which allows MP3 exportation.

FIGURE 11-2   GarageBand

Note: For recording, you can use your computer's microphone or buy a better one at Radio Shack for about thirty dollars. If you are using more than one mic, you'll need a four-channel mixer, which you can purchase for around fifty dollars.

2. **Record the audio, capturing it to GarageBand or Audacity.** Don't worry about mistakes; you can edit those out.

3. **Edit the audio.** Remove the bad stuff and bring all the usable footage together.

4. **Add an opening and closing with a show jingle.** GarageBand comes with some cool jingles and effects you can use for your podcast. Choose "Control » Show Loop Browser," and you can find a variety of sounds. All you need to do is drag and drop them into your track mixer.

5. **Once your audio is recorded, create an RSS feed.** The best way to do this is through FeedBurner.

6. **When your audio and RSS files are completed, upload both to your blog.**

7. **Submit your podcast feed URL to the iTunes Store.** Your podcast will be reviewed by iTunes staff before it goes live in the iTunes Store. Note: If you are an Apple user and have an **iWeb site**, you're all set. In GarageBand, just hit "Share » Export," and the podcast will be sent to your iWeb site ready to be published.

The Importance of Metadata

As with so many other types of web and mobile content, you need to include accurate and findable *metadata* with your podcast in order for it to be found. People can't subscribe to it if they can't find it. A high percentage of people look for podcasts by searching for them, so make sure you get this step right.

Your podcast's metadata should include all of the information that describes your podcast for the potential subscriber, as well as for iTunes searching. The podcast's category and subcategory determine where the podcast will appear. The title, author, description, and up to twelve keywords can be used to determine relevance.

Best Practices for Podcasting

Podcasting can really help online marketing efforts for your business. In some cases, a podcast series may become a new business altogether, as some of the most successful podcast hosts have discovered.

So, what are the best practices when it comes to podcast content creation, marketing, distribution, and monetization? Well, first, know that developing podcast content, building an audience, and attracting advertisers will take serious effort. And it may never happen quite like you hope; it may simply be a great extension of your current marketing efforts. If that's what happens with your podcast, you should still call it a success, no doubt about it.

How well are your podcast shows presented? Is it easy for your audience to interact with the show? What's the online viewing experience like? These are all important questions. If you decide to use audio content like podcasting for your business, you want to get a nice return on your investment—and a nice return on the time you dedicate to the activity.

Here are a few of the practices that separate average podcasts from the really great ones:

1. **Preparing with notes and questions.** Make an outline of what you want to talk about before you start recording. If you are interviewing someone, have your questions in advance. Whatever you do, don't script the entire program; no one wants to hear you reading. It's incredibly boring.

2. **Keeping podcast length short.** Ten to thirty minutes seems to be an appropriate length for a business podcast. Some are sixty minutes long.

3. **Optimizing the podcast.** This is a critical step, as I mentioned earlier. Use the appropriate title, description, and tags, and make sure that you use your keywords in the RSS description.

4. **Having high production values.** We're talking about maximizing sound quality and reducing background noise here. Poor sound quality will turn people off. Remember, you are competing with thousands of podcasts.

5. **Keeping podcasts informative rather than sales-driven.** Don't pitch your products or services. This is pretty much understood by most people, but it needs to be mentioned. Introducing who you are and what your company does is perfectly fine, but again, no one wants to hear a commercial.

6. **Looking for opportunities to send listeners to your website and/or social media profiles.** Although you don't want to actively sell your products and services through your podcast, you should refer listeners to your other online content, such as white papers, e-books, special reports, etc. This is the way you build the relationship, so when people are ready to buy, they come to you; this is the same pattern we've been discussing throughout the book.

7. **Providing show notes.** Describing what you will discuss brings in more listeners and helps the search engines find your podcast content.

8. **Syndicating your podcast.** There are many quality podcast directories, like iTunes and AudioFarm (as well as many others). These directories help get your podcast content out there so it can be found.

9. **Exporting audio from your video content.** Going back to the content-leveraging principle, you probably have a few hours of video that you could pull the audio from and use for a podcast, right? If not, always think in this two-prong approach with your audio and video content. You create it once and use it twice, sometimes for two different audiences entirely. Bonus!

10. **Using cover art for your podcast.** Attractive cover art gets new subscribers for your podcast, plain and simple. Plus, for your podcast to be featured on the podcast main page of the iTunes Store, it's required. Most nice-looking podcast images include an image as well as a title, brand, or source name. A 300x300-pixel JPG is the recommended size and format. Find that quality designer and go to work!

Developing a Strong Bond with Your Audience

The best talk radio hosts are able to create a very strong bond with their audiences because they do certain important things with their voices and the content they produce in order to build instant loyalty. The first thing, of course, is *the sound of their voices*. If you've been told you have a "voice for radio," then maybe podcasting is something you should take seriously. But more important than the actual timbre of your voice is the *friendliness* of your voice. Sounding like a nice, approachable, helpful person will take you far in the podcasting arena.

Your inflection and tone, and your ability to laugh or find humor, are all important too. Your voice can communicate passion and sincerity in a way that your cool e-book never will. We can even "hear" people smile as they speak, and that's very powerful. And if you can throw in the timing and wittiness of a David Letterman or Conan O'Brien, you could have podcasting magic.

So, what's the strategy for developing this unbreakable bond with your online or mobile audience? By using attention, empathy, storytelling, and mirroring. You get **attention** by having a compelling opening to your podcast, by providing substantive, quality content, and by reminding listeners what they will continue to receive in future episodes if they stick with you. Attention is difficult to get in this noisy world, but once you have it, especially in podcasting, chances are you will keep it.

Empathy helps you develop that sense of intimacy with your listeners that forms a strong connection. It's communicating that you understand their challenges or problems. It's presenting your content in a compelling, emotionally and psychologically enriching manner. Reach out to your audience, answer their specific questions, and show you truly care about them.

Next is **storytelling**. Engaging and well used by all the best talk radio hosts, stories are the most effective way for people to see themselves in the situation you are talking about. It also addresses the natural curiosity in people. The right story is always about the listeners, or ties the listeners in somehow. Do this right and you'll become a persuasive podcast storyteller.

Mirroring is a technique in which you demonstrate that you are a kindred spirit to the listener, that you and she are the same, that you're "all in this together." David Ogilvy said it best, I think: "If you're trying to persuade people to do something, or buy something, it seems to me you should use their language, the language they use every day, the language in which they think." Agreed, Master Ogilvy, agreed.

Webinars

Webinars are growing in popularity. Because of technology advancements and lower production costs, companies all over are using webinars to fire up the lead-generation engine. It seems that everywhere you look online there are ads for new web seminar offerings. And some of them are really well done. I know that if I attended all the webinars that looked enticing, I'd have my whole week planned, every week!

As I mentioned earlier, webinars are very popular in the B2B space because they aid in the research phase of vendor selection. The more information companies have before they make a decision, the better. Think about it: Your prospects perhaps don't want to talk to your sales team quite yet, but they are more than willing to hear what you are all about in a no-pressure webinar in which they are among many other prospects. Bottom line: Webinars are a great marketing tool and an effective way to reach your prospects or buyers.

A study by Business.com found that 67 percent of business leaders who rely on social media for business information seek out relevant podcasts or webinars. And RainToday, marketer of tools and information to help grow service businesses, says that "event or conference presentations rate second to referrals and personal awareness as the top method for how professional services companies initially identify the firms they work with."[44]

According to a Forrester Research report, "B2B Marketers' 2010 Budget Trends," webinars are one of the best and most popular ways to generate leads. Forrester found that webinars received more budget than online display ads and even e-mail marketing.[45]

Plus, with a webinar you can target hundreds of people at once. This broad-reaching capability puts webinars in a class all their own. Instead of inviting a few prospects to an in-person event, you can invite hundreds to a virtual one. This is one reason that many

---

[44] Business.com. 2009. "Business Social Media Benchmarking Study—Small Business Decision Makers." http://www.business.com/info/business-social-media-benchmark-study.

[45] Ramos, Laura, with Peter Burris and Zachary Reiss-Davis. 2010. "B2B Marketers' 2010 Budget Trends." Forrester Research, March 23, updated March 29. http://www.forrester.com/rb/Research/b2b_marketers_2010_budget_trends/q/id/56717/t/2?cm_mmc=Forrester-_-Blogs-_-Related%20Research-_-3994.

companies have cut the number of trade shows they attend and exhibit at. There may be no need, when they can simply hold a low-cost, efficiently delivered webinar.

Webinars also provide a great way to reach out to prospects by phone or e-mail, both before and after an event. This is a natural relationship builder. After all the phone calls, e-mails, and the actual webinar, you practically know your prospects!

So, web seminars are educational, social, affordable, and give participants the ability to ask questions, but how can your company really excel at them?

Best Practices for Webinars

So, how can you be among the best of the best in the webinar world? As I mentioned, there are thousands of webinars held every year. You want to become a leading voice in your industry using this online medium. In order to do that, you simply need to follow these best practices.

1. **Deliver solid, high-quality information.** Your audience is looking for valuable content. Too often, webinar attendees are disappointed because they leave feeling like they were sold to rather than educated. So, use case studies, client stories, and real-world applications to express the content.

Don't just focus on the number of leads you'll generate. If your products or services are good enough, they should practically sell themselves in a webinar environment.

2. **You need to market your webinar effectively.** Market the webinar everywhere. Use your in-house e-mail list, and consider renting lists from reputable publishers and industry groups. You should put your event on calendars, and market it via Facebook and LinkedIn (use their event sections). Create an Event Page on Facebook and an Event Invitation in LinkedIn. Activate social-media tools within the virtual-platform environment, allowing attendees to promote your event while it's happening.

Use Twitter. Develop a hashtag to help promote the event, and use it on the day of the webinar to get last-minute sign-ups and post-event downloads. People will retweet what they are hearing, and you can follow the hashtag yourself to take questions from the audience.

All promotions and collateral produced for the event should reflect the pain points of the audience, not how your company sells its products and services. You can also combine your registration with an industry poll or survey, and offer a prize as an incentive. Consider advertising with display ads on industry and partner sites. If you have enough time, ask your audience for input on the agenda.

3. **You need to compensate for not being there live.** Nothing beats a live sales meeting or performance. We all get something intangibly enriching from a face-to-face event. So, with a *virtual* event, you need to compensate. Be sure to rehearse and run through procedures. Ensure that the speaker and moderator are comfortable with

the platform and controls, test all Internet connections and hardware, and review the speaker's slides. Again, presenting online is different from being in front of a live audience. It's more difficult because you can't feed off of the energy of the people; you can't compensate for bad slides or a boring delivery.

4. **Have a backup plan ready in case of technical problems.** In all the webinars I have attended over the years, I would say that 15 percent of them have had a serious technical issue come up. Whether it was the slides not advancing when they should have, a bad phone or Internet connection, or even a speaker who forgets to call in, it *can* happen. The key is to have a contingency plan in place. Be sure to have your speakers' cell phone numbers; also, have their slides printed out so they can present from a hard copy if need be. Have the phone number and e-mail address for your webinar vendor support staff on hand.

Prior to the webinar, have someone on your team dial in to make sure the number is working for participants.

5. **Select the right time and day for your webinar.** Avoid holding your webinar on Mondays or Fridays. The best time of day is 1 pm EST, as this accommodates attendees on the West Coast; but webcasts are typically hosted any time between 11 am and 3 pm EST.

6. **Require speakers to practice.** Have presenters, whether they are in-house experts or third-party speakers, do a live run-through to make sure they sound good and the timing is right. You'll also want to approve the slides to make sure the presentation is not repetitive or boring.

7. **Remind invitees about the event.** As registrations start coming in, follow-up is critical. Send the first reminder one week ahead of time and a second reminder the day before the webcast. And don't forget to send the audio recording to those who registered but forgot to show up. About half of the people who sign up for a free webinar won't attend. Offering a post-conference download via e-mail is key here.

For your PowerPoint presentation, put up a slide that indicates, "The webinar will begin in 10 minutes," so those who log in will know that everything is working correctly. Have the webinar host make an announcement to let attendees know it will start soon and that their audio is working. Also, start two minutes past the hour; this allows the inevitable latecomers to catch the whole event.

8. **Recruit known, respected guest speakers.** Your CEO or CMO might be the obvious choice, but may not be the right pick. Outside speakers can help expand reach and promotion, as they will probably be talking about the event. It also builds credibility and awareness for your products and services without "selling" them directly. Some of your attendees will be impressed that a respected authority in your industry—a third party—is endorsing your company.

9. **Give your attendees something for free.** Don't let your attendees leave empty-handed. Give them the ability to download slides. If this isn't possible, send them the slides. You could also use case studies or a white paper as a giveaway item.

10. **Make registration easy.** Having a nice event-registration site will get attention. Limit the copy to a hundred words or less and use graphics and video to attract attention. Your registration page should be clean and informative, yet inviting. And here is the other key: Minimize the number of fields you require the registrant to complete on the registration form.

Webinar Platform: GoToMeeting (Citrix) or WebEx (Cisco)?

In order to hold an online web seminar event, you need to partner with a vendor that has the software to do it right. There are many platforms to choose from: On24, LiveMeeting, GoToMeeting, WebEx, and more. Personally, I think the two best are GoToMeeting and WebEx. I have used On24 extensively, but found it to be on the pricier side.

According to *PC Magazine*, GoToMeeting (through their GoToWebinar service) is "by far the most polished of all the applications we evaluated."[46] I tend to agree with this assessment. The system has a simple interface, uses an easy registration process, is offered at a very reasonable price, and records events so you can review them later.

FIGURE 11-3   GoToWebinar

---

[46] HubPages. 2011. "GoToMeeting vs WebEx—Which Is Better?" Accessed 2.15.11. http://hubpages.com/hub/GoToMeeting-or-WebEx.

WebEx is also a solid choice. Its conferencing tool is an effective web conferencing solution, but lacks in a few areas. It enables sharing of documentation, presentations, drawings, and applications, just like GoToWebinar. It also can be used through your Wi-Fi supported smartphone browser. But, it's not as user friendly as GoToWebinar. Nontechnical users tend to prefer GoToWebinar to the other meeting solutions.

My advice is to try both and see which one you prefer.

Summary

Audio content is the most underappreciated type of content—by far. With all the emphasis on social media and blogging over the last few years, it seems that audio content, whether it's a web seminar or podcast, has become a lesser priority. But remember, B2B decision makers place a big emphasis on this type of content. They regularly tune in when they are attempting to short list potential vendors for RFP's. And that's important for any company that wants to grow.

Producing a web seminar, in particular, can be much simpler than you may think. You don't have to hold them every week or even every month—four–five times a year is fine. Holding an event every two to four months will still payoff big for your company because of one very important distinction: As long as the information is still up to date, you can use the *recorded audio* over and over again in your lead generation efforts.

So, what topics could you brainstorm for a web seminar or podcast series? Are there opportunities that your competitors have missed? Explore the possibilities and give it a shot. Your prospects are waiting to listen!

CHAPTER 12

Content for Mobile

*M*obility—the ability to go anywhere, do anything, but still be connected to the rest of the world. It is an idea as simple as a flower's bloom but as far-reaching as the cosmos. It supports and nurtures efficient human connection and puts us in the best position to have the greatest impact on our businesses, our communities, and ourselves. Smart mobility truly fosters the best in us.

I saved the best for last for good reason—"mobile" is the future. And it is already here. But how do we harness the power of mobility? How do we connect in the best, most inspired way?

From the very beginning, the computer revolution was about freedom and empowerment. When Steve Jobs talked about *revolution*, he was serious. And this is the promise that mobile computing and mobile content gives us. Like nothing else before it, it is the power that will enable us to finally reach every place we ever wanted to go in business—and in the social world as well.

Of course, the proliferation of mobile phones, especially smartphones, is driving the revolution and giving us the chance to connect in powerful interactions that line up with our customers' preferences and location, in real time. Because we can connect with them *wherever they are*, the connection is super efficient and actionable. Content that is mobilized becomes turbocharged and highly relevant.

Your mobile phone is very personal. Unlike your regular phone or desktop computer, it is rarely shared. Mobile phones have cameras, play videos, and capture voice recordings. Like the web itself, mobile is a *transformative* technology; it can create meaningful one-on-one opportunities to truly engage new audiences. A multichannel mobile strategy will be important now and forever more. And what's the latest data telling us? According to the Nielsen Company, smartphone users are projected to account for more than 50 percent of U.S. wireless subscribers by the end of the year.[47] Gartner predicts that worldwide mobile application sales will increase to 21.6 billion by 2013,

---

[47] Entner, Roger. 2010. "Smartphones to Overtake Feature Phones in U.S. by 2011." Nielsen Wire, March 26. http://blog.nielsen.com/nielsenwire/consumer/smartphones-to-overtake-feature-phones-in-u-s-by-2011/.

up from 4.5 billion in 2010.[48] And according to Kelsey Group, U.S. mobile advertising revenue will be $3.1 billion by 2013, up from $160 million in 2008.[49] Personalized coupons delivered through mobile phones have achieved redemption rates between 15 and 50 percent, which is higher than in other channels.[50] And here is the real kicker: Gartner estimates that **by 2013 more people will be accessing the Internet via mobile phones than on personal computers**.[51] That's pretty incredible.

Mobile content also gives your company the ability to collect powerful analytics data unavailable anywhere else. It is the most personal, targeted, and actionable marketing available today, but of course, there are issues that need to be addressed. As with any other new technology, mobile is evolving right before our eyes. Right now, mobile technology *does not* have a fully accepted standard in place, a standard by which creators can distribute their content easily. There are dozens of platforms on which mobile devices run, each with its own operating system and application requirements, which makes content development a bit complex. The answer, at least for now, seems to be to design for the most common denominator. But, if you have the budget and truly want a universally innovative and engaging presence, you can develop for all the major platforms: iPhone, Android, BlackBerry, and others.

Why is mobile content so important? Because our mobile phones are always with us, they make any message we receive immediately available. And because we use our smart phones to stay connected with the rest of the world, we check them often. This *immediacy* makes mobile marketing an extraordinary option for last-minute or time-sensitive calls to action. The mobile nature of the delivery increases the odds that the recipient is already "out and about" and available to act immediately on information. Mobile content simplifies the interaction between company and customer, making it easy for us to interact with the brands we love.

Mobile marketing is *the new* direct marketing. Why? Because our target market can receive and understand our marketing message directly. Nothing gets in the way. Mobile content is more direct because it is cost effective, scalable, targeted, personal, shareable, and portable. Mobile content can also convert traditional marketing efforts into direct-response campaigns. TV or radio commercials can be made interactive and measurable when combined with a mobile call to action. Plus, the time between the marketer sending the message and recipients acting on it is the shortest of any marketing channel ever conceived. And the effectiveness has been proven. In every study and in every bit of research done so far, the results are conclusive: We are seeing dramatic

[48] Smartface Developer Zone. 2010. "Monetizing Mobile Applications." Last modified December 14. http://developer.smartface.biz/monetizing-mobile-applications-n86.html.

[49] Schonfeld, Erick. 2009. "Mobile Advertising Is Shaping Up to Be All Search." TechCrunch, October 6. http://techcrunch.com/2009/10/06/mobile-advertising-is-shaping-up-to-be-all-search/.

[50] Loyalty360. 2010. "Chip-Enabled Mobile Marketing." Accessed 2/5/11. http://www.loyalty360.org/white_papers/chip-enabled_mobile_marketing/.

[51] Gartner. 2010. "Gartner Highlights Key Predictions for IT Organizations and Users in 2010 and Beyond." Accessed 2/5/11. http://www.gartner.com/it/page.jsp?id=1278413.

improvements in the effectiveness of marketing campaigns. Through improved targeting, better offers, and the latest technology, the conversion numbers are proving that mobile *is real*, very real.

And the future? Mobile marketing and advertising is projected to *nearly triple in the next three years.* So, get ready, strap yourself in, and hop on board. The train is leaving. . . .

Mobile is *mainstream,* and it will be at the forefront of everything that happens in the future.

The Third Screen

In his book, *The Third Screen*, best-selling author and digital pioneer Chuck Martin explains how the age of the smartphone is redefining the role of the consumer, clarifying that marketers must do more than send out a mass ad and hope for the best. They must interact on the customers' terms. Martin does a great job of explaining the role of m-commerce (mobile-powered commerce), mobile video, SMS messaging, location-based marketing, advertising and media, and the new laws of inbound marketing. He links the technological developments of m-commerce to the behavioral changes that accompany them, and reveals how key mobile innovators are becoming the mobile platform providers of the future. If you haven't picked up *The Third Screen* yet, I highly recommend it; it's a great read and a nice complement to the information presented in this chapter.

FIGURE 12-1 *The Third Screen,* by Chuck Martin

Additional Benefits of Mobile Content

Mobile marketing can reduce costs for content aggregators, brands, and mobile marketing companies. In addition, the improved targeting effectiveness and data offered by mobile marketing programs can help establish your company as an innovator and technology leader. So what are the other benefits?

- Reduced costs: Mobile marketing reduces distribution costs through lower printing, delivery, and reconciliation costs, achieved through increased operational efficiencies.
- More effective customer targeting: Mobile campaigns can be targeted efficiently to gain new customers, increase customer loyalty, and cross-sell products. More efficient targeting typically leads to improved conversion.
- Improved analytical data: Mobile marketing allows companies to predict and measure responses to a campaign more accurately. Mobile provides superior authentication, so it can be helpful in checking the rapid proliferation of discount offers.
- Consumer engagement: Mobile marketing connects you with prospects in many cutting-edge ways, including mobile direct marketing, location-based mobile triggers, and mobile-enabled digital free-standing inserts (DFSI) coupon portals.

Mobile Content Features Are Just as Compelling

Modern mobile devices have many important features that have never been available in one single unit before:

- Voice channel
- Data channel
- Larger mobile screen (user interface)
- Mobile speaker (for point-of-sale reader communication)
- Mobile camera to capture visual information (e.g., barcode coupons, images, and text)
- Global positioning system (GPS)/location-based service (LBS) capability
- Accelerometer technology, allowing the device to be orientation-aware
- Bluetooth capability, allowing data exchange with other Bluetooth-capable devices (e.g., to push marketing during the channel scan)
- Wi-Fi capability, allowing the device to recognize local area networks (e.g., to push marketing during the channel scan)
- Mobile web capability (e.g., to download coupons, ads, and offers during web-based sessions)
- Mobile app store access, which allows downloading of value-added apps (e.g., to embed marketing inside a mobile application, usually in return for a discounted app)

- Near field communication (NFC) capability that allows the device to exchange data with other NFC-capable devices (e.g., to enable direct communication with a POS device, a smart poster, or a public transportation kiosk)

Who Is Your Mobile Audience?

Although we are all using mobile devices to improve our day-to-day productivity and efficiency, the progressive mobile user can be a bit different than the average user. Younger and more technologically savvy, these consumers are clearly leading the way and helping all of us improve our ability to connect with quality content. And some of these people could be new to your brand experience. So, who *are* these mobile users? What motivates them to take *action*? Some of the points to consider include:

- How many visitors are coming to my site or app from a mobile device?
- What is the mobile device of choice for these users?
- What pages of my site do they most frequently visit?
- Which content resonates the most with them?
- How can a conversion take place in the mobile environment?

What are the hard facts of mobile content? For one, you have limited "real estate" or space for your content. Buttons are also more difficult to click. Attention spans may be even shorter. Zooming in to better view certain site areas will definitely occur. If a user is entering text for a form or something else, much of the screen will be covered by the keyboard. How will you deal with this issue? No matter what mobile content you develop, these important realities need to be considered.

If you are developing an app or a mobile site, these questions and their answers will be important. Again, your analytics program, whether it's Google Analytics, AdMob, Bango, or some other program, can help determine where you place your energies. More to come on that.

A Mobile Content Strategy

Mobile content development takes time and money. It's a commitment and a strategic move. As we know, there are differences in the types of mobile devices on which your content can potentially run and there are differences in those you can potentially reach. So, you want to start with a carefully thought out strategy before all else. Having a solid plan in place with a realistic timeline will serve your company well in the still evolving mobile environment. Be sure to address basic questions, such as:

- Who are you trying to reach?
- How will they access your content?
- How will they use your content?

- Which of their needs does your content address?
- Will this be a free or paid content service?
- Will you create mobile apps for a specific platform?
- What are your competitors doing?
- What value will mobile bring to your customers?
- How will you make your mobile content sticky and engaging?

Performing a Mobile Content Audit

As for all other types of content, you want to see what's already happening out there and where the potential opportunities lie for your mobile future. By simply checking your website's analytics you may find mobile visitors are already accessing your site. In fact, up to 30 percent of existing websites are getting hit by smartphone searches today.

Be sure to check your site on all types of major mobile platforms, including an iPhone, Android, BlackBerry, etc. You can also use some of the current online tools to see how your website would actually appear on any mobile device.

FIGURE 12-2   iPhone

Both Firefox and Safari offer easy ways to change your user agent and see what your site would look like through other browsers. For Firefox, download Chris Pederick's User Agent Switcher (http://chrispederick.com/work/user-agent-switcher/). For Safari, just enable Developer Mode (go to Preferences, Advanced, and check the "Show Developer" box) and select your user agent from the Develop menu. Be sure to shrink your browser window to the size of your mobile device.

How does your site look? Is there too much there? Is it easy to get around? What about navigation—are your site pages easy to get to? Are buttons clickable? Don't be too surprised if your page is not totally optimized for the mobile environment. This is typical.

As with other types of content, you need to consider *your budget*. On the low side, you could simply add a call to action to your print and web advertising that instructs prospects to send you an SMS text message or visit your mobile site. On the high side, you could develop a mobile application or dedicated site. Regardless, the best course of action is probably a stepped, integrated one.

What Should Your Company Be Thinking About with Mobile Content?

Starting with a strong mobile web presence is a good entry into the space. As the cornerstone of any mobile strategy, it is clearly imperative if you want to connect with mobile users. Your prospects and customers will be searching for you. It's important that you are there and that your site looks good, whether it's a simple presence or a full mobile site. And if you are sending SMS text messages, these messages should include a link to a page where mobile users can discover what you're all about.

What might your mobile content look like? There are a few ways to get there:

1. **Mobile version of your existing site.** If you've been on the mobile version of Facebook or Amazon, you know what a mobile site needs to look like. The key here is to offer features that are similar to those on your Internet website, but adapt them to a handheld format. Think simple and intuitive.

2. **Plug-in-based mobile site.** This may be the easiest way to go with your web content. Blogs and websites based on WordPress, Drupal, or similar open-source platforms can use free plug-ins that format sites for mobile audiences. Practically plug and play, you can be up and running and looking good in the mobile environment very quickly with this option.

3. **Mobile landing pages.** Like any other landing page, these single-page web properties can be created quickly to establish your mobile web presence. Whether you are doing an SMS text campaign, a social media blast, or any other type of campaign, a landing page may be your best bet.

4. **Dedicated mobile site.** A popular option, especially with larger companies that have bigger budgets and longer-range plans in place, these are standalone sites that mimic much of the layout and content of your traditional website, but are mobile friendly. They, of course, look similar to your traditional site but are configured in a way that simplifies the navigation and user experience.

But there should be more to mobile content and your overall mobile content strategy than just your website.

A Good Way to Get Started

Sometimes, the best idea is to simply do some quick tests and judge the reaction. A good way of doing this is by putting together a mock-up mobile page that connects with user needs. By looking at your analytics, you'll see the most highly viewed content in the site. It may be your main services page. It may be an e-book offering. Whatever it is, this represents solid insight into how users will interact and engage with potential mobile content. Where are visitors on the site right before they respond to a call to action? This will be your most relevant content. And in the mobile space, it's where you'll want to focus first.

There are elements you want to be sure you don't miss, including an easy-to-find button where users can switch to the desktop version of the site. The mobile version of your website should not have too much information. Just say "no" to clutter or verbose copy. The most relevant content from your desktop website will be front and center. People want to get in and out quickly. Whether they are looking for local movie times, a hotel, or a restaurant; checking the weather; or performing some other task, they want quick results.

Based on what you are seeing, should you make a mobile version of your website? Budget and business strategy play a key role, of course. But my proposition is this: Even if you aren't seeing a business case or the data isn't telling you anything conclusive, you should definitely consider moving forward with some type of mobile presence. It's that important.

Making Your Website Content Mobile Friendly

If you want to get a jump on your competitors in this space, make your website content mobile friendly. So many companies are nowhere near taking this step, so if you can be a first mover, there is a lot of upside. Keep these following things in mind:

1. **Keep your pages short and compact.** Mobile pages and downloadable content take longer to load. Like web visitors, mobile users don't have time to wait. Giving them just the facts—in brief, consumable chunks—is the best idea here.

2. **Make navigation easy.** Typing on a tiny mobile device keypad is challenging. By making improvements through navigation, you'll ensure a mobile-friendly experience. Ensure that users can get to all the important parts of your website.

3. **Create content that's "touch friendly."** With the iPod, iPad and other mobile devices, the touch screen is a key component. Users will be interacting with your content by using their fingers. Content and links need to be prominent: large, clear, and intuitively placed. Making the user interface as app-like as possible is a good practice.

4. **Go easy on the images.** In the mobile environment, images are big and clumsy and, for the most part, not needed. Strip the images from your mobile site, and you'll find a higher conversion factor and improved user experience. Also, eliminate the flash content and check your form fields—ask for only what is absolutely necessary, perhaps just name and e-mail address.

For those companies that sell thousands of products or have a wide range of important content pages, it's important to drive mobile traffic back to your fully featured website, because that's where all the details and highly specific content will stay. Use your mobile site to whet people's appetites, and then when they get to the desktop version of your site, you can fully deliver the goods.

Other Options:XML and RSS Mobile Websites

Do you have a blog or a news website that is mostly text based? If so, one of the quickest ways to create a mobile version of your website is to use the RSS, ATOM, or XML feeds that might already be in place. Feeds for each page can be ported directly to pages on a mobile subdomain or subdirectory. Give it a shot.

Writing Content for Mobile

We all know that the space we have on our mobile devices is tiny. It's one of the drawbacks of mobile text communication, but it's a reality of the medium. If your traditional site comes up in a mobile search, there is no way people can read it. If it shows up at all, it will be microscopic. So, how do we write for that tiny screen? How do we change the way we say things in order for people to understand what we are saying? With brevity and concise language. Give just the facts, only the facts, and that's it. Use headings, bulleted lists, and commands instead of complete sentences—when writing your mobile content, this is the only way to go.

Mobile means "mini"—it's a miniaturized version of the extended sentence or thought. So, what are the rules of the mobile content writing game?

- The most important information goes at the top of the screen.
- Break up copy into small sections.
- Keep sentences brief.
- Use short words (fewer syllables).
- Don't force users to scroll too much.

Focus on these elements, and you'll get your point across perfectly on a mobile device.

Mobile Represents a Universe of Content Possibilities

One of the great things about mobile is the ability to reach your target market in so many different ways. It's not just about making your site mobile friendly. Utilizing text, voice- and e-mail, video, and more, you have a new opportunity to connect in compelling, practically *revolutionary* ways through the mobile channel. Incorporating mobile into your online marketing program has big potential impact. Your choices are many.

Short Message Service (SMS) Content

Using SMS, you can send short, text-based messages to your audience, which can include links to your website, social media profile, and more. Whether prospects text you back, or even call you, SMS content has proven very effective for companies everywhere.

Multimedia Message Service (MMS) Content

MMS is similar to SMS technology, but can also send content, including images, video, and audio files such as ringtones. If you want to be a forward thinking mobile marketer, lead with this type of content.

Voice

This is one element of a mobile strategy that many companies forget about. I think one of the keys of mobile marketing, along with all web content strategies, is to never forget the power of weaving in traditional tactics, like phone and print. Mobile phones have click-to-call functionality that enables audiences to reach you directly, or to click to request a call from your team.

Applications

Downloaded an app to your iPhone, iPad, or Android lately? Chances are good that you have—probably a few. As one of the hottest trends of the past few years, apps represent a huge opportunity for companies everywhere, and it's not just for B2C. Some marketers have directly integrated campaigns into their audiences' phones by designing and offering a branded mobile app. I'll show you how you can take advantage of this trend.

FIGURE 12-3   iPhone Apps

Location-Based (Proximity) Mobile Marketing

There is lots of new activity in the location-based (proximity) mobile marketing area. With Foursquare, Gowalla, Facebook Places, and other services leading the way, we are the forefront of something very exciting here. Smartphones, which have GPS capability, enable others to know our physical location, if we allow them that access. Progressive companies with retail locations now have the chance to deliver ads to mobile users when they are near their stores, capitalizing on impulse buys and leveraging the power of social gathering, especially in densely populated urban locations.

Content

Let's not forget about the power of branding. Whether you're Starbucks, Jamba Juice, J.Crew, or any other powerful brand, you want to leverage your already powerful connection into the mobile space. This could include e-books, white papers, ringtones, images, videos, and more, all branded and all available in a mobile format.

E-Mail Content

Although it may seem like a no-brainer, e-mail absolutely needs to be considered in the larger mobile environment. As the most popular activity in the mobile space (sometimes taking more time than even the calls we make) e-mail is clearly a *mobile channel*. How can your company maximize and leverage your position with mobile e-mail content?

Mobile Integrates with Everything Else

Whatever your perceptions may be of the mobile space, it's important to start thinking of it in a holistic, comprehensive way. Mobile content, and the marketing that goes along with it, does not succeed in a vacuum. It works best when integrated with other channels and tactics to form a cross-platform strategy.

Mobile applications, websites, SMS promotions, apps—everything you do with mobile—should somehow tie into social media and your other marketing efforts. These are logical connections and are indicative of successful content marketing as a whole.

How are the mobile market leaders doing it? They are integrating mobile apps with television, targeting mobile ads with specific social media campaigns, using barcode calls to action in traditional advertising, and more. They are testing, refining, and most important *connecting* with the market, some of whom may never have been exposed to the brand before.

Mobile content should be promoted on your website, your blog, your YouTube channel—everywhere you have a presence. As you will see, mobile content is the bond that connects all other media. Why? For all the reasons we've covered already, but the clear winner bears repeating: **Our mobile devices are always with us.** Our mobile devices are very personal; they're true extensions and expressions of ourselves. Our phones are with us during the day, at night, and sometimes even while we sleep. Good or bad, they have a permanent place in our lives and are ready for action during all stages of the buying process and at all times of the day.

So, when it comes to your total content marketing strategy, there are important factors that need to be considered in the mobile realm. What goals do you want to achieve with your mobile content? How will you achieve those goals and minimize potential negative impact?

Mobile Applications

So, your site is mobile friendly. You have put together a mobile strategy. Developing an "app" seems pretty interesting. One thing that cannot be denied is that apps are hot—super hot. But what is an app?

An app, short for an "application," is a software program that runs on a smartphone or tablet. Apps allow companies to engage their prospects and customers at any time and from any place; they offer a location-specific, targeted approach that satisfies an immediate need for information and provides total integration with social media and feedback tools.

B2C apps are a given. This is where app development started and has already proven very successful. But B2B apps aren't far behind. There are lots of exciting developments in the B2B mobile app space. Plus, you can have apps for all your audiences: for clients and prospects, certainly, but you can also have separate apps for employees, sales teams, vendors, and more.

Games remain the most popular type of application, but mobile shopping, social networking, utilities, and productivity tool apps continue to grow. Chris Foresman, of Ars Technica, in an article on mobile applications, says that "Predictions for 2013 are 21.6 billion apps sold for a total of $29.5 billion revenue."[52] That's a seriously large market, especially when it didn't exist five years ago.

What's going on in the B2B app space? A consulting business might use an app to allow clients to access the firm's e-books and consultant directory; a recruiting firm can build apps to more easily present candidates to clients and solicit resumes. There are all types of things you could do to reach your target market with a mobile app.

Mobile Applications for B2B

Mobile applications in the B2B space need to engage prospects and help solve customer problems. People use mobile applications much differently than they use websites.

[52] Foresman, Chris. 2010 "Apple Responsible for 99.4% of Mobile App Sales in 2009," Ars Technica, http://arstechnica.com/apple/news/2010/01/apple-responsible-for-994-of-mobile-app-sales-in-2009 .ars.

They are looking for action, movement, results, and, as we've seen with the explosion of mobile games, entertainment. In the mobile B2B space, applications serve to provide quick information or solve problems that your traditional website cannot.

Mobile Advertising Content

Whether users are surfing the mobile web, are using mobile applications, or are playing mobile games, ads are a natural part of the experience. Of course, you have choices with your ad content: You can drive people to your website, to a mobile-specific landing page, or to a download page. A click by a prospect might also place a call through their phone.

As with traditional ad banners, mobile banners are graphics placed on a web page. A conversion occurs when a visitor clicks through to a linked offer. Mobile site owners agree to show the advertisement on their sites in return for payment from the mobile ad network. Mobile display ads can also be included in games and downloadable mobile applications for additional targeted exposure.

If you are developing banner content, it is important to focus the graphic on *your call to action*. Mobile advertising is still new enough that many viewers could be easily confused by seeing a brand message from a company when they are on a different brand's website, so clarity is key to generating a good click-through rate (CTR).

There are important elements to creating effective mobile advertising content. Your mobile advertisement content can entice people to click through to visit your mobile website and download your mobile application or sign up for your alerts. The creative content can be text or display advertising, video, or animation.

As with all things mobile, you have a limited amount of space in which to convey your marketing message. Because your ad is displayed on a very small screen, leave out complex graphics. If you are writing copy for a text-only ad, use common SMS and web abbreviations, otherwise know as "txt spk," to convey your message. This form of shorthand includes words such as "DK" for "don't know," "Gr8" for "great," and "<3" for "love," and will help you get across more in less space.

QR Codes

QR codes (quick response codes) are being used in mobile advertising campaigns all over the world, especially in Asia. Their use in the U.S. market is just picking up now, and will continue to expand in the next couple of years. What are they exactly? QR codes are small square dot matrices, sometimes called 2D bar codes, which can be placed on billboards, packaging, print media, or even on computer screens. Users with QR-enabled phones can capture the bar code by taking a picture of it with their phone's camera. The QR code can open up a whole new world of promotional opportunity: It can load a web page, display a branded message, or add a contact to your address book.

iPhones don't currently come with a QR code reader, but the next-generation iPhone more than likely will. One way around this, however, is by using a QR code app. The best one is QR Reader for the iPhone. It has a large range of usability and sharing options, it looks good, and it's easy to use. For Android, download the Barcode Scanner app for QR Code functionality—it's been rated highly by users.

FIGURE 12-4   QR Code

SMS Text Message Content

Text messaging as we know it, or SMS (for short message service), is one of the best methods of mobile advertising in practice today. With billions of text messages sent and received every day and over 90 percent of them opened, it is the "certified mail" of digital communications. Chalk it up to the magic of mobile, but SMS messages are very effective.

In both B2B and B2C, text messages hold a special opportunity because so many companies have yet to use this marketing medium. And here is the other thing: Including a text offer in an ad is becoming as important as including a phone number and website URL.

But how do you get started? The "bargain basement" approach is offered by companies like MobiQponsis, which automatically sends people text coupons when they are shopping in the vicinity of participating businesses. This method is popular with small retailers, restaurants, and other local businesses, but it does not allow you to capture recipients' cell numbers, which is one of the most important features of successful text-message marketing campaigns.

The next step up is a method used by service providers like Distributive Networks, which ran the Obama text messaging campaign in 2008. The main component of this mobile advertising program is registering for your own proprietary "short code," which is a five- or six-digit phone number that dialers use to access a text marketing campaign. It's great for branding because you can select a vanity short code like APPLE (27753), and you can collect information such as zip codes and birthdates from callers. But these types of campaigns are expensive, and the budget can easily run into the thousands for licensing, activation, and hosting fees.

There is a more popular way: Sharing a short code. Many small businesses use firms like Mobile Commons or HipCricket to advertise their SMS messages in this manner. Going this route can cost as little as a thousand dollars per month.

One of the keys is how you let people know about your texting campaign. That's where your website, social media profiles, blog, and all your off-line advertising vehicles come in. Everywhere you have access to your market is a place to let people know about your texting campaign.

But what types of content resonate in a mobile SMS campaign? How can you get people to take notice and actually want to text you? Here are the most popular ways:

- **Providing exclusive access**—This approach promotes the fact that those who text in will get something that no one else will. Those who participate will be "part of the club" that most people will be left out of.
- **Giving a free item**—This is a classic promotion that advertises "the first 100 people to text in get a free item valued at X."
- **The ask campaign**—Make a straightforward request, for example: "Join Our Text Club. Text ABC to 95780." Advertise it on your website, in print ads, direct mail, and on TV or radio.
- **The incentive**—Whether it's a discount or an upsell, an incentive can work really well. Popular discounts are a percentage off today's purchase. An upgrade would be "buy such and such and we'll give you something free."
- **Holding a contest**—This is a great way to engage customers and to get them thinking about your product: "Win $50 Gift Card. Text ABC to 24570."
- **Showing you value their opinion**—Ask for their vote or provide a survey. If you're running a restaurant, ask customers, "What should our special be?" and tell them to "Text ABC to 24570."

The bottom line? You want to gain trust by offering something of value and then work toward building a relationship. When people are given something valuable—an exclusive VIP pass or privileged information—they respond. And your company wins.

Then you take it one step farther to secure long-term loyalty—you provide a sale, discount, or other promotion **only to your text-message customers**. And because you have access to your customers' mobile phones, a device that is with them all the time and that they respond to more readily than anything else, you have an incredibly strong bond with them. Plus, you can send

FIGURE 12-5 SMS Texts Are Powerful

them customized offers based on their preferences. Don't forget to cross-promote with your website, social media, and all of your off-line and print advertising.

Location-Based Mobile Marketing Content

Stores, restaurants, clubs, and other businesses that rely on local visitors can now leverage mobile marketing because of their ability to target local foot traffic. They can set up location-based Bluetooth broadcasts that send marketing messages directly to consumers when they are in the area. These companies can also develop strategies that incorporate outdoor advertising, to allow users to text in for specials, menus, show times, directions, or other information.

What works? Making your mobile content messaging as specific and actionable as possible. If you are a retailer, provide a cool deal that expires in just a few hours. If you are a restaurant, send out information on your lunch specials. There are lots of things you can do in this channel.

Location-based mobile content is great for real-time events, like baseball games, concerts, and also conferences that are scheduled in the area on the day the message goes out. The best mobile marketers can reach the right consumers when they are in the area and, hopefully, when they want the message. Foursquare is leading the way with location based mobile marketing.

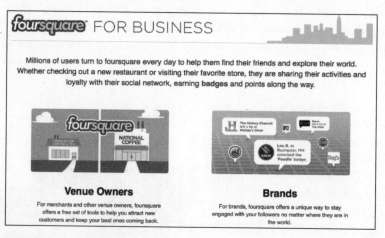

FIGURE 12-6   Foursquare

Key Considerations for Location-Based Mobile Marketing Content

If you want to capitalize on the power of location based mobile marketing, there are some important things to keep in mind when you put together a campaign. Here are the important considerations:

- **A captured target.** Your prospect or customer is already in or near your place of business. This is the true power of the medium.
- **Increased impulse buying.** Real-time delivery of advertising can get people to take action now—for example a message that reads, "Come in within the next 15 minutes and receive 30% off your dinner."
- **Relationship and historical marketing.** You can review past purchasing history to tailor and fine-tune future marketing messages.
- **Psychological nurturing.** Consumers feel like they are part of something that's happening now, that they're wanted for something popular, which inspires brand recognition and loyalty.
- **Increased return on investment (ROI).** Repeat or additional consumer purchases during a visit. Time-based incentives or promotions can be sent to increase the total value of the sale.

How users discover Specials within foursquare

To help our users find Specials, we show them Specials nearby to where they are. For instance, if a user is in your venue, they'll see your Special presented within their foursquare app on their phones. But they don't have to be visiting your place; if that user is nearby, they'll also see your Special, and they 'll know that they can stop by to redeem it.

There are three ways that users can discover your Special within foursquare:

When users are looking at the nearby "Places" tab on their phone, venues that have active Specials are highlighted.

If a user checks in close to your business, they'll see that there is a "Special Nearby." By clicking through, users can get more detail on your Special.

When a user checks in to your business, they'll see that you are offering a Special.

FIGURE 12-7 Example of Location-Based Mobile Ad

Mobile SEO

How do mobile search engines work? Traditional search engines and mobile search engines have many of the same qualities. As with Google's normal search engine functionality, its mobile "spiders" are doing the same thing: reading and categorizing the information available on the web.

Currently, the biggest difference between Google's traditional search engine bots and its mobile search engine bots is that the *mobile bots evaluate your site as if it was being displayed on a mobile device.* If the bots determine that your site will perform well on mobile devices, it will be ranked high in mobile search results. Developing your site or app for specific devices like the iPhone or Android? Mobile search engines can also detect what type of mobile device you are searching from and, in some cases, rank sites according to how well those sites will perform on that specific device.

A critical point to know is that mobile search engines frequently pull their results from *both the traditional and the mobile search engine indexes.* The mobile search engines provide mobile results whenever they can, but mobile pages must still compete against their traditional counterparts to rank well in most mobile searches. Most people assume that when they are searching from a mobile search engine, they will be given only mobile results, but that is not the case. If you want to get "mobile only" search results, you need to click on the mobile link from the search page.

In large part, mobile SEO is very similar to traditional SEO. If you need a refresher, be sure to see Chapter 4. However, to achieve high mobile rankings, it is important to **use conventional mobile designations in your file structure**. If the mobile aspect of your website is on a mobile subdomain, it should be called m. or mobile. If the mobile aspect of your website is on a subdirectory, it should be called /m or /mobile. These are the most common designations, and the search engines understand them as mobile designations.

Mobile Keyword Research

There are differences in keyword strategy for the mobile environment. Whether mobile searchers are running to the grocery store, going out for a night on the town, or traveling to the mountains on vacation, they use keywords that are more action oriented and they are more likely to include verbs, for example "find post office" or "download ringtone." And because they are typically trying to find a specific store, location, or other geographic destination, they also are location specific in their searching behavior, using city names, neighborhoods, or zip codes. So be sure to use these keywords near your other major keywords to improve your visibility in mobile search engines.

Sometimes, branded searches are more common with mobile devices, such as "find Jamba Juice Seattle" or "locate 24 Hour Fitness Las Vegas." Very few people use mobile to research or investigate a product or service. They want to fulfill an immediate request or action.

Integrating Mobile with Your Total Content Marketing Program

The key activity that separates average marketers from the ones who are setting the pace is campaign *integration.* Remember the idea of *leverage* and *sharing* within the content marketing activity? You can get a lot more out of your mobile content when you leverage it against everything else you are doing with your site, blog, and other content channels.

The great thing is that integrating a mobile marketing campaign with an online marketing campaign is actually very easy. In most cases, it simply means promoting your mobile content on your traditional site, your social media profiles, your e-mails, and your blog. It's first about creating awareness that you do, in fact, have a mobile presence. Second, it's a way to incentivize user behavior, especially with location-based mobile marketing. If you want to get more of these types of users, you simply direct them to your mobile site and offer them some great deals through that channel.

Also, those who visit your traditional website are a targeted group. Because they showed interest in your products or services by going to your site in the first place, chances are they will be drawn to your mobile content as well, especially if they are frequent visitors or are a part of your customer loyalty club. And, of course, some people will go to the web to find out more about your mobile offerings.

If you have both a mobile and a traditional website, it is important to let viewers move between the two sites easily. Put a button or link at the top of all your website pages and allow viewers to specify the type of device they are using to view the website.

Next Steps

Mobile content is super hot. The biggest and most well-known brands around the world are embracing it in large numbers. The proliferation of mobile phones, especially smartphones, is driving the evolution of an exciting new capability that benefits everyone: the ability, in real-time, to market specifically to a consumer's preferences and location. Research everywhere is showing dramatic improvements in the effectiveness of offer redemption rates and overall conversion. As a result, mobile marketing and advertising is projected to nearly triple in the next three years.

Mobile is here, it is now, and it is going to be a great ride for any company that embraces its potential content marketing opportunity.

CHAPTER 13

Putting It All Together: Unleashing Your Content Marketing Machine

You made it! Nice work. By getting to this point in the book, you have concluded your first comprehensive lesson in web and mobile content development and content marketing. Content case studies, content best practices, specific how-tos, things to avoid, recommended service vendors, and more—we've covered a lot in the past twelve chapters. You've gotten a taste of all the types of online and mobile content you can develop and the benefits of each. And you've been invited to put all the information through the lens of your own experience, so you can determine how you will use the information in this book, based on the type of business you have, your location, and your available resources.

Some of you may have benefited from every chapter in the book. Perhaps you are new to this stuff. That's great; as I mentioned in the book's introduction, you represent the majority of readers. Others of you may have enjoyed most the information from one or two chapters. Perhaps it was the video and mobile content chapters—those two were very popular with some of my manuscript readers! Whatever you happened to pick up, I'm happy to have been a part of the education. I don't know about you, but I learn new things every day from people everywhere. Learning is an important part of my life; I hope that's true for you, too. We can never learn too much. And to that, let's make a "content toast" right now.

As you've seen through this educational experience, *content* is absolutely red hot. There's no denying that. And it's a big part of what's happening in the web and mobile world. Whether you are a restaurant owner in Denver, a software entrepreneur in Austin, the CMO of a Fortune 100 company in New York, or any other forward-thinking marketer, it is my hope that you have benefited from this education. But here's the thing . . . we aren't quite done yet!

Let's take the next few pages to review the important points we discussed, bring it all together, and put you on a path for *total content marketing success*.

The Content Life Cycle

Earlier in the book, I talked about the *ecosystem* of online and mobile content, or what I called the content "life cycle." I mentioned that online content is a living, breathing thing. It's truly *evergreen* and, in many cases, stays online *forever.* I indicated that your content carries your reputation and your brand with it, in perpetuity.

As you recall, the content life cycle includes:

- Content planning and strategy
- Content creation
- Content marketing/distribution
- Content management/curation

Armed with your newfound knowledge, you can now determine how you will put the content life cycle to use in your organization. But before we go there, let's consider where your company stands with all of this "content stuff."

One thing that troubles me about the current books available on content marketing or content strategy is that most are talking way above most people's heads; the concepts and ideas are presented with too much complexity. After all, thousands of you out there are just seeing the ideas of content marketing for the first time. I know, because I see it when I'm out and about, speaking at business meetings. And I'm not talking about the high-profile industry events, I'm talking about the local business meetings on Main Street, USA—Bob's Hardware, that maybe wants to compete more effectively against the local Home Depot. I'm also talking about all the family-owned and multigenerational companies I've interfaced with, where managers are so busy running their companies that they've missed the content marketing "train." And I'm also referring to companies that are newer, and are staffed with sharp, gifted entrepreneurs who simply have an expertise in another area—engineering, IT, maybe a creative discipline. The fact of the matter is that there are many companies out there that want to understand content marketing, but need to be taught in a way they can grasp easily and then move forward with, without having to spend six months or more getting up to speed. These are the companies that need the education the most. And, as I stated in the beginning, this was one of my objectives with the book—to make it manageable for *all.*

So, with that in mind, let's discuss your ability and readiness to implement the lessons in the book.

Your Stage with the Content Curriculum

Every company is at a different place when it comes to content marketing. A few companies out there are total pros. Some have been at it a long time, but need some brushing up. Others are totally new to it and can't wait to get started. Wherever you are in the process, there are things you need to be doing right now to ensure success.

- **Novice.** At this level, you undoubtedly feel overwhelmed by online marketing and all the content topics we covered, but your commitment to making changes and starting a content marketing program are strong. It may take a couple reads of the book for you to understand and internalize the information; that's to be expected. I recommend you use this book as a handy reference manual and simply pull it out when you need it. For example, when you start blogging for the first time, reread Chapter 8 carefully and take the process step by step. If you are just getting your feet wet with setting up your Facebook page, read Chapter 7 again, and also refer to the blogging chapter. Then, don't forget to check out your competitors to see what they are doing. The rest of the information in this final chapter is very important for you, because careful execution will ensure you start off right.

- **Intermediate.** This stage is where most companies fall. You have a website, perhaps a blog, and maybe a few social media profiles, but you aren't doing much with any of them. You were too busy, didn't see the potential, or have never been inspired to do more with your content. After reading this book, I hope you see that you no longer have an option—you must embrace web and mobile content if you want to succeed against your competitors. It's that simple. And you will! You have all the tools you need now to plan and execute. My advice to you is twofold: Talk to your existing customers and really seek to understand their needs. What are they asking for? Next, carefully study your competitors to see what they have done with content. Once you have accomplished these two tasks, you can prioritize what you need to do to compete more effectively and find opportunities that they may have missed. The reason for these two tasks? *It cuts down your time for development and implementation.* And I realize that *time* may be your most precious resource. The rest of the information in this final chapter is, most certainly, for you as well.

- **Advanced.** Then there are the companies that are out there, developing content and doing it pretty well, but that need to improve some element of their total program. Perhaps you are looking for the latest content strategies used by the most forward-thinking companies, Hopefully, you've learned this from the case studies and research I shared in this book. For the advanced learners, perhaps the ideas and techniques about content leverage and automation proved to be the most valuable for you. I encourage you advanced content marketers to go to my blog, become a subscriber, and continue your education. I handle many of the more advanced and cutting-edge content marketing ideas there. There are many other fantastic blogs and industry news sources that I recommend you check out on a regular basis; two of which are the SEOmoz blog and ClickZ.

Both are absolutely fantastic for any content marketer who is truly committed to the discipline.

With your current level in mind, let's bring back three of the key concepts I discussed in the first chapter: the content marketing machine, the seven-prong content approach, and the eight steps to content success. Now that you have learned all the various content types and have seen how they are being used by other companies, it's time to determine how you will apply these concepts to your current and ongoing marketing program.

The Content Marketing Machine

As you'll recall, the three pillars of web content success are content, design, and usability. Essentially, these are what your content says, how it looks, and its ease of use. All three are important and all three need to be carried out effectively. Taken together, considered thoughtfully, and done right, these three pillars will turn your company into a content marketing machine. And that's what we want. We need to develop a perpetual, totally leveraged, fully automated content connection, lead-generation, and business-growth machine for your company. The rest of the information in this final chapter will give you what you need to make it a reality.

Using the three pillars as the foundation for every piece of content you develop, you'll recall that you need to consider four things:

- Planning the content that you need (strategy)
- What types of content you produce (development)
- Ensuring your prospects and customers see it (marketing)
- Supporting it (management)

As you see, you are now standing face to face with the content life cycle. It's time to make some decisions. But each one you make will be informed by the needs of your customers and prospects and by your commitment to the process.

We learned earlier from the Junta 42/Marketing Profs Study that the top content challenges companies face are producing the *kind* of content that engages prospects and customers, producing *enough* content, and having the *budget* to produce content. For the first two, you should now have a clear picture of how to proceed. By reading this book, absorbing the concepts, and understanding the best practices, you are armed and ready to tackle these obstacles and truly make them *opportunities*. The last one—budget—will hopefully be addressed by all the new prospects you'll attract with your content and who will eventually become your customers. The new income you produce from these paying customers can support your content marketing program ands help grow your company.

Another thing that bears repeating at this point are the *content practices of the best in class companies*. The reason these companies are successful is that they are careful to consider the "stage in the buying cycle" when developing content, they allocate more budget to content marketing than others, and they get lots of support from the owners or upper management of the company. If this sounds like your company, great! Along with your commitment to content development and content marketing, you have much of what you need to be very successful.

For those companies that may not have *budget and company support*, you can easily get these by developing great content that connects with your target audience. Trust me: If you do content marketing right, you **will** impact the bottom line. And if what you are able to do brings in more income for the company, you'll have pretty good evidence when you suggest content marketing expansion.

Let's get back to the content life cycle: **content planning and strategy**, **content creation**, **content marketing/distribution**, and **content management/curation**. It's time to put it to work for your company.

Content Planning and Strategy

As you recall, content strategy is the practice of planning the **development**, **delivery**, and **management** of your web and mobile content. It's a process-driven activity, one that is made up of laying out, masterminding, and scheduling all the content that will be published. It includes strategizing for all the content types we discussed in the book: website copy, e-books, social media content, web videos, blog posts, and all the rest.

Your tactical activities, of course, make up the strategy. If you're like many companies, you'll start with your main website, a blog, your social media profiles, and maybe a digital newsletter. Perhaps you'll have much more than this, but if you have these basic building blocks or cornerstone types of content, you can start building a unified and directed *content strategy* around them. And to ensure they are working, you'll tie certain goals and results to these content tactics and measure them.

Content strategy is all about setting up a *road map* for the creation, delivery, and governance of content that your website users and social network will find valuable. You want to create content strategies that are in line with your business objectives and user goals. You also need to take into consideration your current content assets and your available resources to assemble a content plan that fits them. In addition, you'll plan to make all content for your company:

- Relevant—your content needs to be managed throughout its entire life cycle
- Optimized and sharable—the search engines and social networks are a key channel for your content
- Leverageable—the content needs to serve multiple roles and be used to inform other pieces of the content universe

- Profitable—the success of the content should be partially measured by its impact on your organization's bottom line

Here are the key stages of your content strategy and planning work:

1. **Audit and assessment.** Take a look at everything you have—your site, your blog, old company brochures, everything. Is your current content not in line with user needs or out-of-date? Most companies could make this claim; it's just a fact of business life with today's busy schedules. And you know what? Content marketing is a lot like our personal relationships: We can always do better and improve. With this step, you'll want to review your current content assets and total ecosystem, including:

- Existing content performance (web, social media, SEO, print, etc.)—Where are the areas of opportunity?
- Internal roles and processes—Who is in charge and how does content get produced and distributed?
- Content strategy readiness—Do you have a compelling value proposition and products and services that people want?
- User expectations—What do your prospects and customers want to see from you? What types of content resonate?
- Competitors and influencers—How does the external environment look, with regard to content that others are developing?
- Content supply chain—Where will all the content come from and how will it get to those who can benefit from it?

When your audit is completed, you'll have a new window into the quality of the content you have (or don't have) and into the environmental or organizational impact on its creation, delivery, and governance.

2. **Strategy and integration.** All content needs to serve a purpose. All content should be proactive. Most of all, you need content that supports business objectives and meets your user goals. A quality content strategy exercise will perform this role. In this stage, you need to set up and design content solutions that are specific and measurable. Your content strategy will include detailed recommendations for:

- Messaging—What will the content say and how will it communicate your brand?
- Structure—How will the content be set up? What will it look like?
- Work flow—How will the content get produced and distributed?
- Governance—How will the content be managed on an ongoing basis?

If you're engaged with multiple, ongoing content initiatives, you need to ensure that these are well integrated into your content requirements, schedules, and desired outcomes.

Content Creation

Next is the content development piece, the part that many companies find the most challenging. But you can rest a bit easier: All of the chapters in this book now serve as your guides for the content creation process. Of course, developing something from nothing can be stressful. If you're like 70 percent of the companies out there, you have at least some content already developed. And this existing content will serve as a nice springboard for the rest of your content creation activities.

So, what exactly will your new content be? What will it look like? And who in your organization will put it together? How will they develop it? These are the important questions at this stage of the content life cycle. You'll be considering all of the following types of content (I've put in boldface the ones that are most critical to your success):

- **Website content**
  - Website pages
  - Landing pages
- **Lead-generation content**
  - E-books
  - Articles
  - White papers
  - Case studies
  - Digital magazines
- Press releases/media room content
- Online ad content
- Social media content
- **Blog content**
- **Relationship building content**
  - E-newsletter
  - Autoresponders
  - Other e-mails
- Video content
- Audio content
  - Podcasts
  - Webinars
- **Mobile content**

This extensive list looks daunting, I know. The best course of action, in order to attack it head on, is to determine *which areas you can focus on first*. These are the ones that offer the most potential to connect you with your target market, as determined by your content strategy exercise. Again, every company is unique and every industry is different. Your prospects and customers can be very different from those of even your closest competitors. So, there is no clear-cut way to say which five content types, for example, are the best ones for your company. You will naturally find out as you get involved with the process.

One thing I will recommend is this: Ensure that your website comes first, followed closely by your lead-generation content and relationship-building content. Next is your blogging. These are your primary content types and the ones that everything else can feed.

Your social media content can be populated by your blog posts, at a bare minimum, so even if you just set your profiles up (which doesn't take long) and only occasionally publish to them in the first few months, you'll be all right. Having said that, your social media content is very important, so it is next in line.

After you've got a solid plan to develop these areas of content, I would recommend developing your press releases and video content. These are "extra" types of content that can support your mission, get the word out, and help bring more prospects into your tent. And they can also feed your blog, newsletter, and social media content. Next comes your online ad content and audio content. Like exhibiting at trade shows, these are definitely *not required* to be effective in the content marketing arena, but can help support the overall cause. Last is your mobile content. But let me clarify this point: *Making sure your site is mobile friendly is definitely a top-tier priority.* But all the other mobile content activities—mobile apps, mobile advertising, and the rest—can wait if you lack the budget, people, or time. Mobile is extremely important and, without a doubt, a big part of the future picture of content marketing, but it needs to be done right the first time and it needs to be carefully monitored.

After you've decided which content arenas to develop, you need to put together an editorial and publishing schedule. How do you "calendarize" the content production in order to make sure you allocate the right time and produce it in the correct intervals? Keep reading.

Develop a Content Publishing Schedule

Frequency and recency are two important elements of advertising. They are also important tools in your content marketing aresenal. Increasing how often people see your content and sticking to a publishing schedule will help your efforts considerably.

- **Every day**
  Content activities:
  - Post Twitter updates
  - Post industry news items to Facebook/Twitter/LinkedIn pages
  - Read top twenty-five blogs in your industry and comment
  - Add a chapter or section for one large content project: white paper, e-book, slide presentation, or newsletter

Content support activities

- Check your site and blog analytics, make adjustments
- Check your keyword research
- Refer to your content strategy/plan, if needed
- Start thinking about next month's press release

- **Every week**

  Content activities

  - Record your weekly update video and/or podcast
  - Complete three to four new blog posts (write them all at once and stagger publishing them or write one every other day)
  - Write one guest blog post on a large, complementary blog
  - If you have time, write one article that you can distribute (such as a how-to article or a product/service review)
  - Add a new web page or section to your site
  - Focus on optimizing an existing page that needs help
  - Participate in LinkedIn discussion group comments
  - Add two to three status updates on Facebook (spread throughout the week)

  Content support activities

  - Check your site and blog analytics, make adjustments
  - Check your keyword research
  - Refer to your content strategy/plan, if needed
  - Check on the competition

- **Every month**

  Content activities

  - Publish monthly newsletter
  - Shoot and produce three videos—one from an event, one of an executive providing an industry opinion, and one interviewing someone important in the industry or a customer about their success (do them all in a week or space them out over the month)
  - Upload your latest PowerPoint presentations to SlideShare
  - Request and assemble client testimonials or customer product reviews for the month (*every* client or customer)
  - Write one to two customer case studies
  - Produce a webinar

  Content support activities

  - Check your site and blog analytics, make adjustments
  - Check your keyword research
  - Refer to your content strategy/plan, if needed
  - Check on the competition

- **Every quarter**
  Content activities
  - Write an e-book or white paper (at least ten pages of research-based, quality content)
  - Hold a Facebook or Twitter contest and give away something of value
  - Work on a joint content project with someone of importance in your industry (partnerships)
  - Produce a quarterly update of your industry
  - Consider doing a live video from your office and promote it as such (make the topic compelling)
  - Work on something big and important like a mobile app, microsite, Facebook app, widget or . . . a book (yes, that's right, a book is the ultimate in content development!)

  Content support activities
  - Check your site and blog analytics, make adjustments
  - Check your keyword research
  - Refer to your content strategy/plan, if needed
  - Check on the competition

Need Content Ideas?

Stuck for content topics or tactics you can implement? Need some ideas for the content creation step? Hopefully, you've gathered enough content-starters from the chapters of this book, but I thought it would be a good idea to add just a few more, for good measure. After all, you can never have *too many* good ideas in the fine art of content marketing.

Whether you are a rookie and need some inspiration or have "done it all" with content and are seeking some fresh ideas or consider yourself a great content developer but not the best brainstormer, I understand. We all need some help in this area once in a while. Here you go:

1. Take your most popular e-book or your best blog posts, add a few images, put it into PowerPoint, and then record it with Camtasia for a YouTube video.
2. Use a blog post to discuss a challenge that your company faced and how you overcame it. People love true stories.
3. Take a webinar or series of podcasts, get them transcribed, and offer it as an e-book or white paper.
4. Comment on other blogs from your industry. Be original and interesting (think one or two solid paragraphs, not just a line or two). And then keep a copy of all of them so you can compile and repackage them as an e-book.

5. Develop some content that showcases the genius of industry figures you respect and admire. And then use it as a springboard to partner with them.
6. Develop a buyer's guide for your products and services based on the feedback you get from your customers.
7. Write an industry report on a hot topic that is backed up by solid research from respected industry associations. Post it on your blog and your social media profiles and put it in your newsletter.
8. Do you have some strong opinions and something interesting to say? Feel like things need to change in your industry? Write a twenty-page manifesto that reflects your best rants.
9. Review topics and items relevant to your industry, and make your reviews thoughtful, fair, and informative. Surprise people by using three to four long paragraphs to review every facet of the subject of your review: a product or service, a book, a webinar, a podcast, a video, an event you attended.
10. Use your video camera to record something that reflects your best self and then apply that to your products and services, a business issue, or a customer request. If you're funny, use your humor. If you're the serious type, make your presentation authoritative. If you're a "ham," then do something totally different or a little bit crazy (within reason). Then put the video up on your YouTube channel.
11. Turn your digital newsletter into a paper version and send it out through regular mail.
12. Write a white paper that attempts to tackle the most controversial or challenging issue in your industry.
13. Create a free "course" delivered by e-mail autoresponder.
14. Offer a free teleclass to build interest in your business (record it so you will have another type of content to offer).
15. Compile your top thirty blog posts into an e-book.

Start with One Big Idea, Then Develop It in Chunks

If you want to come up with more than *a hundred* solid content topics in short order, do this: As a leading authority in your industry, behave as if you are going to *write a book*. Whether it's the industry "bible," a how-to book, a review of the best service providers, a collection of opinions from other industry leaders, or something else, this book would be a definitive guide for prospects, customers, and partners.

How do you do it? Simply sit down with a piece of paper and brainstorm all the chapters and subchapters that would make up the book. If you need help with this step, start at the very top with the title. Then break it down to the three most important sections of the book, followed by the twelve chapters that will make up the book, followed by the ten headings that make up each chapter. Add all this together, and you will have *120 new content ideas* for blog posts, videos, newsletter articles, or any other type of content you wish to develop. This recipe for web or mobile content has been used countless times by thousands of content marketers. It works for many reasons, but most interestingly because it reflects Newton's First Law of Motion, which essentially states that: *An object in motion will remain in motion unless acted upon by an external force.*

How does Newton's Law apply to content creation? Your book idea is the object in motion. An idea generates other ideas because it represents motion, and the energy, inspiration, and discovery that takes place keeps you on the task of generating more ideas. The great thing about this approach, if you stay with it, is that you will not only get a book out of it, but a potential webinar series, a video program, enough blog posts to last six months, and more. Add in industry news and updates that you could offer, customer case studies, and other book ideas down the road, and you have content that will last you *a lifetime*.

Repurposing Content—Maximize the Leverage

Don't forget the leverage aspect of your content! Every white paper, webinar, case study, video, podcast, or other piece of content you create can work for other campaigns. The process is actually simple. Record your webinars, then use the links in a lead-generation effort. Compile your website articles into a cool, new e-book. Repurpose and reuse what you already have in place. This will save you tremendous time and will put your content in new channels, which could attract new prospects.

Need some more specific, tried-and-true ideas?

1. **Use testimonials and case studies for banner ads.** Despite what you might think, you have clients who are willing to share their testimonials or offer a case study. All you have to do is ask! Once you get a few, make them really work for you by incorporating them into a banner advertisement for your company. Let's face it, there is nothing more effective than our best customers' words of praise. You can also use these treasured testimonials or case studies as material for traditional ads in magazines or newspapers, or as television commercials or radio spots.

2. **Transform product datasheets or user guides into videos.** Close the deal once and for all with your buyers in the later stages of the buying cycle by turning your product datasheets, technical spec docs, or user guides into video content. You can take this visual and auditory magic and put it on your site, your blog, your YouTube channel, and your Facebook page. Do it right, and your conversion numbers will improve. I guarantee it!

3. **Create videos from speaking engagements.** Again, there's power in video. People love to hear you *and* see you. It's an easy way for them to consume the information

without working too hard. So, the next time you are speaking anywhere—whether it's a big industry event or at your local Rotary club—be sure to bring your video camera and tripod and get your presentation recorded. Your video will be seen by many more people than those who saw it live.

4. **Use past media attention or blog interviews as content for e-mails or tweets.** Make your outreach to new prospects easy by sending them stuff they want. If you did a recent interview with a well-known blog or received some media attention from your local paper, radio station, or a television news program, make it work twice as hard for you: Build lead-nurturing e-mails or tweets simply by sharing a link to this coverage. It works. I've done it myself many times in the past.

Content Marketing and Distribution

So, you have a content strategy and multiple types of content ready to deliver—now it comes down to *getting it to the people*. Well, one thing I need to reiterate right now: **Optimizing content for search and for social media will go a long way toward achieving your content distribution and marketing objectives.** Why? *Because if people can find it on their own, your distribution job will be complete!* That's right, this stage is the best part of the entire content life cycle because, unlike marketers of old, you don't need to push it to your audience and *make them* consume it. When they find it, they will choose to consume it on their own; then, if they like what they read, viewed, or heard, they will contact you. Your job with this stage? Number one, to ensure that the content is optimized and shareable. And number two, to have your distribution infrastructure set up for maximum effectiveness. The first, we have covered in depth. But the infrastructure piece we have only covered in pieces. So, let's discuss that now. The content we will use as an example is your brand spanking new white paper titled, "Everything You Ever Wanted to Know About Content Distribution." How's that for relevant and appropriate? The finished PDF file is sitting there on your desktop and in hard copy on your desk staring at you. And it is a work of genius. Lots of great content filled with solid research and smart editorial. But no one, absolutely no one, except your internal team, knows about it yet. It's time to get it out there. How do you do that? Here is my ten-step recommendation:

1. You post it on your website with no strings attached. It's free and you require no personal information from prospects (you'll use your second white paper or an expanded version of this one to do that).
2. You blog about it.
3. You e-mail your in-house database.
4. You post it on your social media profiles.
5. You publish a press release (pitch it to the media too).

6. You create an ad campaign using banner and text ads.
7. You reach out to popular and respected bloggers in your industry and get them to blog about it.
8. You mention it in your next monthly newsletter.
9. You use it as a basis for a webinar or podcast episode.
10. You produce a video about it.

Get the idea? By performing each of these steps, in no particular order, you are unleashing your content into the online and mobile universe for all to see. And again, like Newton's First Law of Motion, *putting the content in motion* so that it will not only stay in motion, but pick up steam and go viral across these many content channels, which actually reflects Newton's Second Law of Motion, which says, roughly, that: **Acceleration is produced when a force acts on a mass.** Your "mass" is the white paper. The "force" is the positive reaction and sharing of your white paper. And the acceleration is the viral spread. It's really that simple: Quality content, distributed correctly, connects every time.

The one thing to remember is this: The competition for attention has never been greater. Is your content really *that good*? It absolutely needs to be. There will almost always be other types of content available that will be similar or even identical to your content. There are few barriers to entry in the online medium, but there are companies that do content better than others. What you need to do is make your content the best and distribute it more effectively than anyone else. And, of course, as with anything, pray for a little luck to come your way. You never really know what will go viral anymore.

One way around the competitive aspect is to *stay on top of your keyword research*. See what's trending or popular right now in your industry and then search these phrases to see what types of reports, white papers, e-books, or other content items are out there that may be using the popular keywords in their title. If you see an opportunity, jump on it! It could be your *eureka* moment.

Content Management

Auditing, planning, developing, and then distributing content is one thing. Managing it is quite another. Depending on how much content you have, what it communicates, and where it is "housed," there are important decisions that need to be made. How and why new content is being created are important questions to address in this stage. Content always needs to be *working* for your company, serving an important role with prospects, customers, and other users.

For content to remain accurate, relevant, and valuable, it's important to develop specific governance policies, standards, and guidelines. These can inform and even define your:

- Content-related roles and responsibilities
- Decision-making processes around content
- Content governance tools

What happens after the content is launched? Who will follow up on inquiries, comments, replies, and requests for service? How will the content get revised or updated when the time comes? Who will be in charge of archiving content? Make sure, when putting together your content strategy, that you follow through with all of these important steps. It is a commitment and a process that involves a group of dedicated team members. You'll need time for planning and management of the strategy.

The two important ways of managing content to see whether it is still relevant are : by *measuring* **the content using your analytics program** and by **staying on top of the latest industry news** to see if your content reflects the current technology and tastes.

Content Curation

You may have heard the word *curation* in recent months in reference to online content and wondered, "What could this possibly mean?" Content curation is the process of finding and categorizing content from multiple sources and making it available to your audience. As a complementary piece to the content creation process, it can help make you a valued resource in the minds of your prospects and customers. Curate important, substantive content well, and you can build trust with your audience. The key is to focus on unique topic areas and to become the most trusted source with these subjects.

Google and other search engines have done this for years through content *aggregation*, but this process is done by computers that find the best links to make the content experience more fulfilling. Search can only get you so far, though. Humans curate content. You can hand select the content out there that you think is the best, just as if you were a curator for the Museum of Modern Art in New York, finding the best paintings to present to visitors.

My opinion is that content curation is secondary to content creation. But finding great content from a range of sources is a natural by-product of your involvement in your industry, and sharing that content with your audience could help you build relationships—and, in the end, it may help you sell more goods and services. Your prospects need help sorting through the content that is exploding all around them. Do that job for them, and it will pay off. Information is power, and if you give that to your customers, they will more than likely pay you back for it.

Current Trends in Content Marketing

What are the current trends in content marketing? Which strategies will provide you with the biggest benefit for the time invested?

1. Social media marketing is getting huge.
2. Mobile marketing becomes the real deal.
3. Content marketing expands into new venues.
4. Online retail continues to take market share from other channels.
5. Integrated marketing comes of age.
6. Location-based services are growing.
7. Target market segmentation and targeting are driving more dollars to content marketing.
8. *Quality* of content is taking precedence over quantity—it really makes a difference now.
9. User experience is becoming more important than ever.
10. Content marketing is super hot.

How will your company embrace each of these trends? Will you focus a bit of energy on each of them or go full bore with just a couple? Much of this depends on the type of company you have, your specific content needs, and your current resources.

Content Marketing Best Practices

I'm going to end the book with an important section that I think will provide a lasting takeaway for you and your future content-building empire: content marketing's best practices.

1. **Source content from everywhere within your company.** You never know who in your company will rise to become an expert. Great content can come from anywhere in your organization and by actively seeking it out, you'll get unique viewpoints on the same issue. Whether it's your product development team, your director of IT, or even the customer service reps, your company's employees are a natural source of compelling blog posts, video interviews, or white papers. Tap them.

2. **Align the "pain points" of your prospects with content "cures."** Relevance is everything. And so is addressing your prospects' pain. Remember the list of human motivations: the need to feel secure, loved, respected? If you can tap into these needs and solve a troubling issue, you will turn into a trusted provider. This idea can be difficult when we are all in love with our products and services, but we all know by now that people are really turned off by self-important promotion or opinion. If people think you can address their needs, you'll get their business.

3. **Develop content that appeals to different types of decision makers.** In the B2B space, purchase decisions are usually made by a group of people. Content that connects with the VP of Information Technology may not connect with the chief marketing officer, yet both are involved with making the buying decision. So, perhaps

you provide a technical spec sheet with considerations for IT needs and show that to the VP, then put together a marketing plan that incorporates a social media strategy for the CMO.

You can also build out a specific type of content, a technique used on many websites today: "buyer persona" modules, which use a "character" that matches the personality of your target audience to help them understand the value proposition in their terms, from a point of view that they understand.

4. **Develop content for all stages in the buying cycle.** There is the researching stage, the gathering information stage and the ready to buy stage.

Researching: thought leadership is important: blog posts, white papers, and e-books help here. You can also align your company with someone respected in your industry for a webinar offering.

Gathering information: prospects want to know the ways that you will meet specific challenges they have. Data sheets, case studies, and comparisons to the competition are all great for this stage.

Ready to buy: these folks will be reviewing multiple proposals for companies on their short list. Make sure your proposal is solid. A long list of testimonial content also works great here.

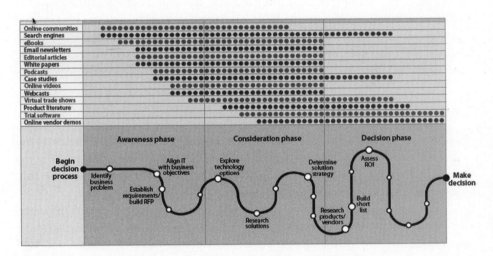

FIGURE 13-1   Source: Google/TechTarget Media Consumption Report, 2009.

5. **Develop great content in all the different formats and channels.** This is a repeat from previous mentions in the book, but it definitely belongs on this list. Some of your prospects like reading about you through a white paper or your blog posts, others like

to see and hear you through video, and some may want to "get to know you" on an informal basis through your Facebook page. Appeal to all of them, all the time.

6. **Use social media to build, connect, and grow relationships.** Your prospects and customers on Twitter, Facebook, and LinkedIn want you to engage them in dialogue and conversation. They may want to do some small talk before they even consider buying from you. Make sure you make it a compelling, two-way conversation.

7. **Seek to educate your prospects with compelling content.** People like to learn. When they learn something of value without having to pay anything for it, they feel connected and are typically loyal to the one who educated them. And they almost always go back for more. *Be* that teacher for your prospects. *Be* the information provider they trust. Remember, buyers today conduct massive amounts of research on the web before they buy. Seek to educate your customers, and your company will serve as their lifelong teacher—and as the place where they ultimately buy stuff.

8. **Measure your content marketing progress!** Measure, measure, measure. It's what separates the best content marketers from the rest of the pack. Each content goal should be tied to a success metric. But be careful; this isn't always easy. Your ultimate measure is **demand generation, or conversion**. Measuring this can be tricky. Was it a white paper that closed the deal or was it a combination of your prospect's exposure to five different content types? Or was it a phone call from your top salesperson? For content marketing to demonstrate ROI, the metrics you use to evaluate strategy and your content campaigns need to be meaningfully related to demand generation. Doing this will ensure accurate analytics and provide great data for future content marketing campaigns.

Some Final Thoughts

As we come to a close, I want to leave you with this thought. It's a simple idea that I feel will work really well for your company, no matter what types of content marketing you engage in. In fact, it's the same way I closed my first book, *Content Rich*. And it is this: *Make your prospective customers feel like they are buying from a friend.*

Your goal with your content is to build relationships and attain greater influence. But you also want to reduce your customer acquisition costs, improve your customer loyalty rate, and, overall, increase each customer's lifetime value. In addition, you want to learn something from your customers. You want this to be a true give-and-take relationship, a genuine *partnership*. This is an important distinction between successful content marketers and unsuccessful content marketers.

With social networking expanding at an incredible rate and with a more personal approach becoming popular in business, I think the relationships we have with our customers will continue to grow and become more important with time. As you know by now, the goal of your business should not be solely to get the sale, but to develop a relationship with each and every customer—a mutually beneficial relationship that will lead to more sales, testimonials, and referrals over the years.

By seeing your customers as friends, as part of the family, you will be exposed to wonderfully new and unexpected surprises that will provide lasting value and personal satisfaction. As I mentioned in the beginning of the book, content can empower people everywhere to have a voice. And content tells the story of your product or service and propels it into the hearts and minds of your prospects, customers, and others.

When you propel your content into their hearts you have just made a friend and quite possibly, *a customer for life.*

Friends Communicate with Each Other

The hallmark of a solid friendship is effective, two-way communication, not just talking or hearing, but *listening*. You can't build a friendship by e-mailing your list every other month and pitching them with your latest products or services. To make friends with your customers, you need to communicate on a personal level.

So, commit to communicating with them at least once a week via your blog and social media channels. Heck, pick up the phone and give them a good old-fashioned call! This will keep the conversation going and connect you on a deeper level. It will also make them feel valued, like they are on the inside of something very cool.

Friends Are There Through Thick and Thin

Isn't it true that our best friends give us the benefit of the doubt? No matter what happens, they let us slide sometimes, it's just part of the deal. In fact, the best of friends will never leave your side. By developing friendships with your customers, you have a relationship based on honesty and trust.

Customers will not suddenly jump to a competitor of yours if they feel a true connection with your company. Being available and personable and truly caring for them will go a very long way. You only get what you give, right? So, ask them to be in your advisory groups. Seek their opinions on anything and everything. Hold an event for all of your customers. Building a community with your customers will give you their loyalty.

That's a Wrap!

You've completed the book, and, hopefully, have come away from the experience with some great information, but the real work is just beginning. Now is the time to put these content development and content marketing ideas into practice. So, sit down with your team and start coming up with some ideas. Plan a robust and comprehensive content strategy. Grow your web and mobile presence through powerful, persuasive content. Ensure that your content is search engine optimized and shareable through social media. Differentiate your content from your competitors' so you stand out. *Connect* with your prospects. Ask yourself: What content can I develop today to make a big impact tomorrow?

As I bid you a fond *written* farewell, please know that I really appreciate you picking up this book. I treasure the relationships I have with all of my readers. And if the opportunity comes up, I would love to meet you in person, or at least via e-mail or my blog, or perhaps Twitter or Facebook.

Be on the lookout for me . . . the *Content Is Currency* book tour may be coming to a town near you! In addition, I may be speaking on the topic in a hotel lobby or corporate boardroom in your city. I'd love to have you join us; there's nothing quite like face-to-face learning. Plus, we have a lot of fun at our events.

May your websites, blogs, social media presence, newsletters, videos, and more serve you well, and may your businesses be successful. May the rich content you build truly become currency and put you well on your way to industry dominance!

Thanks for reading!

Index